CLIMBING THE

MISSISSIPPI RIVER
BRIDGE BY BRIDGE

VOLUME TWO
Minnesota

Written and Illustrated by
Mary Charlotte Aubry Costello

This book is dedicated to the Sisters of Humility–
Sister Clarice Eberdt, M.A.
Sister Maria Trinitas Rand, M.A.
Sister Kathleen Eberdt, Ph.D.
who were indispensable in its preparation and completion.

[handwritten: Siblings. All three nums taught at Marycrest College, Davenport, Iowa, in the '60s.]

CLIMBING THE MISSISSIPPI RIVER BRIDGE BY BRIDGE
  Volume 2– All the Minnesota bridges across the
                  Mississippi River from the Iowa border to Lake Itasca,
                  the source of the Mississippi River

Copyright© 2002 by Mary Charlotte Aubry Costello
All rights are reserved including the right of reproduction
in whole or part in any form.

Publisher • Mary C. Costello
Desktop Designer • Bob Grove
Printer • Von Hoffman Graphics, Inc.
Illustrator • Mary C. Costello

Library of Congress Catalog Card Number 94-096856
ISBN 0-9644518-2-4 Softcover
ISBN 0-9644518-3-2 Hardcover

First Edition: March 2002

MANUFACTURED IN THE UNITED STATES OF AMERICA

COVER

This is the Hennepin Avenue Bridge in Minneapolis , Minnesota, the
site of the first bridge across the Mississippi River. It is the fourth bridge
in this location, a beautiful modern suspension span, in keeping with the
original bridge, built in 1855, which was a suspension as well.

Contents

PART FOUR: AMID LAKES AND FORESTS
(Baxter to Beltrami County Map)

PART FIVE: RAILS TO ROCKS
(County Road 12 to Source of Mississippi Map)

Appendix

Introduction

If you were to travel the length of the Mighty Mississippi, you would pass under 219* bridges. Volume I took us under 86 of these magnificent structures from New Orleans to the edge of Minnesota. In this volume we travel the length of Minnesota up to the very headwaters of the river. We pass under 135 well-traveled bridges.

The state of Minnesota is unique in many ways. Some of Minnesota's unusual features are explained in legend. Paul Bunyan, the legendary giant logger, was delivered by five giant storks. Babe, a blue ox, helped the lumberjack by dragging a water wagon that sprinkled water on the forest path to ice it in winter, thus facilitating the hauling of huge logs from the crowded woods. The many lakes in the state were caused (according to legend) by the Blue Ox's every step and are a reminder of the giant and his pet ox. Legend also explains that Lake Itasca, the source of the Mississippi River, was formed when the wagon leaked, and filled the lake. The overflow ran down the land to New Orleans carving out the Mississippi River.

Recorded history of the state and river is almost as fascinating. Hernando DeSoto discovered the Mississippi River in 1541 for his homeland, Spain.--Father Jacques Marquette, 35 years of age and much loved by the Indians, and Captain Louis Joliet, 27, discovered Machinac Island in Michigan. After finding the river at its confluence with the Wisconsin River, in 1673, they sailed south on it to where the Spanish claimed ownership. They then returned. Their allegiance was to France.--Robert LaSalle traced the river's course in 1682 from the point where the Wisconsin River meets the Mississippi to the mouth at the Gulf of Mexico and claimed the region for France.--Henry Schoolcraft in 1832 officially "discovered" the Headwaters at Lake Itasca though he was not the first white person to see it.--Father Hennepin's Italian companion, Tonti, in 1680 saw the source of the river when he was hunting separately with the Indians who told him it was the beginning of the Mississippi.--And in 1805, a trader, William Morrison. saw the source at Itasca but it was called Elk Lake at the time. The Indians also told him it was the source.--Father Louis Hennepin is the first recorded white visitor to see the Falls of Saint Anthony in what is now in Minneapolis and named the falls after his favorite saint, St. Anthony of Padua, in the 1680's.

Geographically there are 600 miles of river from St. Paul to the headwaters at Itasca. The route is curving, twisting and is made up of oxbows and few straight areas. "The Mississippi River is the crookedest great waterway in the world," said Willard Price in his book The Amazing Mississippi. The river passes through small and large lakes including Lake Pepin, Lake Bemidji , and Lake Winnibigoshish to name a few. Springs are in evidence in the north where the river forms a large question mark (going north and then east before heading south). Groundwater accounts for two-thirds of the river's flow.** Giant stands of trees in the forests and in parks, such as Itasca State Park, speak well for the conservationists after the initial "free" logging that depleted many areas. Wildlife and rare plants abound in the almost pristine area near the source as it drops 500 feet of elevation to St. Cloud . (See "Stairway of Water" diagram) From Lake Itasca to Cass Lake there are 242 kinds of birds, 23 species of reptiles and amphibians and 57 species of mammals according to the "Mississippi Headwaters River Trail" guide.

The Mississippi River bridges are a varied group from a row of rocks and a single half-log in the Itasca State Park to award-winning deck-arch spans in Minneapolis. There are mystery bridges, privately owned bridges, bridges that work as entertainment centers, pedestrian and bike bridges, both low and high railroad bridges. Many styles of bridge structure are represented in this final section of the Mississippi and can make the state of Minnesota proud.

I am sad to see my part in this "show and tell" come to an end, but I will always be grateful to have had this opportunity to commune with the third longest river in the world.

---

* The total number of bridges is 221, but one would not be able to canoe under the log and rock bridges. Therefore, 219 spans is accurate here.

** In the area between Lake Itasca and Cass Lake this statement is true says the Minnesota DNR as stated in "Mississippi Headwater River Trail" (map, brochure), column 5.

Preface

It all began about twenty-six years ago with a teaching unit on the "Local Mississippi River Bridges". As an elementary school art teacher in Davenport, Iowa, I learned from other teacher's investigations about the Quad-City bridges and taught my students about them. They studied and drew the bridges and finally created a model bridge they, personally, would like to see built. Each student was his/her own designer/engineer/builder. An enormous display in the school hallway of every kind of bridge in all stages of professionalism culminated the unit. The fifth graders as a whole loved the project, and I developed a "love affair" with the Mississippi and its bridges.

With my interest in bridges aroused--actually growing year by year--and with time made available to me by early retirement, I decided to write the bridge book that I often challenged my students to write. Since there is no book written about all the bridges on the Great Mississippi--the only exception being one written in the late nineteenth century of the bridges between St. Paul and St. Louis (Warren 1878), long since outdated,-- I felt there was a need for such a researched publication. To enhance the written record, illustrations of each span seemed a requisite and, with my art background, I was eager to take up that challenge.

Therefore, I left teaching and traveled the entire length of the Mississippi River alone, visiting and sketching each bridge from Lake Itasca, Minnesota, to New Orleans, Louisiana. Originally my intent was to write this book for children. However, as I discovered a tremendous interest in my project from people all along the river, and as I became more fascinated with bridge stories and structures myself, the concept of my book changed and expanded to include adults.

My personal experiences are an integral part of the Mississippi story making the book a blend of history, facts, personal observations and experiences. My intent is to make people more aware of the beauty, unique features, style and history of "their" bridge. Although some bridges may be deteriorating and in need of replacement, their place in the area history is recognized and appreciated.

As I prepared for my bridge tour, I knew it would be exciting, but never did I think it would be as exhilarating and enjoyable as it became.

My plan was to take sketchpad, camera, binoculars and traveling clothes in my little red Datsun, first to the north, and then to the south.

I had contacted people all along the way concerning possible lodging. One friend had a summer cabin in Cullen Lake, Minnesota, another a "loft" at O'Brian Lake in northern Minnesota. I had two daughters in Minneapolis and so it went. When "in the field", sometimes distance or darkness meant a local motel.

Although I traveled from north to south on the Mississippi, I have reversed the order in my book, putting the larger and more impressive bridges at the beginning.

My state maps were vital aids in finding bridges, but often it was necessary to question strangers. Whenever I arrived on the spot, I photographed the bridge, then sketched it. Finally I took notes on the colors, sounds, surroundings, and incidents that happened while I sketched.

After three weeks of driving and sketching up north, I went south. By September of 1986, I had finished the major part of my traveling, though I have gone north five more times for missed or new bridges.

Surrounded by three stuffed sketchbooks of drawings, photos, notes, and articles, I sat down to the computer. Sometimes I spent the normal eight-hour day before that wonder machine, the computer; other times I started very early in the morning or ended very late at night. The telephone was an important part of my spare-bedroom "office" equipment.

From countless interviews with engineers, DOT personnel, bridge designers, construction workers, railroad administrators, bridge-tenders, historians, librarians, tourist-center staff and citizens living along the river, I learned statistics that couldn't be found anywhere in print. The bridge histories have come from newspaper articles written, for the most part, when the bridges were constructed. Minnesota DOT, railroad companies (BNSF, CP, and UP) the Coast Guard, Corps of Engineers, city libraries, and Historical Societie's were helpful sources.

Redrawing the 135 sketches from my originals and from on-site photos took about two-and-a-half years. This task was every bit as enjoyable as the writing had been.

In the years of writing and illustrating my bridge book, I have learned so much, traveled so far, and made so many new friends that I would gladly experience it again. Climbing the Mississippi River Bridge By Bridge has been a labor of love.

Acknowledgements

I wish to thank all the people who have helped create this book. Especially my thanks goes to my family who answer whenever I call for help no matter what it might be--computer problems, terminology or support. Thanks in particular to Sister Kathleen Eberdt, CHM, for critiquing all of my sketches and for proofing copy when asked--forsaking her own needs in order to help me. Thanks to the beloved, late Sister Maria Trinitas Rand, CHM, for her early proofing of the entire book. I am very grateful to Marcella Kennedy, Transportation Specialist with the MNDOT, whom I called everyday for weeks for information. Thanks to the men of the railroads who were so very cooperative and helpful: from the BNSF Pat Hyatt, Gary Strelcheck and Nicholas Mraz; from the UP, Paul Welsch, Tom Dunn and J.R. Iwinski; and from the CP, Stephen Hill. To Charlotte Fogle, Crosslake, Minnesota, thanks for being both hostess and photographer when I needed you. For 16 years Ben Thoma, at Itasca State Park, has provided answers, pictures and information, Thanks, Ben! Also this past year Connie Cox certainly has been gracious and helpful. I want to thank Kevin Nelson, Wabasha Street Bridge engineer, for his delightful tour of this new structure, pictures and his continuing help. I am grateful to Jim Stoutland and Kevin Anderson both from MNDOT, to Matt Lang formerly of St. Paul DOT, to Lloyd Larson formerly with Bemidji DOT to Bemidji's former Assistant Highway Engineer, Westley Djoney, to Tracy Moe formerly with St. Paul Public Works Department and finally to Ron Deiss, Archeologist with the Rock Island Army Corps of Engineers.

Special thanks to
Harold Sandberg
for his overwhelming support and patience
while carefully critiquing all the drawings
and copy for both volumes

PART ONE

PART ONE
Land of the Indian Princess

*T*his Minnesota area of the Upper Mississippi Valley is dominated by striking features-it has the highest cliffs as well as the widest part of the Great River.

Fantastic glacier-cut cliffs solidly border the river valley from LaCrosse, Wisconsin, to Newport, Minnesota. Grandad Bluff, Sugar Loaf Mountain, Barn Bluff and Maiden Rock are well-known landmarks along these shores. The river's highest precipice is at Eagles Bluff in Wisconsin at 1,100 feet above sea level.

Here, also, one finds the beginning of a new trend for this never-to-be-outdone river as it short-cuts its way through numerous lakes. The first lake we see when traveling north is Lake Pepin. Here the Mississippi expands to almost a three-mile width (14,520 feet, or 2.75 miles), its widest point. Below, at Lansing, Iowa, the river from shore to shore across islands and sloughs is 14,350 feet (2.7 miles), slightly less wide.

Hiawatha Valley, as most of this area is commonly known, is unique in having many Indian-named towns along its shores. Wabasha (Wah-pah-sha) and Red Wing were Sioux Indian Chiefs, and Winona was Red Wing's eldest daughter. Lacrosse was an Indian ballgame.* All of these Indian names are appropriate along the river, for it was Ojibway Indians who named the "Mississippi", a title meaning "the Great River." Often told in the region are legends of Indian princesses, such as Winona, a princess who jumped from Maiden Rock (above Lake Pepin) to her death because she was not allowed to marry the brave of her choice.

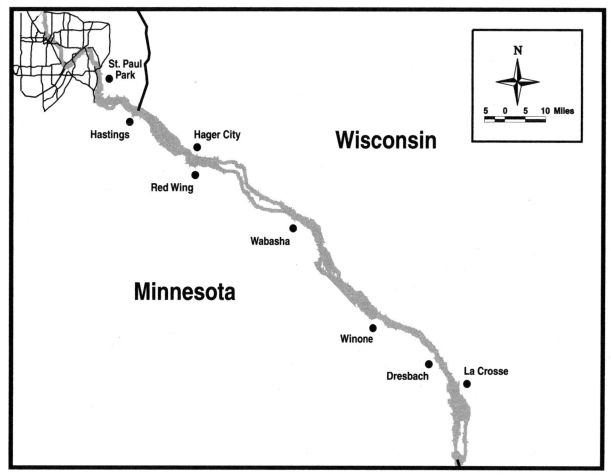

*The game of lacrosse used a ball and a stick. The game received its name because of the stick, which resembles a "cross" such as is carried by a bishop.

Cass Street Bridge, LaCrosse, Wisconsin, US61

I first saw this bridge in the evening light from the sandy beach of Pettibone Park. The change of lighting in twelve hours caused the rich blue span of the evening to change appearance. In the morning light the bridge's blue color seemed lighter and the piers better defined. The evening light had silhouetted the trusses, though I could tell they were blue. The piers were in greater shadow in the evening and the water was much richer in color. After experiencing my evening and early morning views of the Cass Street Bridge, I felt I understood a little better the Nineteenth Century Impressionist painters who studied the effects of light on color and shapes. The US 61 bridge changed character from "dramatic" to "innocent" overnight.

From this structure I found out what the engineer, Jim Turk, meant when he said, "You can recognize a cantilever when you know what to look for." I know that the US 61 bridge is not a continuous truss, as I originally thought, because there is a change in the truss pattern at the ends of the center span. A close look reveals a double diagonal. Therefore, it is a cantilever bridge which had been built out from each side toward the middle, using no scaffolding, with the center span elevated into place between.

The concrete piers of the Cass Street Bridge reflect a touch of the Art Deco Period* popular in the 1930's. The simple relief on the end of the square column rises two-thirds of the way up the outside ends to an arrow-like point. The two shafts of each pier are connected with a narrow top band, and a horizontally stretched "x" creates a "cut-work" effect which is attractive from any angle.

Two other features of the US 61 bridge make it different--the roadway and the parapets. After crossing the two-lane bridge, I understood at least one reason for the 30 mph speed limit; the bridge was slippery even though it was dry. The woman at the Tourist Information Center said the problem had been worse and has been partially corrected. The steel grid deck has the advantage of being light in weight and keeps unwanted snow or insects from collecting; but it is sometimes slippery because tires polish the steel bars.

The railings beside the sidewalks of the Cass Street Bridge are unusual and beautiful in design. There are few other parapets like them along the river. The supports are sturdy square posts of steel with panels between, consisting of two long and three short metal bars used alternately. The short poles are supported at top and bottom by long horizontal bars. The arrangement is very attractive.

The 1890 bridge, built on the same spot as today's high truss span, was declared "the longest swingspan in the world" during its day. No information on the old swingspan's length was available.

When I arrived at the Cass Street Bridge, a young woman and a friend walking in the park gave me directions and even made me a map for getting to the LaCrosse motels. Their concern was an example of Mississippi rivertown friendliness.

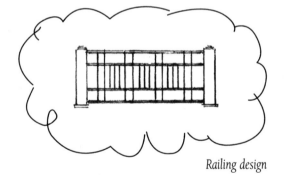

Railing design

Use:
US 61, Wisconsin SR 16 and local traffic

Location:
Between LaCrosse business district and Pettibone Island, Wisconsin

Style:
3-span cantilever truss with deck-truss approaches

Length:
Channel span - 462 feet clear
            - 475 feet total
Total length - 2531 feet

Width:
2 lanes plus 2 sidewalks

Clearance:
67 feet MLW

Date completed:
July 1939 or 1940; replaced 1890 swingspan

Designed by:
Wisconsin DOT

Bridge:
#B-32-0300 Wisconsin

Owner:
Wisconsin DOT

*In 1925, the Paris Arts Decoratifs Exhibition (whence the name Art Deco) introduced decoration not applied to surfaces, for the most part, but achieved with lines and planes divided into shapes and motifs by sculpting.

Cass Street Bridge, La Crosse, Wisconsin

Mary C. Costello

LaCrosse-LaCrescent West Channel Highway Bridge, US 61

A huge tree in Pettibone Park shaded the 1931 LaCrosse-LaCrescent West Channel Bridge when I first saw it. The lines of the trusses, the deck and the walkway were all softened in late afternoon shadows. Most older truss bridges are narrow, high and cold appearing, but this one was quite the opposite. This old span was not elevated but started at ground level, was "low-roofed" and seemed wide. As a bonus, it was freshly painted. Only one other place on the Mississippi River gave me this feeling--the St. Paul Park Bridge in Minnesota. It, too, had a friendly tree at one end.

However, the old span definitely needed replacing. "It was held up by signs!" said Tom Kratt, construction manager on the new bridge. Two matching bridges have taken its place.

The 1992 built crossings at LaCrosse-LaCrescent are very plain, even generic in the Mississippi River bridge world today. Though they are two, side by side, with different bridge numbers, I am treating them as one. The "teen-styled" piers are close but not connected. The westbound span was completed in 1992 and the eastbound was expected to be completed the following year. However, because of the big flood of '93, was delayed until '94. Although the engineer told me that no trees were removed except a pine that was taken to another location when building the newer bridge, I have not been able to locate where I felt that warm feeling. The closest thing to it was the Sportsman's boat ramp from which location I drew. Maybe no one but I have missed the old span.

Use:
City, park and highways US 14, 61 and SR 16 traffic

Location:
Between LaCrescent, Minnesota and Pettibone Island, Wisconsin

Style:
7-span prestressed concrete girder

Length:
Channel span - 105 feet clear
                        - 108 feet total
Total length   - 760 feet

Width:
2 lanes, 49 feet total, with a 5-foot sidewalk on each bridge

Clearance:
12.5 feet MLW

Date completed:
1992 westbound and 1993 eastbound; both replaced 1931 truss span; 1890 original bridge built

Designed by:
Owen Ayres & Associates, Madison, Wisconsin

Bridge:
In Wisconsin - #B-32-0164 eastbound span; #B-32-0165 westbound; in Minnesota #27018 eastbound and #27017 westbound (Houston County, Minnesota)

Owner:
Wisconsin owns the westbound, and Minnesota, the eastbound.

West Channel Highway Bridge, La Crosse

Mary C. Costello

7

LaCrosse-LaCrescent Canadian Pacific Railroad, Main Channel Bridge

*H*ere at the Canadian Pacific Railroad Bridge I had an unusual experience. At almost suppertime I parked and was photographing the swingspan bridge when a man came down the wooden steps onto the embankment. His name was Bill Knutsen and, as an insurance adjuster, he was looking at the damage a boat had recently inflicted on the wooden sheer fence. In conversation I discovered that he was very interested in bridges and trains. He even suggested some people for me to contact.

A train crossed the bridge. Then with the turnspan open, a boat passed through. As we talked, the span slowly and quietly closed. The bridge operator came out to the end of the movable span with a sledge hammer and pounded the track in place. I later found he has a red light that goes on in his office that tells him when the track is not lined up properly. Mr. Knutson called to him, introduced me and then left.

Norm Brownell, the bridge tender, invited me out to his bridge office because he had a train due in five minutes. His office was only one span out over the river--not too scary--but I walked the railroad ties with care. No sooner had I entered that full cubicle, than Mr. Brownell saw something below the bridge that caught his attention. A rowboat was floating without anyone in it. He said he was going to call to an approaching cabin cruiser if the pilot didn't do something about it first. He closed the screen door and went out to call over the rail. I watched from the window in the operator's office. It was at this point that he noticed three teenage boys swimming from the long protection pier below. He then became truly upset because he is responsible for anything that might happen at the bridge.

"Is that your boat?" he yelled. The boys pretended ignorance. When he suggested, "The one floating away with the current," one youth immediately climbed to the bridge roadbed and ran along the tracks to the steps and down along the shore. A second boy started to swim for the boat. The last one climbed up the round "cell" and onto the bridge, dripping wet and barefooted, following his friend. Mr. Brownell yelled something to the last fellow, but he had gone in chase of the boat also.

I could tell the bridge tender's concern. At that moment he received notice via radio that the expected train had arrived. We saw the boys retrieve the boat; the first "land-runner" swam out to catch it. The incident was over within five minutes.

The Canadian Pacific train passed right by the tender's office. I tried to photograph it but managed only a blur. The picture of the end of the caboose turned out better, but was of little value to me.

All I saw of the CP Railroad Bridge on that day were the three fixed spans of Parker truss--one humpback and two flattops--along with the big turnspan, but from the Corps of Engineers I learned that there was another Mississipppi River bridge on the other side of the island. I will treat that bridge separately on the following page; however, none could be more exciting than this main channel railroad bridge had been.

Use:
Canadian Pacific Railroad traffic and Amtrak

Location:
Between LaCrescent, Minnesota, and LaCrosse, Wisconsin; two miles above the highway bridge

Style:
Swingspan with one humpback and two flat-top fixed through-trusses

Length:
Channel span - 150 feet clear
            - 178 feet total, half swingspan
Total length - 1042 feet

Width:
1 track, 20 feet

Clearance:
21.9 feet MLW

Date completed: December 1876; partially rebuilt May 1928; in 1998 the Coast Guard ordered the swing-span be replaced with a liftspan (work not begun as of end of 2001)

Designed by:
Chicago, Milwaukee, St. Paul & Pacific Railroad Company

Bridge:
#L4-B

Owner:
Canadian Pacific Railroad

Unique feat:
One of the first 15 bridges across the Mississippi River

Canadian Pacific Main Channel Railroad Bridge, La Crosse

Mary C. Costello

9

East Channel Railroad Bridge, LaCrosse, Wisconsin

*O*riginally this East Channel was the main channel, wrote Brevet Major General G.K.Warren in <u>Bridging the Mississippi River Between St. Paul and St. Louis</u> and called it the "old channel." The Milwaukee and St. Paul Railroad Company planned to locate their bridge across the southern end of Minnesota Island with the main low water channel on the Wisconsin side. "The Island divides the channel almost equally,"noted Warren,"... the main low-water channel could be kept permanent on either side of this island."

So in 1875-76, when the M.& St.P Railroad Bridge was built, the main channel was changed from the east to the west channel. A dam was built at the head of Minnesota Island 1.5 miles above the bridge to cut off or slow down the water flow to the east channel to insure navigation of boats and rafts on the new main channel.

The 5-span iron through-truss bridge over the "old channel" remained just that until 2001, but was upgraded to steel and pin-connected trusses in 1905 and/or 1928. In 1995 just one of the trusses was replaced with a through-plate girder. However, by 2001, after two years of work, the other four through-trusses also were replaced with TPG's. It was expected that two 74-foot long through-plate girders would take the place of each truss and that four new piers would be added. But, after hearing local organization's input, the railroad (now the Canadian Pacific Railroad) was required to provide a wider span for recreational crafts at the east end of the bridge where there is a deeper channel. Therefore, the eastern two trusses became 1-74 foot and 2-111 feet TPG's instead of 4-74 foot TPG's. This required one less new pier and the removal of one original pier. All remaining piers were encased up to 16" in concrete.

After taking a lunch break at a Hardee's in LaCrosse, I was refreshed and I remembered two things that the bridge tender had told me earlier. First he had said, "The East Channel Bridge is around the curve in the tracks. It's right there." The other statement was to the effect that no trains were scheduled to come until about 4:00 p.m.

It was 2:30 before I made up my mind to return and walk the French Slough Bridge and track to the East Channel Bridge. With water bottle in hand, I began my trek. There were no buildings along the raised four-and-a-half block long embankment, but there were the remains of drought-ravaged crops in the clearings. I hurried because of the four o'clock deadline. From tie to railroad tie I stepped and finally came to the end of the curve. There the bridge was--50 feet ahead with its five matching through-truss spans (obviously before the changes) which I drew.

All that was visible at the other end were trees. Beyond them across Minnesota Island, I knew, was the main channel railroad bridge that I had completed earlier.

I finished my sketching, beat the 4:00 p.m. train, and made my destination well before dark.

Use:
Canadian Pacific (former Soo Line) trains plus Amtrak

Location:
One mile south of I-90, connecting Minnesota Island and LaCrosse, Wisconsin

Style:
10-span open-deck through-plate girder

Length:
Channel span - 105 feet clear
      - 111 feet total
Total length - 764 feet

Width:
Single track, 18 feet

Clearance:
21.6 feet MLW

Date completed: 2001 renovated, 1928 updated,1905 pin-connected trusses and swingspan, original span 1876

Designed by:
Canadian Pacific design office

Bridge:
#L4A

Owner:
Canadian Pacific Railroad

Canadian Pacific East Channel Railroad Bridge, La Crosse

Mary C. Costello

Canadian Pacific Railroad Bridge at LaCrosse, French Slough

In December 1876 the LaCrosse Railway Bridge was open for travel (one of the first 15 bridges across the Mississippi River), according to G.K.Warren's <u>Report on Bridging the Mississippi River Between St. Paul, Minneapolis and St. Louis, Missouri.</u> It was located between the city of LaCrosse, Wisconsin and the State of Minnesota. The Milwaukee and St. Paul Railway Company was authorized in 1872 to build a bridge and were allowed to choose the location, even though the city of LaCrosse opposed the site. It is the present bridge site, a distance of four to four and one-half miles between the main bluffs.

Starting at North LaCrosse there was a 1420 foot embankment to the Black River (not included here because it is not the Mississippi River). Six hundred feet of pile trestle preceeded the 310 feet of the Black River Bridge pivot span. Then there were a 1000 feet of trestling to the French Slough. According to Brevet Major General Warren, the bents of this trestling were 16 feet apart and rested on four piles sawed off about three feet above the surface of the ground. At first the French Slough was crossed on trestling, but the railway company proposed building a 100-foot truss on stone piers, which it appears the railway did.

In 1905 a pin-connected through-truss span over the French Slough replaced the earlier through-truss, and in 1998 was converted to two 82-foot open-deck through-plate-girders. The rest of the spans (eight of them) are plate girders below the deck. A new pier, required between the new girder spans, is open in the center bottom in contrast to the others which are solid. These solid piers in 1998 were actually jacketed with concrete, making them appear new, when actually some date back to 1876. "They are masonry block or timber mats set on timber piling," says Stephen Hill, Manager Projects in U.S., in a recent publication about the replacement of trusses on the Canadian Pacific Bridges in LaCrosse, Wisconsin.

A float out/float in method of replacing the truss with the girder was put in action. "Pumps were used to raise the truss by taking water out of the lift barge for the float out, and to fill the lowering barges after floating in the new TPG's."[1] The process took 15 hours and required the scheduled Amtrak train to detour but was completed in time for two freight trains and the next Amtrak train to cross.

Use:
Allows the CP trains to cross the French Slough at LaCrosse

Location:
Between LaCrosse, Wisconsin, and La Crescent, Minnesota

Style:
10 spans of 8 deep deck-plate girders and 2 through-plate girders

Length:
Channel span - 72 feet clear
            - 82 feet total
Total length - 812 feet

Width:
Single track, 18 feet

Clearance:
21 feet MLW

Date completed:
November 1998 replaced 1905 pin-connected truss, 164 feet long, with a through-plate-girder; 1876 was original span

Designed by:
Canadian Pacific design office in Calgary did renovations; originally the Milwaukee and St. Paul Railway Company designed

Bridge:
L2

Owners:
Canadian Pacific Railroad

Unique feat:
A part of the first 15 bridges to cross the Mississippi River

Canadian Pacific French Slough Railroad Bridge, LaCrosse

Mary C. Costello

13

Dresbach, Minnesota, Highway Bridge, I-90

*T*he Mississippi River is glistening in the sun, the summer wind is blowing, and the wild yellow trefoil "pockets" are scattered throughout the grass. I am on the grounds of the Interstate Highway Tourist Center, enjoying the view of Dresbach's long girder bridge that took seven years to build.

As I crossed the bridge, I felt as if I were on a sunken race track, even though the bridge is a deck girder, not a half-through. The railing is open concrete placed on a curb, but one cannot see the river for the speed of the traffic and the height of the bridge. The lanes of traffic, two in each direction, are separated by a median composed of a concrete step with a corrugated steel top and a heavy steel bar raised on posts above that. I felt almost claustrophobic. However, I have been over the Dresbach Bridge since and have not had that feeling. It must have been the heavy clouds hanging overhead and fast traffic that produced the sensation I experienced on my first crossing of the Dresbach span.

From the outside, the I-90 Highway Bridge is much more attractive. A blue-grey color, the ribbed girder is very deep over the main channel and for a span on either side. The deepest points are over the T-shaped ("hammerhead") piers. The girders arch between these piers then straighten out and become half the depth from there to the Wisconsin end of the bridge-extending over eight 170-foot-long spans.

From the highest part of the bridge there is a long 2.4% grade down to Wisconsin. At this point of the Mississippi, the Minnesota shores are higher than the Wisconsin side.

This Interstate 90 Bridge helps to link Boston, Cleveland, and Chicago to the West Coast. It is in an area where there is more land than water because of all the islands. Most of the islands here, however, are between bodies of water other than the Mississippi--Round Lake, French Lake and Black River. This single bridge crosses both the main and back channels of the Mississippi River. The one bridge does double duty.

I looked closely at the pretty little trefoil flowers hiding in the grass at my feet. They have fine detail, smoothness and beauty that humans, with all their knowledge of engineering and electronics, cannot match. Each plant has five center-opened pockets, like the soft little plastic coin purses my children used to have. I could not help thinking that man can make large and magnificent bridges but only God can make a tiny trefoil.

Use:
Highway I-90 traffic

Location:
Between Dresbach, Minnesota, and north LaCrosse, Wisconsin

Style:
12-span continuous plate-girder

Length:
Channel span - 411 feet clear
               - 450 feet total
Total length - 2,490 feet

Width:
4 lanes plus 4-foot median, 67.5 feet total

Clearance:
62 feet MLW

Date completed: October 1967

Designed by:
Wisconsin DOT, bridge section

Bridge:
#B-32-0045 Wisconsin, 9320 Winona County, Minnesota

Owner:
Wisconsin and Minnesota Departments of Transportation

Highway I-90 Bridge, Dresbach, Minnesota   *Mary C. Costello*

*H*ere is a bridge with four and maybe five lives--better than most bridge chances for survival, though not so numerous as a cat's lives.

No longer in use as a highway bridge, the old Winona "Wagon Bridge" is still in place and still very attractive. This bridge has been a recreational spot on Latsch Island for fishing, walking, or just viewing the beauty of the Mississippi, the Wisconsin channel, in particular. For a few years it was used as a bikepath but now it is officially closed though some people still walk on it. There is plenty to see from here--houseboats, wharves and picturesque elevated river-shanties. The city of Winona is committed to restoring the Old Wagon Bridge to vehicular use to Agahaming Park. Money is being raised for that purpose.

When it was completed in 1917, the concrete bridge replaced a wooden span as the Wisconsin channel crossing and approach to the high 1892 truss bridge. The two totally different spans (concrete arch and steel truss) were connected but had a ramp and stairway to the Latsch Island beach below. When the old steel truss span was removed in 1942 because the new highway bridge was completed slightly to the west, the metal from the main channel bridge went into "the war-effort." (Scrap metal, as we know, was recycled to make weapons during World War II.) However, the concrete bridge was left standing because of the lack of manpower at the time to complete the job of removal. This was the beginning of its second life. The concrete bridge, having crossed part of the island to meet the old metal structure, was left with its end "in the air" until 1947. It must have been used, however, during those five years with its concrete ramp and stairway as a means for getting down to the island "bathhouse" and park grounds from Wisconsin. In 1947 the arch bridge was dropped 320 feet to the ground, making the overall span more attractive and usable as a thoroughfare for cars. Again the bridge received a new life.

The 1,229-foot long bridge in Winona has twelve open-spandrel concrete arches crossing the Wisconsin channel and eleven interesting approach spans over Latsch Island. This southern deck-girder approach is a unique cantilever design.

"Each pair of girders spans two piers and is cantilevered beyond both piers to meet the next set of girders. The girders have straight lower edges between the supporting piers and half-arches on the cantilevered ends, giving the long approach the appearance of an alternating arch-girder-arch-girder rhythm." (Frame 1988, 1)

The main-span deck of this Mississippi River back channel bridge rests on spandrel columns and an arched curtain wall above the columns. In contrast, what appear on the approach to be solid arch spandrels are actually girders with heavy concrete brackets and inscribed panels. The second to the last bridge girder-arch as seen from Latsch Island Park is especially charming, with a wide paved path passing under it. This is a beautiful bridge and I am glad the city has voted to preserve it (its fourth life). It has not made the National Register list yet, though it has been considered for this award.

One of the attractive features of the structure is the neo-classic concrete railing. The top cap extends over the rest of the parapet, forming a horizontal band the full length of the bridge. The open-balustrade design consists of a wide post and simple cast-concrete balusters between. The vertical shadows caused by these "windows" break the strong horizontal line of the railing. The later-designed approach railing has five oval openings in a solid wall instead of balustrades.

The narrow deck of the Old Wagon Bridge has a walk on one side and a high curbing on the other. Cars may no longer drive on the deck. Only bikes now ride its roadway.

Two boys, about 10 years old, fishing on a dock east of the Wagon Bridge, answered my questions about the local bridges. Then they asked me the time because they were due home at four. "It is 3:15," I told them. Worried about being late, one of them ingeniously made a sundial by drawing a circle in the dirt and adding a stick in the center. This improvised dial would very adequately indicate the passage of time.

While I was taking the boys' picture from the boardwalk leading to the landing pier, a strange noise like a siren followed by a hissing sound in the marshes alongside the boardwalk made me think of snakes and helped me decide it was time for me to leave.

Use:
Formerly part of Highway 75; officially closed to use

Located:
Over the Mississippi River North Channel, between Latsch Island, Minnesota (formerly called "Island 72", now Agahaming Park) and Wisconsin

Style:
12-span reinforced-concrete open-spandrel continuous-rib-arch and 11 pairs of deck girder approach spans

Length:
Channel span - 35.5 feet clear
- 72 feet total
Total length - 1,229 feet

Width:
2 lanes, 17 1/2-foot roadway and one 5-foot sidewalk

Clearance:
32 feet MLW (approximately)

Date completed:
December 1917 (as a part of 1892 high bridge); saved when the high bridge was removed and in 1947 was brought to the ground; originally a wooden bridge built in 1887; ferry service before that

Designed by:
Unknown (but built by O'Hagen & Lake, with supervising engineer H.E.Wolf of St. Paul)

Bridge:
#4260 Minnesota

Owner:
City of Winona

Toll:
Until 1923 as a part of main span

Unique feat:
Potential for National Register nomination in Minnesota

"Old Wagon Bridge," Winona, Minnesota

Mary C. Costello

17

Main Channel Highway Bridge, Winona, Minnesota

Coming down from the tree-filled, 600-foot high bluff, one cannot help being awed by this long, flat expanse of city stretched out below. Winona parallels the island-riddled Mississippi River, with the bridge crossing it near the middle of town. "The city is named after the beautiful Sioux Indian princess, Wenonah, eldest daughter of Chief Wah-pah-sha," a peace-maker during the Sioux Indian Uprising of 1862. In the 1800's Winona became an important river and railroad transportation center.

My daughter had said I would like Winona and I did for a number of reasons. In town I saw a boy at a cardtable selling lemonade, which recalled old memories and made me feel akin. When I drove over the end-to-end bridges to Wisconsin, I discovered Latsch Island. On the island I found a clearing under trees from which I could view the main bridge and enjoy another kind of greeting. The "Winona," a white sternwheeler with yellow roof and red paddlewheel, passed by and, because of its wake, a mother and two baby ducks came into the little cove by me. They stayed long enough for me to sketch them. How could I not like this kind of reception?

The bridge looked beautiful in the sun-the part of it, that is, that I could see. The total length of the crossing here in Winona is 4,500 feet, including two bridges over the river and one over the train tracks. This silver-colored main channel structure is composed of twenty-three spans, nine of which are trusses. The middle three are through-trusses and the rest deck-trusses. On the far west end is a long concrete girder approach and to the east, out of my view, is a long earthen dike road crossing over the island.

In December of 1941, when World War II was declared, this new Winona Bridge was not finished. In fact, the steel superstructure had just started to rise on the bridge. However, construction was hastened, and it was completed in November of 1942, despite labor shortages, difficulties in obtaining materials, and high water.

The Mississippi crossings here date back to the 1800's. A ferryboat pulled by ropes made the crossing then. The first bridge was completed in 1891 and formally opened in July of 1892. It was a toll bridge from its inception until 1 December 1923, when the toll booth was burned in celebration of the bridge becoming free. Built in "the horse and buggy days," the bridge was not too dangerous until the automobile became a viable method of transportation. Then, at least, the Wisconsin end was considered "death road." Therefore, in 1916, the east end was rebuilt straight, with a new concrete deck-arch structure. It had a concrete road that formed a junction with Wisconsin Highway 35. Though in 1916 this new portion was "an approach to the high steel-trussed wagon bridge," today it is a free-standing bridge on its own. The steel portion of the old bridge was removed in 1942 and reused for the war effort, when the cantilever through-truss bridge was completed.

From my island cove, I heard sounds of a large hawk and the "ding, ding, clang, clang" of a train backing up behind me, or so I thought. In reality, it was Old Man River playing tricks--carrying the sound from the other side of the channel.

Use:
Wisconsin 54, Minnesota 43 and local traffic

Location:
Between Winona, Minnesota, and Wisconsin near Fountain City

Style:
3-span cantilever through-truss

Length:
Channel span - 420 feet clear
             - 450 feet total
Total length   - 2290 feet

Width:
2 lanes total 31 feet, plus one 5-foot sidewalk

Clearance:
64 feet MLW

Date completed:
21 November 1942; widened deck 1986; replaced 1892 truss span and earlier ferry

Designed by:
Minnesota DOT, Mr. Overholt, squad leader

Bridge:
#5900 Minnesota

Owner:
Minnesota DOT

Main Channel Highway Bridge, Winona

Mary C. Costello

19

North Channel Bridge, Winona, Minnesota

The North Channel Bridge is a structure of great simplicity. I viewed it from Latsch Island, opposite the main channel bridge, on a late August afternoon.

After crossing the first Winona Bridge, I saw a short earthen dike and then the "North Channel Bridge." The bridges, unlike the river here, go almost directly north and south, with Wisconsin on the north end. The state boundaries split this smaller channel; therefore, this bridge was built jointly by Minnesota and Wisconsin, though the federal government contributed half the expense.

I see little relationship between the two Winona bridges The North bridge has no high superstructure. Rather, it is low and straight with ten 101-foot long spans of concrete girders. The "n"-shaped concrete piers are short since no large boats use this back channel. They are very white, attractive and sturdy-looking. Under them appears to be a good spot for fishermen--quiet, undisturbed with the permanent piers to attract the fish, or at least so my brother thinks.

Standing behind the houses on the Latsch Island north shore, I watched the late afternoon sun cast shadows on the piers. The only sound I heard was a dog barking. The water was rippling so the reflections were not perfect. The tall silver lightpoles on either side of the bridge added height and repeated the curve of the pier. It was a pleasant, peaceful scene--the kind you would like to sit and enjoy, with feet dangling in the river.

Use:
Highway 54, Wisconsin, 43 Minnesota and local traffic

Location:
Between Winona Main Channel Bridge and Wisconsin

Style:
10-span prestressed concrete girder

Length:
Channel span - 97 feet clear
- 101 feet total
Total length - 1008 feet

Width:
2 lanes, plus one 9.5 foot sidewalk; 61 feet total

Clearance:
20 feet MLW

Date completed:
1997 remodeled to concrete deck girder span, widened deck; in 1975 new deck lighting;1942 steel deck girder span replaced the original 1891 bridge

Designed by:
Minnesota DOT, Bridge Section

Bridge:
#B-06-0752 Wisconsin, or #5930 Minnesota

Owner:
Minnesota and Wisconsin Departments of Transportation

North Channel Highway Bridge, Winona

Mary C. Costello

Wabasha Highway Bridge, Wabasha, Minnesota, SR 60

When word got around that there was a new bridge at Wabasha, only daredevils were unhappy. Completed in the fall of 1988, it replaced the 1931 nineteen-foot-wide bridge. The old span was "not for the timid," as a 1966 newspaper article stated. On the Wabasha side there was an unbelievable S-shaped approach before a single high 402-foot-long truss span. From this pinnacle, which was the height of the tall flour company elevators, the bridge flattened out, then descended into Wisconsin. Though many trucks had been stuck on it, there had been few accidents on the bridge--drivers were too scared to take any chances. From the foot of this narrow structure a road leads across 2 1/2 miles of dike and four Mississippi slough bridges into the town of Nelson, Wisconsin.

"The new bridge is another truss span...to keep the height down," remarked Quentin Crouch, Public Affairs Coordinator with the Minnesota DOT. "The piers would need to be extremely large to support a bridge without trusses. Then the support, such as a girder, would be below the deck, making the roadway still higher in order to keep the same clearance." The higher the bridge, he indicated, the steeper the descent or the more spread out the bridge would be. All in all, the answer was a truss span.

The method for erecting this 1988 bridge was unique to the Midwest. The 470-foot truss span was erected on falsework on two barges in a quiet spot out of the current and navigation channel. On October 14, 1987, when the Warren-Truss-designed structure was completed, the main river channel was blocked and engineers floated the barge sideways with its huge new span. It was higher than the piers, on purpose. To lower it, they flooded the barges. When it was perfectly positioned, they flooded the barges more and removed the falsework and barges completely. Everything went so smoothly that instead of taking one and a half or two days to accomplish, it took from 7:30 a.m. to 3:30 p.m. By 5:15, the first barge went under the new span. Some of the media arrived too late.

The new interstate bridge is wider than its predecessor but equally high, extending into Wisconsin to meet the same dike road from a slight angle--no other change. In Wabasha, however, the structure for the first time extends into town several blocks. For that reason, a "noise wall" was erected on the approach with an architectural surface treatment over Main Street. This textured double arch above the road looks like an ideal spot for a city logo, slogan or special event sign --though the DOTs might not agree.

The eagles and other wildlife of the Wabasha area had a part in this bridge. Because Lake Pepin is just about 3 miles to the north, its rushing waters seldom allow the river to freeze-over here at Wabasha. This means that wildlife, including the eagles, stay here all winter to feed. For that reason the bridge contract read that there would be "no noisy work between December l and March l." However, the weather was so mild in December 1986 that the river further north didn't freeze and the wildlife didn't come to Wabasha as usual. By special arrangement with the Fish and Wildlife Service, therefore, the men driving the pilings for the piers were able to continue work until December 25 and finished the pier foundations that sped the bridge by four months--a fine Christmas present to the area.

Use:
Minnesota 60, Wisconsin 25 and local traffic

Location:
Between Wabasha, Minnesota and Nelson, Wisconsin

Style:
A single steel through-truss plus concrete girder approaches

Length:
Channel span - 465 feet clear
               - 470 feet total
Total length   - 2,462 feet

Width:
2 lanes plus 8-foot shoulders for pedestrians and bikers

Clearance:
62 feet MLW

Date completed:
Fall 1988; replaced 1931 through-truss which charged a toll from 1931-1947; the 1931 span replaced a ferry service started in 1862

Designed by:
Toltz, King, Duval, Anderson & Associates, St. Paul

Bridge:
#79000 Minnesota, #B-6-0079 Wisconsin

Owner:
Minnesota and Wisconsin Departments of Transportation

State Road 60 Highway Bridge, Wabasha

Mary C. Costello

23

#1 "Pontoon Slough Bridge", Nelson, Wisconsin, SR 25

*T*his first Mississippi River backwater bridge is on the "Dike Road" from Wabasha to Nelson, over what is known as "Pontoon Slough." The name comes from the fact that this was the location of a railroad pontoon bridge until 1940. The area today is a National Wildlife and Fish Refuge and has a paved parking area provided to the east of the two-lane approach road.

The 1940 bridge added color to the area west of the high blue-green hills of Wisconsin. Its "open-box" railing, painted orange,--probably a primer--enlivened what would otherwise have been a very normal-appearing 8-span girder bridge. It would be nice if the bright color remained. Below the pure white concrete curb, deck and girder, are seven very angular piers. Each pier consists of a top rectangle in concrete with eight square precast concrete legs below. This is one of the few bridges so designed on the Mississippi; most piers are round pipe piles filled with concrete. The first and last supports are in line with the rest, but from the side, they angle forward or back. There are square downspouts below the road above each of the open spans, painted white to match the concrete girder. The heavy riprap at the ends under the bridge is intermingled with lavender and white thistles and coarse-leafed wildflowers.

The slough water was strewn with yellow-green algae, especially between the first and second piers, possibly scattered by boats going through. This would no doubt be a good fishing spot, but a sign close-by says, "No Fishing or Diving from the Bridge."

Use:
Minnesota 60 or Wisconsin 25 & local traffic

Location:
Between Wabasha, Minnesota, and Nelson, Wisconsin, over Pontoon Slough

Style:
8-span prestressed concrete girder

Length:
Channel span - 67 feet clear
            - 70 feet total
Total length - 558 feet

Width:
2 lanes, 28-foot roadway

Clearance:
10.5 to 11 feet MLW

Date completed:
1956; new concrete deck 1978; location of 1940 pontoon bridge

Designed by:
Wisconsin DOT, bridge section

Bridge:
#B-06-0024

Owner:
Wisconsin DOT

#1 Pontoon Slough Bridge, Nelson, Wisconsin

Mary C. Costello

25

#2 "Indian or Beef Slough Bridge," Nelson, Wisconsin, SR 25

*T*he second bridge on the "Dike Road" is also a deck girder made of concrete. It is described as almost a twin to the last bridge and close to the same length. Both have seven precast bents (stiff piers) 14 inches square, but the horizontal caps were cast-in-place. Indian or Beef Slough is longer by four inches than Pontoon Slough. It, too, has eight spans of 70-foot lengths, with the first and last slightly different.

When I arrived on the scene, the silver railings, called "single Z's" by the Wisconsin DOT, were being sandblasted and painted orange. These guard rails looked to me like a long square pipe with one side split in the middle and opened for fastening. White dust rose from the truck as it went along one lane doing the work. Two young women, one at either end of the bridge, directed cars onto the structure. It was hot work in the open sun with distant trees offering no relief.

The river here is more coated with yellowish-green scum, possibly because of a tree-filled island infringing on the south. This makes the water less free to flow. A few cars were parked on the Indian Slough Landing, to the east of the bridge. Through the parking area came two fishermen, about 9 and 10 years old. I asked if they had caught anything. Their answer was negative, but they didn't seem discouraged.-- There is always tomorrow!

Use:
Minnesota 60, Wisconsin 25 and local traffic

Location:
Between Wabasha, Minnesota, and Nelson, Wisconsin, over Indian Slough on Dike Road

Style:
8-span prestressed concrete girder

Length:
Channel span - 67 feet clear
              - 70 feet total
Total length - 562 feet

Width:
2 lanes, 28-foot roadway

Clearance:
10.5 to 11 feet MLW

Date completed:
1956

Designer:
Wisconsin DOT, Bridge Section

Bridge:
#B-06-0021

Owner:
Wisconsin DOT

#2 Indian or Beef Slough Bridge, Nelson

Mary C. Costello

#3 Slough Bridge, Nelson, Wisconsin, SR 25

*T*his is the third slough bridge between Wabasha and Nelson, Wisconsin. It is smaller than the last two by about 150 feet and has only five piers. There are other differences. The legs are round, 12 inches in diameter, and are concrete-filled metal to help break up ice. The concrete pier tops have a step on one side, unlike newer models. Most noticeably, the girder is steel instead of concrete. The railings are alike on these slough bridges, but this one was awaiting its turn to be painted when I saw it.

This #3 Slough Bridge (no name seems to have been given) was built in 1955, a year before the last two slough bridges, and has a "bituminous overlay," commonly called blacktop. A two-and-a-half foot curb is used on all four of these Highway 25 bridges. The banks underneath have both large and small riprap to prevent ground erosion. Wildflowers proliferate.

These "Nelson Bottoms," as the area is called, have thousands of acres of woods where deer abound--maybe more deer "harvested" each year than at any other place in the nation. These numerous Mississippi backwaters also produce fabulous walleyes, northern, and some of the biggest largemouth bass which hide under the lily pads. In fact, these backwaters are known as the "home of the small-mouth bass," says a Nelson promotion article.

The Wisconsin skyline was getting closer and the bluffs higher as I continued my journey. I was amazed at the amount of traffic on this road in the middle of the week and of the day--not heavy but constant between the two states.

Use:
Minnesota 60, Wisconsin 25 and local traffic

Location:
Between Wabasha, Minnesota, and Nelson, Wisconsin, on Dike Road

Style:
6-span steel deck girder

Length:
Channel span - 64 feet clear
           - 67 feet total
Total length - 407 feet

Width:
2 lanes, 28-foot roadway

Clearance:
11 feet MLW approximately

Date completed:
1955

Designer:
Wisconsin DOT, Bridge Section

Bridge:
#B-06-0020

Owner:
Wisconsin Department of Transportation

#3 Slough Bridge, Nelson

Mary C. Costello

29

4 Slough Bridge, Nelson, Wisconsin, SR 25

Nearest the small town of Nelson is the smallest of the two-and-a-half-mile-long series of slough bridges. Number 4 Slough Bridge, for want of a better name, is the last bridge in the series and the only one with a structure above the deck.

This Mississippi backwater bridge is a single span, 120 feet long, and is supported by a low "pony" truss in the Warren pattern. The railing consists of two steel bars secured to the side trusses. After over forty years of service the bridge looks very good, but like its companions, was in line for painting when I sketched it. Two signs on the west bridge entrance are for the safety of all. One says "No Fishing from Bridge" and the other "Reduced Speed Ahead, 25 MPH."

As I sketched, I saw a curious thing on the side of the bridge. Hanging from the bottom chord of the south truss were four lines going into the water--one thick, one knotted like a rope, and the other two fine, like fishing line. There was no one around, so it was a puzzle. How were they hung? Was it from a boat below, or by taking a chance on the truss itself? Was someone coming back or were the lines abandoned? These were my greatest problems at the end of the string of bridges, but ones I would have to leave for someone else to solve.

Use:
Minnesota 60, Wisconsin 25 and local traffic

Location:
Between Wabasha, Minnesota, and Nelson, Wisconsin

Style:
Single span steel pony truss

Length:
Channel span -   117 feet clear
                    120 feet total
Total length -   139 feet

Width:
2 lanes, 28-foot roadway

Clearance:
6-8 feet MLW approximately

Date completed:
1955

Designer:
Wisconsin DOT, Bridge Section

Bridge:
#B-06-0019

Owner:
Wisconsin Department of Transportation

#4 Slough Bridge, Nelson

Mary C. Costello

31

Dedicated by President Eisenhower in 1960, the Red Wing Bridge was named "Hiawatha" after the scenic Hiawatha Valley that extends from Hastings to LaCrosse, and the Indian legend made popular by Longfellow. Eisenhower referred to the original American Indian Chief Hiawatha, who lived 400 years ago and who started the first "United Nations" of the five Iroquois tribes to stop bloodshed. Popularly, however, the span is called the "Eisenhower Bridge."

The Hiawatha Bridge replaced the 1896 span, a 370-foot single truss span bridge. About 1,000 feet north of where that old bridge stood, this span begins. Starting high on Red Wing rocky terrain, the 1960 span crosses the present Canadian Pacific Railroad tracks and the main channel of the Mississippi, then descends gradually to a tree-covered island and Mud Lake Dike.

In constructing the new silver cantilever truss bridge, a unique method of hoisting the 400-ton, 288-foot center span was used. Three deck barges, lashed together, floated the center section into position, where it was raised sixty feet into the air by a pair of "two-drum skagit hoists." This took only thirty minutes, but it took three-and-one-half hours to "pin" the section into place with eight hanger pins, each twelve inches in diameter and weighing 1,250 pounds.

The through-truss here at Red Wing is a Warren truss design. The diagonal I-beams are solid, but the diagonal boxes have holes to permit bolted or riveted fabrication, plus inspection and painting, said H.R.Sandberg, chairman of the board of Alfred Benesch and Company, designers of the bridge. The horizontal I-beams have 2x5-inch holes for drainage of water. Another engineer informed me that the reason for holes is that beams in compression require a certain size but can be of less weight. The holes make the beams lighter.

The portal overhead-design could not be simpler than the V that spreads from one side of the Red Wing Bridge to the other, inside a rectangle. The piers, too, have a simple construction--an arched opening between rounded columns.

This bridge is in the town of Red Wing, named after the chief of the friendly Dakota Indians whom the American Government called Sioux. All members of this Indian dynasty wore the wing of the wild swan dyed scarlet; consequently, they were called "Wings of Scarlet" or Red Wing.

The town of Red Wing, at the head of Lake Pepin, the widest part of the Mississippi, is especially memorable for me because of "Barn Bluff," a solitary mountain of rock just rising out of the flat ground but shaped like a gigantic barn. Located by the edge of the river and the business district, Barn Bluff is also near the bridge. Barn Bluff is an inspiring sight not to be forgotten.

Sketching from Levee Park at 7 a.m., I found the river was peaceful and smooth as glass except for the closest edge. This is unusual. Maybe some of the peace desired by Chief Hiawatha has rubbed off on the river which flows under his bridge.

Use:
US Highway 63 and local traffic

Location:
Over the main channel between Red Wing, Minnesota, and Island 24 in Wisconsin

Style:
3-span through-truss cantilever

Length:
Channel span - 421 feet clear
            - 432 feet total
Total length - 1,631 feet

Width:
30 feet plus 2 1/2-foot safety walk on each side

Clearance:
64 feet MLW

Date completed:
November 1960; 1896 first bridge built here

Designed by:
Alfred Benesch and Company, Chicago

Bridge:
#9040 Minnesota, B-47-0027 Wisconsin

Owner:
Wisconsin and Minnesota Departments of Transportation

"Hiawatha" Highway Bridge, Red Wing, Minnesota

Mary C. Costello

33

Hager City, Wisconsin Highway Bridge, Back Channel, US 63

"*A* fresh-looking blue bridge in flat, green country" is how I remember this bridge. The area felt like what I, a city girl, think country on a summer morning should feel. It was clutter-free, fresh-smelling, and as green as any Irishman could ask. The island grounds were low and rolling with groups of trees here and there. Though the Wisconsin terrain, according to Warren's topography map, changed to great heights once it crossed the river, I didn't go any farther than the bridge.

This Hager City Bridge is over the Wisconsin Mississippi River Channel at the north end of the US 63 bridge crossing. The river at this point between Minnesota and Wisconsin is split into two distinct channels by a large island. Red Wing is at the south end, and Hager City, formerly called Trenton, is at the north end of the crossing.

The bridge is short, with seven spans of royal blue steel girders. The three main spans are deep and ridged rather than short and plain, as are the ends. All the piers are solid concrete slabs with both the upstream and downstream ends rounded and thicker than the middle.

The parapet is a low concrete wall with four-foot long openings at the bottom for drainage and one foot of concrete before the next six-inch high opening. Above the concrete are two heavy horizontal pipes in a curved steel support.

I had parked on a shaded hill at the end of the bridge. The traffic is fast in the area, and the hill blocked my view of oncoming cars out of Hager City. It seemed dangerous to take off from a standstill as I headed back to Red Wing. It was not very busy when I left, otherwise, I think I would have had trouble.

On the other side of the river channel, after one crosses the bridge, was a camping area. This island would seem an ideal secluded spot to spend a night, next to the placid Mississippi River, yet close to the cities via the attractive nearby bridge.

Use:
US 63 and local traffic

Location:
Between Hager City, Wisconsin, and Island 24 near Red Wing, Minnesota, over the Wisconsin Channel

Style:
7-span steel plate-girder

Length:
Channel span - 140 feet clear
          - 150 feet total
Total length - 739 feet

Width:
2 lanes

Clearance:
18 feet MLW

Date completed:
September 1960; replaced a 5-span through truss span; original bridge 1889, an elderly man remembers, or 1896 said Red Wing

Designed by:
Wisconsin DOT

Bridge:
#B-47-0023

Owner:
Wisconsin Department of Transportation

Back Channel Highway Bridge, Hager City, Wisconsin

Mary C. Costello

Hastings Vertical Lift Railroad Bridge, Minnesota

*O*ne of the three lift spans on the Mississippi is here at Hastings, Minnesota. (The others are at Hannibal, Missouri, and in St. Paul, Minnesota.) In 1871 a swingspan was built on this same spot, and part of that bridge is still incorporated in this 1981 bridge. On the opposite bank are 20 spans of railroad trestle which follow the river north.

Standing by a small memorial park an older couple were enjoying the river view. They informed me about the railroad bridge's previous style but disagreed as to when it was converted to a lift. It is amazing how time plays tricks on us. The couple, though, spoke with great pride and enthusiasm about their bridges. There was no need for my "bridge-promoting" here-the elderly natives were already "sold."

The Vertical-Lift Bridge has two flat-top spans at one end, all Warren,-style trusses, however, the lift span is longer than the other two put together. The top of the vertical lift span is slightly arched and again is almost twice the height of the other spans. In the center of the bridge is the old bridge tender's house that is used for lift machinery, while another one has been built on the ground for the person in control. The two tall lift-apparatuses are partly concrete and partly steel. The giant counterbalance inside of each is concrete, as are the top and an inner wall. The inside of the pulley wall is perpendicular but the outer or back wall is steel and angles at the bottom for support.

The new piers support these lift pulleys. The other piers are the 1871 originals of "magnesium limestone found in the vicinity, mostly from Barn Bluff at Red Wing," says Major General Warren in his 1878 book of the bridges of his time. The piers have five-and-a-half-foot triangular-shaped ends, both upstream and downstream, to break the ice and cut the water.

Warren, in his book, claimed that coming from the north, the single channel makes a sharp turn just before the Hastings Bridge--only 1,800 feet of warning, meaning potential disaster. It is a big surprise for riverboat pilots unfamiliar with the river. This situation remains the same today.

The Hastings Bridge was in its normal resting position as I sketched, and the only activity I saw consisted of a railroad engine, two boxcars and a caboose crossing the bridge. I would like to have seen the vertical-lift rise to allow a tall boat to pass here at one of the narrowest points on the navigable river (400 feet, according to Warren). However, boats were one thing I couldn't plan!

Use:
Canadian Pacific (former Soo Line) trains & Amtrak

Location:
Between Hastings, Minnesota, and Washington County, Wisconsin

Style:
Vertical lift through-truss

Length:
Channel span - 307 feet clear
          - 324 feet total
Total length - 1755 feet

Width:
Single track

Clearance:
60 feet MLW with span lifted; 21.9 feet otherwise

Date complete:
1981; replaces 1871 swingspan reconstructed in 1928

Designed by:
Howard, Needles, Tammen & Bergendoff

Bridge:
#L-268

Owner:
Canadian Pacific Railroad

Unique feat:
Location of one of Warren's original 15 bridges across the Mississippi in 1871

Vertical Lift Railroad Bridge, Hastings, Minnesota

Mary C. Costello

37

Hastings Highway Bridge, US 61, Hastings, Minnesota

I was impressed with my first view of the 1951 Hastings Bridge. As I came into town, I saw many trees and hills, and all of a sudden a giant silver "roller coaster" loomed ahead. It really made me sit up straight. What I actually saw was the arched superstructure for this through-truss bridge--with its high rolling 514-foot center and two dipping 226-foot side spans of Warren design trusses.

Uniquely, Sverdrup and Parcel designed both steel and concrete girders to support the approaches. The five north approach spans are supported by steel deck plate-girders, but the five shorter spans to the south are continuous concrete deck girders.

This Hastings bridge is a short distance west of where the famous "Old Spiral" structure formerly was located. Any article about the Hastings bridges must have a prelude about the old 1895 span. Some people claimed it was the only such spiral bridge in the world, and quite definitely it was the only one in the country. People came from all over the world to see it. The landmark bridge was built in this configuration in order for it to end in the business district rather than bypass it, as it would otherwise have done. The bridge arched over the main channel as any ordinary single through-truss span. However, at the end of that superstructure, over a corner of land 120 feet by 60 feet, the spiral started and made one complete circle. The descent was five feet for every 100 feet of distance. The Spiral Bridge was a third of a mile long, 18 feet wide, and had a 5-foot wide walk. The citizens of Hastings hated to see the old bridge torn down when the "new" bridge was built. (Anyone who would like to see this kind of ramp today can find one on the 1983 Luling, Louisiana Bridge described in Volume I.)

Trivia about the old bridge is interesting. At its opening, a horse-drawn buggy was the first vehicle to cross. Four people claim to have designed the bridge, one of them a convict in a state prison, but perhaps the most convincing is Lawrence H. Johnson. Near the end of its use (in the 1940's)

the bridge was so weak that a school bus exceeded the four-ton limit, and the children had to walk the bridge while the bus driver drove the bus across and met the children at the other end. Finally, in the bicentennial year, 1976, a Spiral Bridge Monument was erected on Sibley Street at the approximate site of the old bridge.

For 45 years before the Spiral Bridge was built, a rope ferry transported pedestrians, vehicles, and live-stock across the river. With the spiral bridge lasting until 1951, the residents were well served for 100 years before today's "giant roller coaster" bridge replaced it.

Use:
US 61 and local traffic

Location:
Hastings to Washington County, Minnesota

Style:
3-span continuous steel through truss, arched

Length:
Channel span - 350 feet clear
            - 502 feet total
Total length - 1,857 feet

Width:
32-foot road plus one sidewalk

Clearance:
63.8 feet MLW

Date completed:
November 1951; replaced the 1895 Spiral Bridge which replaced the 1850 rope ferry; soon will be replaced under the Truman-Hobbs Bill (to provide funds)

Designed by:
Sverdrup and Parcel

Bridge:
#5895 Minnesota

Owner:
Minnesota DOT

US 61 Highway Bridge, Hastings

Mary C. Costello

Inver Grove Heights Railroad/Highway Bridge, Minnesota

Wouldn't it be fun to own a Mississippi River Bridge? Wouldn't it be even more enjoyable to own an auto/train bridge and have it make money? This is exactly what Al Roman and Associates were able to do after the Rock Island Railroad Bridge closed in 1980.

Between Inver Grove Heights and St. Paul Park in Minnesota is a bridge purchased early on by the Chicago, Rock Island and Pacific Railroad for both cars and trains. It was interesting to me for many reasons. First, its owner, the CRI & P, was the railroad for which my father worked for forty years. Secondly, the only other bridge owned by that railroad across the Mississippi is in Davenport, Iowa, my home town. It, too, is a double decker of which there are a limited number on the Mississippi. Finally, the bridge was low and inviting, with people on board giving it a personal touch--one person collecting tolls, the other operating the swing span.

In the 1930's, it is said that when John Dillinger, bank robber and murderer, was attempting to escape from the police, he led the officers on a chase across this railroad bridge and then doubled back. The bridge opened for a boat after his second crossing, and thus he was able to elude his followers.

In March of 1980, this CRI & P Bridge closed because the railroad went bankrupt. People were forced to drive seven and a half miles north to I-494 or eighteen to twenty miles south to Hastings. For those needing to cross the river for work or other reasons, this was inconvenient until Mr. Roman bought the bridge and opened the roadway two and a half years later. Special legislation had to be passed in Minnesota for an individual to buy the bridge, and was the only bridge in Minnesota that charged a toll. The bridge was open twenty-four hours a day for vehicular traffic, and when the river was navigable, a bridge operator was on duty for the same length of time. Although the traffic had been reduced from 4000 cars that used it daily before the first closing,

about 2000 crossed it daily before this last shutdown.

Unusual features of the bridge are its overall style and railing. Many railroad bridges, have through-trusses for their trains but this bridge has through-trusses for cars only. Beyond the pin-connected rim-bearing Baltimore truss swingspan, the bridge is flat-topped, with two kinds of truss-es--Pratt at the St. Paul Park end, and Inver Grove Heights end has a Vierendeel truss pattern, said William Gardner, director of bridge operations. This railroad/highway bridge is certainly different. A wooden auto-guard railing on the lower deck, composed of three face boards and a flat cap, is not found on any other Mississippi vehicular bridge that I can recall.

Another distinctive element of this Minnesota bridge is the short St. Paul Park approach. At this threshold is a high plate-deck girder with fancy brackets below, mounted on very sturdy beams anchored in stone piers below. Entering from this end there is a sharp left turn onto the bridge, a straight ride across the swingspan to the other end which stops abruptly and forks to the right to exit so one must be ready. The end wall has taken many a hit. There was a two-ton limit and 20 mph speed limit which people didn't mind considering the bridge is only 18 feet wide. The train tracks have a deep, 54-inch deck plate-girder on the east end, continuing beyond the lower deck because the bridge is high. However, on the west end the bridge tracks exit on raised ground. The tollhouse is located on the ground at this west end approach.

Mr. Al Roman indicated on the telephone that although trains have not used his bridge since the Rock Island left the world of railroads, there is a chance that this situation could change in the future. Meanwhile, 75 cents per car kept his books in the black until the day in June 1999 when a bad beam was found and conflicting inspection results are keeping the bridge closed.

Use:
Formerly county road 38 and local traffic

Location:
Between Inver Grove Heights and St. Paul Park, Minnesota

Style:
Double deck through-truss swingspan, 18 through-truss auto spans and a deep deck plate-girder train deck

Length:
Channel span - 192 feet clear
             - 442 feet total
Total length - 1661 feet

Width:
2 lanes, 18 feet total and single train track above

Clearance:
19 feet MLW

Date completed:
1895; 1927 repairs; 1970 remodeled after deck fire; 1980 railroad bankrupt; 1982 refurbished for takeover; closed June 1999

Designed by:
Unknown, possibly Pittsburgh Bridge Company who built it

Bridge:
#5600 Minnesota

Owner:
J.A.R. Bridge, Incorporated

Toll:
75 cents until closed; in 1895, 25 cents for double team, driver and family

Unique feat:
Was only toll bridge in Minnesota; one of three privately owned Mississippi River bridges [2]

Railroad/Highway Bridge, Inver Grove Heights, Minnesota

Mary C. Costello

41

PART *T*WO

PART *T*WO
A Familyof Bridges

After plunging over a series of rapids and dropping sixty-five feet at St. Anthony Falls, the Mississippi takes on the character of a rushing river. This is where it all began- that is, the big river, the first bridge and the cities of St.Paul and Minneapolis. The Falls provided the power for the pioneer industries, saw milling and flour milling , and the first suspension bridge provided the means for transporting people, thus contributing to the growth of Minneapolis and St.Paul.

With 33 bridges in the Twin-Cities one can imagine, and correctly so, that the bridges are close together in the business districts. The river averages about 700 feet wide and the elevation of the sides varies. From Fort Snelling to "the Falls," the river has cut a gorge and the bridges are mostly cliff to cliff or in one case like a slide (Wabasha Street Bridge). From the Upper St. Anthony Falls Lock and Dam, the river is 420 feet higher above sea level than it is at St. Louis. This fact is easier to comprehend when one sees the U.S.Army Corps of Engineers' "Stairway of Water" chart illustrating the river with the lock and dam system "steps" to make the drop less drastic and problem-causing.*

Beginning with the 1883 Stone Arch Span, railroad bridges comprise over a third of all the Twin-Cities bridges. However, it is the unusual and attractive highway bridges of the 1920's that "stand out" for their design, unique to the area. The open-spandrel reinforced-concrete arch spans dominate the bridges in the metropolitan area and are "the first really sophisticated American program of concrete highway bridge construction," says David Plowden, bridge historian. He has appropriately given them the title, "A Family of Bridges."

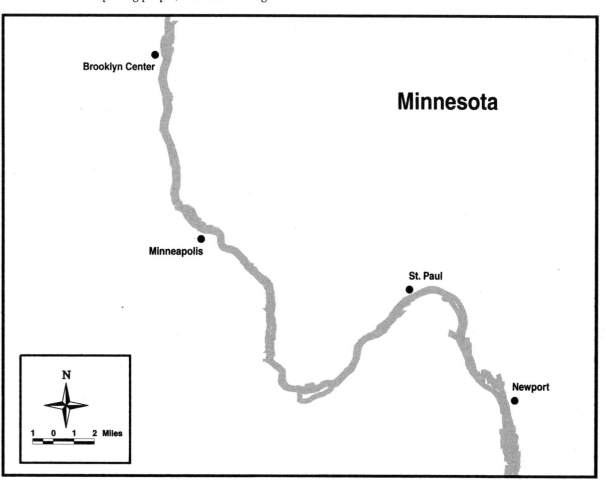

*See chart, in appendix.

**Within the span of this map there are 36 bridges -- 23 in Minneapolis (Ford Parkway through Camden) and 10 in St. Paul (the Beltway through Fort Snelling)

45

Newport, Minnesota, "Wakota" Highway Bridge, I-494

*T*his I-494 Bridge is located between two St. Paul sub-urbs, South St. Paul and Newport. It is a part of the highway system that loops the Twin Cities. When built in 1982, the bridge was located opposite the C.M.St.P. & P. Railroad Depot in Newport, but today has an industrial area at both ends--in South St.Paul the span faces a power plant, pumping station, and warehouse.

The name "Wakota" is a blend of the names of the two counties--Washington and Dakota--on either side of the span. Originally and for about 20 years until 1979, people called the span the "Stockyard Bridge" or "Stinky Bridge" because of the closeness of the stockyards and the water sewerage treatment plant which created an unpleasant odor. That all changed in 1979 when both the stockyards and treatment plant were removed.

As I looked at its light blue-grey profile, I saw nothing unusual about the I-494 bridge. This is the fifth and last single tied-arch bridge on the Mighty River going north. The plate girders on either side of the superstructure curve gently underneath, being deeper at the pier area for extra strength.

The Newport Highway Bridge has two kinds of piers. The piers at the ends of the arch consist of four tall, evenly-spaced rectangular columns of concrete connected at the top and bottom. The rest of the piers are arranged differently-- one pillar on either end and two close together below the middle of bridge roadway, thus leaving two rectangular open-ings.

A dramatic change is planned--two new bridges are to be built here soon to replace the "Wakota." The DOT says the present bridge cannot take care of the increasing traffic on I-494 and therefore will be replaced. Construction will start in 2001 or 2002. The new girder spans will have four lanes each way, with the first one taking six years to built. At the time it is completed, the old bridge will be torn down and the first span used till the second is completed.

Use:
Highway I-494 traffic

Location:
Between Newport and South St.Paul

Style:
A single steel tied-arch span with 11 plate-girder spans

Length:
Channel span - 407 feet clear
⠀⠀⠀⠀⠀⠀⠀⠀⠀ - 421 feet total
Total length - 1,870 feet

Width:
4 lanes, 48 feet total with 3-foot sidewalk on each side

Clearance:
64 feet MLW

Date completed:
November 1959; 1988 acceleration lanes rebuilt, widened and overlaid deck

Designed by:
Sverdrup & Parcel, St. Louis

Bridge:
#5993 Minnesota

Owner:
Minnesota DOT

Unique feat:
First tied-arch bridge in the state; named in a contest

"Wakota" Highway Bridge, Newport, Minnesota

Mary C. Costello

Union Pacific Railroad "Beltline" Bridge, by Pig's Eye Lake

*T*he city does not intrude on the river here--nor hardly does the bridge. This short swingspan has many trees, weeds, and dead timber close by. On one side of the river the "Hoffman Bridge" (as the railroad calls it) is several blocks from the nearest road, and on the other side is miles from anything but the Sewage Treatment Plant and Pig's Eye Road. I tried both approaches.

Starting in St. Paul first, I took hours driving, asking at a highway cafe, and finally parking my car and walking. There were many train tracks to cross, a fence to go through, then a curved track to follow toward the river. The way was mostly sand and gravel and only a path in places. At one point there was a choice of routes, though either one would have taken me to the bridge. When I arrived, there were two cars and uncontrolled greenery all around. It was time for a bridge-tender shift change--the reason for two cars. On the bank in front of me were washed-up trees looking like huge white bones. The bridge consisted of a flat-top span, a swingspan and over backwater eight girder spans hidden by undergrowth. There was a long wooden guard pier or fender running parallel to the river channel to protect the large mechanized swingspan pier and the swingspan itself, when it is open for a boat to go through. On the South St. Paul side of the river, running parallel with it, was a guide fence or "sheer boom," which guides the river traffic into the proper channel when passing through the drawspan. Closer to land was a sheer fence.

As I sketched, the main span slid open to let the "Sophie Rose," a fast barge with only one tow, sail through. The bridge operator certainly had been communicating by radio because there was no audible sound that a boat was coming, though the operator could have seen her. The experienced pilot knew well what to do and "ran the bridge span" free and easy.

The "Beltline" turnspan (so called because it is near the St. Paul city limits) is a Warren truss on an octagonal center pier. The color was a greyed-black basically, though patched up, with the tender's house the same color and appearing small. The other piers are stone, rectangular in shape, and become bigger at the bottom. There were barges all along the opposite shore.

On the way back to my car, trains were active on the many tracks. A diesel, engine #4146, pulling three freight cars, crossed my path, but it was not headed for the bridge.

Closeby was Pig's Eye Lake, the largest rookery for black-crowned night herons in the country, (according to Breming and Watson in "A Gathering of Waters") but I saw none of the large slender birds.

It has been said that this is the area in which the city of St. Paul started. A man with one eye was evicted from where he was living and started a tavern or saloon here. People settled around his place of business and it became known as "Pig's Eye," the first name of the city.

Use:
Union Pacific trains

Location:
Between South St.Paul (suburb) and St. Paul, by Pig's Eye Road and Hoffman Avenue

Style:
A through-truss swingspan, a single flat-top span and eight girder spans on the East over two islands and backwater

Length:
Channel span - 179 feet clear
                      - 401 feet total
Total length   - 1275 feet

Width:
Single track, 18 feet

Clearance:
20 feet MLW

Date Completed:
September 1982, a reconstruction of the Chicago Great Western Railroad; rebuilt earlier in 1925 and again in 1951 after flood; originally St.Paul Bridge and Terminal Railway Bridge built in 1910

Designed by:
Sverdrup and Parcel, St. Louis

Bridge:
#K-526.82A

Owner:
Union Pacific Railroad

Union Pacific "Beltline" Railroad Bridge, St. Paul   Mary C. Costello

Lafayette Street Highway Bridge, St. Paul, SR 56

Of the 33 Mississippi River Bridges in the Twin Cities, this Lafayette Street Bridge is the second longest, being exceeded by the Washington Avenue Bridge, which is 6,336 feet. It is constructed above the old St. Paul railyards to the city's new suburbs and industrial parks. The bridge crosses major highways, principal streets, and several warehouses, as well as Old Man River.

In building the new, the old is sometimes sadly lost. This is what happened in St. Paul. In preparing the nearby approach streets for the Lafayette Street Bridge, an experimental bridge built in 1905 by C.A.P. Turner was removed. It was a flat slab resting upon mushroom-capped columns for support, a design Turner invented. The innovative bridge wasn't over the Mississippi; rather, it was to carry Lafayette Avenue over the Soo Lines Railroad. However, this span was destroyed to make way for the Lafayette Bridge approach. This is the second time we've heard of Mr. Turner. In Volume I he designed the old Moline/Arsenal Bridge. I expect to see more Turner bridge designs in Minneapolis.

I stood next to a foundry that had stacks of metal concave sheeting and other metal forms and strips. From here I could see a stone wall under the bridge on the other side of the river, built to keep the "Roaring Monster" out when it goes on a rampage.

The bridge is a medium-blue steel girder, a girder three times deeper where the bridge crosses the river, since this is where greater strength is needed. There are four hammerhead piers (or, as I call them, "he-man" piers) under the deep girder. Only two are in the water. The 24 other piers are longer to make up for the thinner girders above them. Designed in the shape of double T's, these piers have narrower legs. I took three end-to-end pictures to try to catch the whole bridge, but even then I could not capture the entire long structure.

Above the solid but ridged concrete railing are tapered light poles with only one arm projecting over the road. They look on some photos to be so close that if laid end to end they would equal the length of the bridge.

Really, they would equal only less than a third. Perhaps they are not closer than most, but the long bridge has room for more lights.

The first bridge inside the Twin Cities coming from the south, the Lafayette Street Bridge rises over all that one might like to bypass to arrive at a spot about a mile from St. Paul's business district and State Capitol. The bridge serves its purpose well.

Use:
US 52, SR 56 and 3 plus city traffic to suburbs

Location:
East Seventh Street to Airport Road west

Style:
29-span welded steel plate-girder

Length:
Channel span - 350 feet clear
- 362 feet total
Total length - 3375 feet

Width:
4 wide lanes, 4-foot median, 67 feet total

Clearance:
51 feet MLW

Date completed:
November 1968; widened and new deck in 1992

Designed by:
Ellerbe Associates, St. Paul

Bridge:
#9800 Minnesota

Owner:
Minnesota DOT

Layfayette Street Bridge, St. Paul

Mary C. Costello

Robert Street Highway Bridge, St. Paul, US 52

At its opening, the Robert Street Bridge was suggested as a "Gateway to St. Paul," the way the St. Louis Arch is a "Gateway to the West." It certainly is attractive in its own right. The center arch is askewed on the river, and other bridges, buildings, and an island surround the Robert Street Bridge so closely that they obscure its view, at least in part, so that the title "Gateway" never was accepted.

The Robert Street Bridge is a beautiful 264-foot "rainbow arch span," the largest of its kind in Minnesota, and it cost $2.5 million when built between 1924 and 1926. The designer had a multitude of concerns. The bridge had to clear not only Old Man River's boat traffic but also a railroad bridge underneath, the tracks to the city's Union Depot, and a busy manufacturing plant. The engineers stated, "No money has been spent to beautify the bridge." The design was aesthetically complete in itself.

Formally opened on 6 August 1926, the bridge was named in honor of Captain Louis Robert (1811-1874), a fur trader who arrived in St. Paul in 1843 and joined in its political and business life. The bridge's massive concrete arch is on both sides of the road and is therefore called "half-through." There is no overhead connection because of the shallow depth of the side arches. This style structure is one of a kind on the Mississippi River. According to Compton's Encyclopedia, 1976, Volume 4, "In the half-through arch the road cuts through the arch. Its middle section is hung from the arch and its outer sections are supported by the arch." As this indicates, the heavy concrete arch hangers suspend the center platform of the bridge. The hollow arch appears to be made up of separate rectangular sections of concrete, each of which has three little openings that look like windows and add to the textural effect of the giant structure. They are just indentations in the concrete, I am told; if they were windows, however, what a view would be possible!

There are seven other spans called deck arches. Each span has an arch supporting the deck above. The open spaces above these arches, called spandrels, contain four straight concrete posts which add interesting shadows and design.

The next most attractive feature of this Robert Street Bridge is its piers. The two center ones, really gigantic rectangular columns, have for decoration three grooves topped with a single large embossed circle in art deco style. The smaller piers have two grooves and a smaller circle with the arches fitting snuggly between.

The guard rail on the bridge is very attractive. It has solid concrete posts ending in a protruding scroll. Each post coincides with spandrel columns below and on the main span with the hangers above. What a well-planned design! Between the posts are a top and bottom concrete rail, spaced out with short, sturdy concrete balusters and a concrete cross with a center diamond-shaped opening.

The original bridge on the site, built in 1886, was a narrow seventeen-span iron truss structure which had to be removed to provide clearance below for tracks entering the newly raised and just-completed Union Depot rail yard.

I was sorry to find the one-of-a-kind arch of the Robert Street Bridge so hidden from view on the busy west side because it is one of the beauties of the Mississippi River "bridge world." I would like to think of it as the "Gateway Bridge into the Upper Mississippi River."

Use:
City and US 52 traffic

Location:
Connects St. Paul and South St. Paul

Style:
17-span concrete half-through arch plus seven deck arches

Length:
Channel span - 158 feet clear
     - 264 feet total
Total length - 1,429 feet

Width:
4 lanes plus two 9 1/2-foot sidewalks, 80 feet total

Clearance:
62 feet MLW

Date completed:
August 6, 1926; replaced 1886 iron truss span; new deck and railing in 1989

Designed by:
Toltz, King & Day

Bridge:
#9036 Minnesota

Owner:
Minnesota DOT

Unique feat:
Only half-through arch bridge on the Mississippi River

Robert Street Bridge, St. Paul

Mary C. Costello

53

Chicago & Northwestern, Now Union Pacific Lift Bridge, St .Paul

*T*his is only one of three vertical-lift bridges on the whole Mississippi River, formerly owned by the Chicago & Northwestern Railroad, now by the Union Pacific.

In 1885 there was a swingspan bridge in this location, but in 1913 it was replaced by the present bridge to provide for heavier railroad equipment. Then in 1925 the north end of the bridge was raised 16 feet in order to tie in with new high-level tracks in the nearby depot yard. It is at this point today that the railroad bridge with a 30 degree skew goes under the Robert Street Bridge before continuing north.

This bridge has eight spans with one 192-foot long vertical lift span to provide clearance for river shipping. The south approach has plate-girder spans, each 79 feet long. The vertical lift is electrically operated, designed with a possible 45-foot elevation in 1963. By 1973, however, there was a "37-foot limit--no more." Age was showing. Just as old people cannot move so well as they did when younger, so this bridge was not able to rise so high with its aging parts.

While I was there, the bridge lifted on the 105-foot high towers and a barge passed through. The bridge operator was in a small red building with blue-green trim on the very top of the liftspan. Just to arrive at work meant he had to walk a narrow plank catwalk on a trestle and then climb two flights of stairs...all high over the river.

"He throws a lever that activates a warning signal below to stop approaching trains before he raises the bridge," wrote Craig Borck of the bridge tender, Louis Bouska. (27 May 1973,"St. Paul Sunday Pioneer Press")

I don't remember hearing the warning signal, nor do I know if it would carry over the water to Navy Island, where I first observed the bridge. Radio communication is used extensively between bridge and boat, but I could also imagine the towboat pilot signaling with one long blast of his horn and the bridge operator answering in the same fashion, meaning that the bridge could be opened. With either communication method, within five minutes the bridge would be raised by two General Electric 20-horsepower crane motors counterweighted by two 220-ton concrete rectangles located in the towers. The weights come down when the bridge rises. If the bridge cannot be opened because a train is on it or within the block, four short blasts tell the boat captain to wait.

One can watch from the Robert Street Bridge walk or from Kellogg Boulevard as the lift of the Union Pacific Bridge rises and falls to let large boats through, which could be as many as 18 to 20 times a day.

Use:
Union Pacific Railroad

Location:
In St. Paul, near and partly under the Robert Street Bridge

Style:
A vertical-lift bridge with plate-girders on each side

Length:
Channel span - 158 feet clear
             - 192 feet total
Total length - 940 feet

Width:
Single track, 21.9 feet

Clearance:
72 feet MLW

Date completed:
21 April 1913; reconstructed in 1925; in 1885 a swingspan stood here

Designed by:
Waddell & Harrington, Kansas City, Missouri
Bridge:
#L332

Owner:
Union Pacific Railroad 1996; originally Chicago Great Western then the Chicago & Northwestern Railroad

Unique feat:
One of only three vertical-lift spans on the Mississippi River (others at Hannibal, Volume 1, #38, and Hastings, Volume 2, #17)

Union Pacific Lift Bridge, St. Paul

Mary C. Costello

53

*O*bviously the name,"Raspberry Island" came about when the island was first acquired from the Indians because of the great number of raspberry bushes growing on it. The name has remained ever since even though during WWII the Navy Department had a building on the island and people started calling it "Navy Island." The name was never officially changed.

This attractive though small bridge is the only land-link for vehicles and pedestrians to Raspberry Island. Unusual as it sounds, the bridge is handicapped accessible. The span has ties with the Harriet Island Trail System and River Walk.

Raspberry Island Bridge is a 5-span concrete slab bridge only 325 feet long, over a 300-foot backwater. The bridge has no beams but a cast-in-place concrete deck 42 inches thick at the piers and 18 inches thick elsewhere. The accessories, if they can be called that, are known designs in this area. The luminaries are the single St. Paul standard globe style mounted on each pillar above a pier, and one large with four smaller globes at each bridge entrance. The ornamental railings are the St.Paul standard railing design with posts and balustrades painted a wine color to coordinate with mother-bridge above's trim. The entire bridge is painted "Antique Lace," an off-white to stand out from the Wabasha Bridge's warmer color.

On Raspberry Island itself (shaped like a boat), there are always activities to enjoy--a new glass arch bandshell, the Minnesota Boat Club, established in 1870, a rowing club in existence since 1850, fishing (big northern pike are caught by the bridge), the St. Paul Yacht Club, an attractive park and even stairtowers to climb to the Wabasha Bridge--a wonderful Sunday afternoon outing for the family.

The bridge and island were not always so glorious and glamorous. The first span over the back channel was a truss which was washed out before 1949. On my first visit to the spot I saw the remodeled bridge-a 12-span single-lane white steel beam bridge used mostly by boaters or fishermen. There was a plank floor and raised boardwalk on one side for pedestrians. It had a wooden railing and braced pilings for piers. If two cars met, I'm sure one had to back up. I parked elsewhere.There was a pretty grassy park in the middle of the island with parking, but I did not venture that far.

Today's bridge is a tremendous improvement along with the many new facilities on the island to enjoy. St.Paul is to be commended.

Use:
Access to Raspberry Island Park and Minnesota Boat Club

Location:
St. Paul, Minnesota, south bank downtown

Style:
5-span continuous concrete slab

Length:
Channel span - 70 feet clear
               - 75 feet total
Total length   - 325 feet

Width:
Two lanes, 27.3 feet, people can walk

Clearance:
20.8 feet MLW

Date completed:
November 2001; replaced one-lane steel beam span remodeled in 1969; built as timber beam, 1949; original truss span date unknown

Designed by:
City of St. Paul, Public Works Department

Bridge:
#62580

Owner:
City of St. Paul

Raspberry Island Bridge, St. Paul

Mary C. Costello

Wabasha Street Bridge, St.Paul, Minnesota

Spectacular! is the word to describe the new Wabasha Street Bridge in St. Paul. It serves the needs of almost everyone--the river watcher with its six lookouts; the bikers with a bicycle lane in each direction; the street person with a plaza at each end; young couples with the dramatic lighting on the bridge and grand opening parties they have had; walkers with the 12-foot walkways; exercisers with the stairtowers down to the island below; artists with the ornamental grillwork and overall pallet of colors; as well as for the average motorist crossing the Mississippi on the split road.

Kevin Nelson, Project Manager for the Wabasha Street Bridge, gave me a tour of the new span. He pointed out the elegant red concrete walk in pattern--not painted or surfaced but the color of the cement. He explained that the Sandstone Yellow color of the walls of the bridge, rock like poured walls and plaza were painted to even-out the concrete color. Accent colors like the green patina color repeats the St. Paul Cathedral spires in town and the terra cotta roof color seen on houses in the area are used on the railing and the very modern bridge luminaries. At night the girders and piers are lit and search-lights signal special events at the bridge. I was very disappointed that I could not make the September 12th party which was the third to be so held. Later the stairtowers were added and the lookout points completed with safe railings all around. I was very impressed.

The Wabasha Street Bridge was named after the Indian Chief indirectly (the same as mentioned in Bridge #10) and directly after the street on which it is located. The history of the St. Paul reveals that in 1850 a private ferry carried settlers across the Mississippi River to Indian territory which later became West St. Paul. The first bridge was completed here in 1859. It was a Howe Truss span of wood and iron, 18 feet wide, with a toll charged at first to help make bond interest payments. By 1876 the channel span was remade of iron and in 1890 half of the bridge was replaced. It was another ten years before the southern half was redone and 1955 was the last time the bridge was remodeled before the present bridge was constructed. The old truss span served the city well for almost 100 years--removed in 1996 as it was showing signs of age. What has replaced it certainly shows a new era of time when crossing the river is almost secondary to the pleasures of the citizenry.

Use:
Local traffic

Location:
Between St.Paul's West side and the downtown business district

Style:
3-span segmental concrete box girder

Length:
Channel span - 341 feet clear
　　　　　　 - 396.5 feet total
Total length - 1252.5 feet

Width:
59 feet each bridge, including a 12-foot walk per bridge

Clearance:
52 feet MLW

Date completed:
November 2001, useable in 1998; replaced a 7-span cantilever deck truss remodeled and widened 1955; original bridge 1859; in 1876 replaced an iron span; the north half of bridge replaced in 1890, and the south half in 1900; used a ferry in 1850

Designer:
TKDA

Bridge:
#62555

Owner:
City of St. Paul

Unique Feat:
The location of one of the first 15 bridges to cross the Mississippi River. Bridge acts as a St. Paul "entertainment center" when closed to traffic--plazas at ends for bands; room for dancing and refreshment booths.

Wabasha Street Bridge, St. Paul

Mary C. Costello

Smith Avenue "High Bridge," St. Paul, Minnesota, SR 149

A task force of local citizens had a big hand in planning this St. Paul Bridge. The 1986 Smith Avenue Bridge has a single "inverted arch" of steel below the deck. This was chosen over concrete because of less expense and shorter construction time. Besides the center arch, there are two half-arches starting from the same center pier whose outward thrust helps carry the rest of the bridge. Standard plate-girders serve the remainder of the bridge, all of which is painted brown. The bridge has two 12-foot traffic lanes, each with an 8-foot shoulder and two 7-foot walkways--two because the citizens could not agree which single-side would be best. A unique feature is a small overlook at both ends, using iron railings from the old bridge. I found it interesting that the old piers could not be used because they didn't go deep enough and wouldn't support the weight of the new bridge, which is twice as heavy as the old. The center arch was cantilevered out from the river piers until the last segment was put into place.

The replaced 95-year-old "High Bridge" represented the "highest attainment of engineering skills" in its day. It had a 4% grade (the same as the new span) and rose 123 feet above low water. It was a deck-truss pin-and-eye-bar type construction--a type that has a tendency to fall down, though this one survived almost 100 years. In fact, the old 28-span St. Paul bridge was a half-mile long and one of the oldest bridges of its type in the country. The spindly, fragile-looking, wrought-iron bridge had a long, interesting history. In 1901, it was learned that one of the bridge's center 250-foot spans was slipping from its foundation. It was repaired secretly at a cost of $200 so as not to alarm the citizens.

In 1904 a tornado blew part of the old bridge down, which revealed that parts had been improperly bolted together. The destroyed parts were rebuilt, and the old Smith Avenue High Bridge survived until 1958 when extensive renovation was done, including a new deck. In 1977, the old High Bridge was closed 6 weeks for repairs. The intention was to leave the span in place until the last few months before the new bridge was completed, but safety required that it be removed in July of 1984.

Interesting trivia concerning the new Smith Avenue Bridge are as follows: the decorative lampposts have double lights and round milky-white glass shades; the pier footings were placed using a special cement mix that dries underwater; the two underwater piers cost $2 million each; and workers were paid more than $20 an hour compared with 34 cents an hour for the earlier 1889 bridge. The deck is of a salt-resistant concrete. To prevent cracking under stress the I-beam tension ties have steel cables encased in tubes, two above and two below the beams. To accommodate the lengthening and shortening caused by the hot and cold temperatures, the steel piers flex up to 21 inches on the north end of the bridge and 15 inches on the south. Because of all the above, the engineers say the 1987 bridge is "one of the most remarkable structures built in many years." To enhance its beauty and help celebrate its opening, decorative lights were added to the graceful steel arch and lighted for the first time in late July of 1987. The citizen task force along with many others can take a bow for a job well done on this newest Smith Avenue High Bridge.

Use:
Local & SR 149 traffic

Location:
Between Cherokee Heights and West 7th Street in St.Paul

Style:
One deck-tied steel box-arch, two half-arches and eight plate-girder spans

Length:
Channel span - 440 feet clear
- 520 feet total
Total length - 2760 feet

Width:
Two lanes 12 feet each, 8-foot shoulders & two 7-foot sidewalks

Clearance:
149 feet MLW (high because of typography)

Date completed:
July 1987; replaced the old deck-truss High Bridge of 1889, which was struck by a tornado in 1904, had wooden deck replaced by concrete 1958; 1888 first span

Designer:
Strgar, Roscoe, Fausch, Inc. of Minneapolis

Bridge:
#62090 Minnesota

Owner:
Minnesota DOT

Unique Feat:
1889 span was on National Register of Historic Places; in 1888 Andrew Carnegie Keystone Bridge Company sent the bridge to St.Paul in a million pieces with a 388-page instruction book.

Smith Avenue Bridge, St. Paul

Mary C. Costello

"Omaha Swingspan" Railroad Bridge, St. Paul

*T*he "Omaha Swingspan" is the most unusual bridge on the Mississippi River. The original design was the normal balanced and symmetrical moveable span. Once the bridge was built, however, the person who owned the property adjacent to it did not want the swingspan to cross his land. His objection resulted in the owner's removing most of one end of the turnspan and replacing it with the concrete shell to keep the span balanced. J.W. Iwinski, former Assistant Chief Engineer of Structures for the Chicago & Northwestern Railroad, (now Union Pacific) called the concrete shell a "bobtail".

The Omaha Swingspan has a Pratt designed through-truss turnspan and girder support the rest of the way. In 1947, a 55-foot steel girder replaced 50 feet of timber trestle on the south side of the bridge where the counterweight rests.

Ten of the piers are alike--solid concrete rectangles with pointed ends. Only the turnspan pier is different; it is octagonal and shorter because the turning mechanism at the top makes up the difference. The long sheer-fence on the north side of the turnspan is carefully built of wooden beams and long wooden poles, some driven straight down in the water and some angled for support. This fence is to protect that main pier and its important mechanical parts.

I arrived on the isolated bridge scene about 7:50 a.m. The valley on both sides of the river make the railroad crossing straight and easy. For a while all I heard were birds singing until a woman in a car arrived. At first I thought she was delivering a lunch--she carried a brown paper bag. Suddenly I realized she was the replacement bridge-tender. From the operator who was leaving, I received information about the history and the use of this particular bridge. He said that there is an average of ten trains a day crossing, but they no longer keep schedules. He also added that the bridge acquired its name because originally the western destination of the trains was Omaha.

The original railroad crossing, at or near this location above Pickerel Lake, was completed in 1869 by the St. Paul and Sioux City Railroad Company. The wooden Howe Truss span crossed at an angle as does the Omaha Bridge today. The early bridge was an 8-span drawbridge referred to as the "St. Paul Railroad Bridge" in G.K. Warren's book entitled Report on Bridging the Mississippi River Between St. Paul, Minnesota, and St. Louis, Missouri when there were only 15 bridges spanning the great river.

The draw was "opened and closed by men with levers,"[1] reported Warren, page 71. After just 6 years, because of decay in the original pine chords, the whole superstructure, except for the draw, was replaced in 1876-77. The reason is said to be "the want of care in the timber selection and the use of oak wedges in the pine chords. The acid of the sap in the oak wedges is said to have caused decay in the pine chords." Warren also notes that the right draw was unsafe, never used by steamers descending the river, because of a sandbar that had formed. All of this is interesting background material on today's bridge that is so unique.

Use:
Union Pacific Railroad formerly Chicago and Northwestern Railroad

Location:
Between end of Randolph Avenue and James Street in St. Paul, Minnesota

Style:
A "bobtail" swingspan and ten girder spans

Length:
Channel span - 160 feet clear
        - 185 feet total
        Swingspan is 260 feet, with 75 feet on short side
Total length - 1055 feet

Width:
One track

Clearance:
22 feet MLW

Date completed:
1916, replaced 1877 wooden span; 1947 the 55-foot girder replaced 4-span timber trestle; made bobtail May 1948; original 1869 bridge was wooden swingspan

Designer:
I. F. Stern, Chicago

Bridge:
#15

Owner:
Union Pacific; formerly (before 1996) Chicago and Northwestern Railroad; when built Chicago, St. Paul, Minneapolis and Omaha Railroad; orignal 1869 bridge owner St. Paul and Sioux City Railroad Company

Unique feat:
Location of one of the first 15 bridges across the Mississippi River

Union Pacific "Omaha Swingspan" Railroad Bridge, St. Paul

Mary C. Costello

63

Lexington Avenue Bridge, St. Paul, I-35E

*O*ne of the most hidden Twin City Bridges is the Lexington Avenue Bridge. It can be seen from Highway 13 only in stolen glimpses. From the Yacht Club in Lilydale where I stood the silver span was quite visible. Called the "standard variety interstate bridge," it appeared very attractive and dramatic in the early morning sunlight, with its streamlined-appearing, welded plate-girder. The strong light rays made the structure look fresh and white in front of the olive greens and dark shadows of the trees, the cloud-free blue sky, and the crisp reflections in the placid river. In reality the bridge is riveted steel--a silver color.

The bridge piers are composed of two sections--a concrete lower section almost square and narrower than the upper section. It is this top section that gives the bridge character--like a flat-chested human upper-torso. The bridge's plate-girders over the river are straight and deep, but over ground they are less than half that depth. The important guard railings along the sides are more open than many railings, with pipes and concrete posts about six feet apart. .

The Lexington Avenue area citizens were upset about this bridge being built because of the impact of trucks on their neighborhood. It was a nice residential area. Their fierce opposition temporarily stalled the construction beyond the bridge's northern abutment that would connect with I-35. Whether related or not, today there is a 45 mph speed limit on the bridge.

The "Joe, Al, Jim II Shiely" towboat pushed barges of sand and gravel past me and went to pick up an empty barge docked on the side. It was interesting to watch the process. I didn't feel I was in a big city at all while I was there.

Use:
Local traffic and I-35E

Location:
Between West 7th Street in St. Paul and the Village

Style:
7-span riveted steel plate-girder

Length:
Channel span - 330 feet clear
- 340 feet total
Total length - 1406 feet

Width:
Two 29-foot roadways or 4 lanes with a 4-foot median

Clearance: 64 feet MLW

Date completed:
December 1964; connection to I-35E in 1990; plan is to replace the bridge with a wider one-no date given

Designer: Walter Butler Engineering Company, St. Paul

Bridge:
#9330 Minnesota

Owner:
Minnesota DOT

Lexington Avenue Bridge, St. Paul

Mary C. Costello

Fort Snelling Highway Bridge, St. Paul, SR 5

"A bridge between two tunnels!" and "A giant table between cliffs!" These are descriptions of the West 7th Street Bridge, most often referred to as the Fort Snelling Bridge. The 1961 span built to replace the old crossing was not to disturb the old Fort Snelling, an historic landmark. In order to do this, the span burrows 340 feet under the fort area, crossing the Mississippi and low river valley before entering the high St. Paul bluff. The tunnel top is covered with four feet of concrete, three feet of dirt, and finally sod to preserve the old fort appearance.

Three bridges have been built in this location. The first, a wooden one, was built in 1880 by and for the government primarily to service Fort Snelling. It was replaced in 1909 by a span with two steel deck-arches. Attractive as that structure was, because of its fading strength, in 1939 the U.S.Government refused to provide funds for the Fort Snelling Bridge upkeep. It was considered "unsafe." Only 5-ton loads and speeds of 15 mph were allowed. By an act of Congress the bridge was turned over to the state of Minnesota, which replaced the 52-year-old construction with the present four-lane steel-girder structure slightly north of the old span. Comparing statistics, I was surprised to find that the old Fort Snelling Bridge was higher above the water-100 feet as compared to 88 feet today--and had a wider channel span--321 feet compared to 258 feet on today's bridge.

The river seemed narrow and distant-looking from the bluff. I later found that between St. Paul and Fort Snelling the mighty river is only 320 feet wide.

I was on the Mississippi River Boulevard and could see very little of the piers because of all the trees below. Thanks to an artist's conception of the structure drawn in 1960, I later found there are 6 piers, but only two of them are in the water. The piers are tall columns of the double "T" variety, connected at the bottom with a heavy base. Unusual is the fact that the two main piers are placed parallel to the Mighty Mississippi's bank, at an oblique angle to the bridge. The guard rail is composed of two steel pipes which run through bands of steel approximately every six feet. Below is a concrete wall with a four-foot elongated drainage hole in every section.

Things were happening all around as I stood on the lookout point watching. A river road passed under the bridge in front of me. Workmen had the bridge roadway partially blocked so they could repair it early that Saturday morning. Possibly they later repainted the grey steel girder much in need. I was especially aware of all the traffic on the bridge because the ground I stood on shook with the movement.

Use:
Minnesota Highway 5 and local traffic

Location:
Connects W. 7th Street in St. Paul and Fort Snelling

Style:
7-span steel girder

Length:
Channel span - 258 feet clear
            - 300 feet total
Total length - 1198 feet

Width:
4 lanes, one 8-foot walkway, and a 4-foot median; 73 feet total

Clearance:
88 feet MLW

Date completed:
November 1961; replaced 1909 steel deck arch; 1986 walk added; original 1880 wooden through-truss span

Designed by:
Sverdrup and Parcel, St. Louis

Bridge:
#9300 Minnesota

Owner:
Minnesota DOT

Unique feat:
Only Mississippi highway bridge that has a tunnel at both ends. (Two others have tunnels at one end - #38 Hannibal and #72 Dubuque, both railroad bridges in Volume I)

Fort Snelling Highway, St. Paul

Mary C. Costello

67

This bridge, commonly known as the Ford Bridge because of its proximity to the Ford Plant in St. Paul, is a beautiful foretaste of what is to come in bridge designs in the rest of the Twin City area.

It has five open-spandrel, reinforced concrete rib-arches --three 300 feet wide and the other two 139 feet each. It was cleverly designed for easy access to all parts of the bridge for inspection purposes. This made it possible to cross the river walking on the ribs--a situation graffiti artists have discovered. In 1973 the roadway was widened to four lanes and new sidewalks and new railings were added. Originally the structure had a 40-foot-wide road and nine-foot sidewalks. The road today is 50 feet wide, with four-foot walkways.

Although the bridge is very similar in overall design to the Third Avenue and Cedar or Tenth Avenue Bridges, this span has distinct, elaborate detail. Each of the vertical spandrels is round with an added band of concrete near the top, in line all across the bridge. In addition to this, the spandrels are connected to each other with small arches. In other words, there are 17 small round arches repeating the shape of the larger arch below. In line with each spandrel column are wide concrete brackets that attach under the bridge deck for design and support. The roar of water from the dam close by dominated the sound.

In 1938, the bridge designer/engineer, M.S.Grytbak, reported that the Highland-Ford Bridge was built with very exact and carefully monitored materials. There was a mixing plant on the Minneapolis side which used bulk cement, sieved the aggregate, and measured the amount of water in the sand two or three times a day, every hour on rainy days. The mix was different for different parts of the bridge, depending sometimes on the speed with which it took to set.

The giant concrete pillar piers start directly below the deck. Each has three recessed lines and two embossed circles in the space above the line decoration. In front of the pier is a semicircle of concrete to cut through the water on the north side and prevent whirlpools and eddies on the south. These do not go all the way to the edge of the concrete rib so may be more decorative than helpful. This design is typical of the period between 1925 and the early thirties after the Paris Arts Decoratifs Exhibition, and is commonly called Art Deco.

The bridge when it was built was nicknamed "Highway to the Sky," but I have seen others for which the title seems more appropriate, for example the bridge at Luling, Louisiana, or even the new Smith Avenue Bridge in St. Paul. What a difference the times make.

After drawing the Ford Bridge, including my daughter and grandson, I was driving slowly, peering through the trees, to find the next bridge. A woman in a grey car saw my Iowa license and stopped next to me to ask if I was looking for something. She speedily led me along the Mississippi River Boulevard, past the almost solid-green growth riverside, the pretty old-style lamppost/streetlights and elegant homes, to the next lookout point. I was both enchanted with the drive and grateful for the assistance. The Twin-Cities produce beautiful people as well as beautiful bridges.

Use:
Intercity traffic and CSAH 42

Location:
From Ford Parkway, St.Paul, to 46th Street, Minneapolis

Style:
5-span open-spandrel concrete rib deck-arch

Length:
Channel span - 188 feet clear
- 200 feet total
Total length - 1,523 feet, plus 1,000-foot paved approach on Minneapolis side

Width:
4 lanes or 40 feet wide, plus 9-foot sidewalks; 64 feet total

Clearance:
55 feet MLW

Date completed:
1927; widened 1973

Designed by:
M.S.Grytbak, St.Paul engineer

Bridge:
#3575 Minnesota

Owner:
Shared by city of St.Paul and Hennepin County

Ford Parkway Bridge, St. Paul

Mary C. Costello

69

Lake Street Bridge, Minneapolis/St.Paul, SR 212

Started in 1989, the new Lake Street Bridge was meant to replace the frail-looking 100-year-old span. The citizen planning committee was hoping for an arch bridge and surprisingly got their wish. However, it was the last one of this style to gain Minnesota DOT approval.[2] Instead of metal, as was the centurion bridge, the new Lake Street Bridge is concrete, 85% paid for by federal money and 15% by the state. The committee thought that it should be ready by 1990, at which time the bridge would be returned to Twin Cities' ownership.

The bridge was being done in two halves allowing the old bridge to remain until half of the new one was complete and could accommodate traffic. However, an accident killed one man when one of the two new arch spans collapsed. It was a sad time and construction was delayed and an investigation ensued.

The new bridge was ultimately completed in the fall of 1992. Decorative but functional modern carriage lamps were placed inside the sidewalk close to the street with bright candle-power. Also unusual are the chimney-like stone structures with wooden seating added beside the bridge entryways.

The original Lake Street Bridge was an attractive deck-arch, though wrought-iron, finished in 1889. Before its demise it was the oldest highway bridge, next to the Eads in St.Louis (1874), still in use on the Mississippi River. This two-arch bridge span was not so instantly impressive as its neighbor the Ford Bridge, even though they were the same style. The difference was the material and color. The greyed-black iron of the old Lake Street Bridge was almost lost from sight against a background of trees.

The Minneapolis Tribune stated in an editorial at the time the old Lake Street Bridge was built that it was "foolish extravagance," since there were seven other bridges across the river already. Quite to the contrary, the first Lake Street Bridge became a major corridor between the two cities.

In fact, in 1905, only 17 years after it was completed, the bridge was already too narrow for traffic. Therefore, a third arch, this time of steel, was added down the center of the bridge without moving the other arches. The deck was widened from 18 to 33 feet, allowing streetcar tracks to go down the middle. The spandrels were pin-connected diagonals that zigzagged between the arch and the deck. Each 456-foot arch span was structurally independent, according to the Industrial Guide.

The original Lake Street Bridge served Minneapolis and St. Paul for a century, but life began anew in 1992 with the concrete deck-arch span--set for another 100 years.

Use:
Local auto traffic, bus service, CSAH 35, and SR 212

Location:
Between Lake Street in Minneapolis and Marshall Avenue in St. Paul

Style:
2-span concrete deck-arch

Length:
Channel arch - 300 feet clear
              - 555.5 feet total
Total length - 1484 feet

Width:
4 lanes, 76 feet, with shoulder/bike lane and sidewalks on both sides

Clearance:
66 feet MLW

Date completed:
15 October 1992; replaced 1889 iron deck-arch span which was widened and reinforced with steel arches built down the center in 1905 to accommodate streetcars

Designer:
Howard, Needles, Tammen, Bergendorf

Bridge:
#62082

Owner:
Ramsey and Hennepin Counties

Lake/Marshall Bridge, Minneapolis/St. Paul

Mary C. Costello

71

Canadian Pacific "High" Railroad Bridge, Minneapolis

*T*rains on this "Old Milwaukee Road" Bridge look like a trapeze act performing high atop the trusses--with no protection. Beginning here, this bridge style is typical of the Twin City area railroad bridges. This high deck-truss span crossed the white-looking river in front of me with the Minneapolis skyline behind. The design of the structure was unusual to an Iowan, since in our area railroad bridges are mostly through-trusses.

The bridge looked very small from a distance, but I could see the three spans of "pin-connected Baltimore style trusses"--a truss form commonly used for heavy railroad loads, states the Industrial Archeology Guide. It was built in 1902 with double tracks for the Chicago, Milwaukee, St. Paul and Pacific Railroad.

A Soo Line freight came from across the river as I drove under the approach on the river road at the end of the high span. I saw its two heavy diagonal end-beams and lighter verticals, like legs going to the ground. After the bridge leaves the water, deep girders on steel bents become the style. Also I found that the tall, solid stone piers in the water are rounded on the corners and have a narrow concrete cap on which the deck-trusses rest.

Looking at my bridge photo through the magnifying glass, the bridge looks like a giant transparent ruler over the great waters. Because the diagonals within the spans are lighter weight, only the heavy trussed verticals stand out-like inch marks. A shorter vertical between every two of the above, for extra deck strength, says Harold Sandberg, Chairman of the Board at Alfred Benesch and Company, forms what could be a half-inch indications on that rule. This truss appearance is rare on the Mississippi.

Downtown buildings in the distance gave me a better understanding of where I was. On the opposite bank I could see a triangular, white, sandy inlet in a solid mass of trees. That, combined with the greenery in front of me, made me feel as if I were in the countryside. An unusual houseboat was moored on the left and a train crossed the bridge as I drew. At the last minute a canoe with three people on board headed north on the colorless, reflection-free river. I would have liked to be one of them. What a different view I would have enjoyed!

Use:
Canadian Pacific (former Soo Line) railroad traffic

Location:
Between Franklin Avenue and Lake Street Bridges in Minneapolis

Style:
3-span steel deck-truss bridge

Length:
Channel span - 310 feet clear
- 324 feet total
Total length - 1061 feet

Width:
2 tracks, 22 feet

Clearance:
76 feet MLW

Date completed:
1902, for Chicago, Milwaukee, St. Paul & Pacific Railroad

Designed by:
American Bridge Company

Bridge:
L3-32

Owner:
Canadian Pacific Railroad; originally "Old Milwaukee Road"

Canadian Pacific High Railroad Bridge, Minneapolis

Mary C. Costello

Cappelen Memorial or Franklin Avenue Bridge, Minneapolis

*T*he Cappelen Bridge was considered one of the three most beautiful bridges in America in 1939, along with the Washington Memorial Bridge, New York City, and the Arlington Bridge in Washington, D.C. Occasionally its beauty is reflected perfectly in the river--but obviously not from my point of view.

The Franklin Avenue Bridge, as it was originally called, is an open-spandrel concrete arch bridge whose history is intertwined with its designer.

Norwegian-born Frederick Wm. Cappelen was Minneapolis' city engineer from 1866 to 1896 and from 1912 to 1922. (It was an elected office). Cappelen either built or supervised nearly all the large bridges in Minneapolis during his time in office. Because of the popularity of the automobile after the First World War, need for more bridges in the Twin Cities became apparent, a need that was partially satisfied with the Franklin Avenue Bridge. Cappelen had a number of problems to overcome with his design: the heavy traffic on the river since the construction of Lock and Dam #1 (1917), just two years before the bridge was started; the fact that the dam raised the water to a constant "high water" level needed to be dealt with; the high bluffs on either side of the river and the tall boat traffic, which required a 50-foot bridge clearance; and finally, the need for the span to be at least 300 feet wide. Cappelen's proposed response to these issues was this daring 5-span, 400-foot center-arch bridge of solid concrete. The structure took four years to build and, unfortunately, before the bridge was finished Frederick Cappelen died. A fellow countryman, Kristoffer Olsen Oustad, completed the designs and engineered the bridge to completion. The bridge has since been named in Cappelen's honor.

At the time, the Franklin Avenue Bridge was the largest solid concrete arch-span in the world. That title remained until 1931, when Pittsburg built the Westinghouse Memorial Bridge with a 460-foot span.

By 1971, the 48-year-old bridge showed its age and was scheduled to be rebuilt. Since the local engineers agreed that the bridge was too "heavy" in appearance, every other spandrel was removed, but otherwise the original design was followed. The roadway was dismantled to the concrete arches and was rebuilt ten feet wider. Cappelen's two-ribbed open-spandrel bridge with its beautiful proportion and simple detail fits in well with the park and residences surrounding it.

Use:
City and CSAH 5 traffic

Location:
On Franklin Avenue between River Road East and River Parkway West in Minneapolis

Style:
5-span reinforced concrete rib-arch

Length:
Channel span - 275 feet clear
                     - 400 feet total
Total length   - 1054 feet

Width:
4 lanes, 50 feet total

Clearance:
55 feet MLW

Date completed:
7 December 1923 dedicated; remodeled in 1971

Designed by:
Frederick Wm. Cappelen; (Kristoffer Olsen Oustad finished at Cappelen's death)

Bridge:
#2441 Minnesota

Owner:
Hennepin County

Unique feat:
400-foot center span was longest in world when built; Plowden praised its beauty in his book, Bridges.

Cappelen Memorial or Franklin Avenue Bridge, Minneapolis   *Mary C. Costello*

75

Dartmouth Avenue Bridge, Minneapolis, I-94

Adjectives such as "uninspired design" and "functional" are used to describe the Dartmouth Avenue Bridge. These are not meant to downplay the bridge, but are a fact in contrast to the beautiful structures nearby. Nick Westbrook, researcher with the Minnesota Historical Library, states that this bridge is a convenient, speedy way for people to go from the heart of one city to the heart of the other thus bringing together the two cities.

The I-94 Bridge is a welded box-girder span that has a slightly arched appearance from the side. The busy four lanes of highway bridge traffic require bypasses for cross traffic. Minnesota built an overpass for East River Road traffic, and the West River Parkway goes underneath the span closer to river-level.

In October of 1963, Illinois or Mississippi River watchers were treated to the sight of the 148-ton box girders being transported along the river by barge from Gary, Indiana, where they were fabricated. There were two huge 125-foot-long, 21-foot-deep and 3-foot-wide sections, the largest single pieces of material ever to travel the Mississippi up to this time. "In passing through the Illinois canal, the barges had to be partially sunk so the girders could clear overhead bridges."

When I was photographing and sketching the bridge, I found the work difficult from the east side because trees and other growth were in the way. I crossed the Cappelen Bridge and found, beside the bridge's end, a nicely-landscaped grassy area with a good Dartmouth Bridge view.

The Dartmouth Avenue Bridge's two main concrete piers consist of two tapered columns, connected at the top, and resting on large oblong bases in the water. There are also three more simple, two-column-only piers on the west side before the abutment.

For a guard-rail, the Dartmouth Bridge has a concrete wall along the edge of the road, with elongated drainage holes underneath and a steel pipe that passes through a curved vertical support on top.

Perhaps the Dartmouth Avenue Bridge is not among the most beautiful of Mississippi bridges, but certainly it has proven its worth to inter-city commuters.

Use:
I-94 traffic

Location:
Slightly north of Franklin Avenue in Minneapolis

Style:
6-span welded box-girder

Length:
Channel span - 286 feet clear
- 340 feet total
Total length - 1001 feet

Width:
4 lanes with median; 141-feet total

Clearance:
64 feet MLW

Date completed:
Fall 1964; repaired 1976; 1994 remodeled

Designed by:
Parsons, Brinckerhoff, Quade and Douglas

Bridge:
#9350 Minnesota

Owner:
Minnesota DOT

Dartmouth Avenue Bridge, Minneapolis

Mary C. Costello

Washington Avenue Highway/Pedestrian Bridge

*F*rom a distance the Washington Avenue Bridge in Minneapolis is one of the most intriguing modern bridges that I have seen on the river. The structure is a unique two-deck 5-span steel girder bridge, which unites the two campuses of the University of Minnesota that the river has split.

The designers from St. Louis, Sverdrup & Parcel, proposed two 29-foot roadways for vehicles and an 8-foot divider strip between them. This median would contain a single row of columns supporting an "umbrella" upper level bike/walkway for pedestrians. The final decision changed only the road width, to two 24-foot roadways.

It was Saturday, when I drove along the river road. I was south of the bridge at a turn in the river where the only moving object was a canoe. From here I first saw the Washington Bridge. I was surprised to see that the superstructure had two decks of windows. I thought how unusual and attractive the silver bridge appeared. I was anxious to know more about this unique span.

The plaza and wide walkway for the University students are about 100 feet above the river at bluff level. Walks line both sides of the upper deck of the bridge with large round "lollipop-like" lights, a fair-weather corridor to classes. In the center of this bridge-deck is a thirty-five-foot-wide enclosed passage with glassed-in walls and sliding doors to keep out the elements. The exposed heat pipes keep the temperature from getting below 32 degrees. Students can go from the campus on one side of the river to the other without climbing steps or facing inclement weather.

The vehicular deck is below. It cuts into the west bank of the Mississippi River and below the surface of the University's west campus. The depressed road goes under Cedar Street before rising. It all looked attractive in the architectural drawings and from a distant side view. When I drove on this lower bridge road, however, what a surprise! The bridge served its purpose. There was room, and it was fast and no doubt safe, but I thought the passage dark and depressing. It is strange because my view from the river had me imagining the bridge to be unusually bright and pleasant, with light coming in through the glassless windows.

From the river, there appeared to be only one pier in the water, but there are really two. The River Road goes under the west end of the bridge, which has two shorter piers on high ground. The other piers are three square columns connected simply at top and bottom. The bottom is larger all around and the ends are rounded. This substructure had to be strong enough to support two decks.

The smallest girder on the bridge is ten feet deep and is welded steel weighing 28 tons. The largest center girder weighs 65 tons and had to be delivered from the structural steel company by river barge. The center girder has a shallow arch in its design that no doubt gives it more strength and greater beauty.

The predecessor of the Washington Avenue Bridge, the 76-year-old iron truss bridge, built in 1889, was removed after the new span was in use. It had been closed to trucks and buses as early as 1954. The 37-foot-wide span was down to three-ton loads maximum. In its "heyday" it carried "interurban electric streetcar lines" and was recognized by the government as the head of the big river channel. In mid-life it was struck by lightning and its floor burned. In its old age it was on the verge of condemnation but held on until the young two-level bridge could take over. Then the aged structure was purposely weakened, nudged and dropped into the river before being salvaged.

Use:
Upper deck for pedestrians or bikes; lower level for vehicles, US 12

Location:
Joins the University of Minnesota campuses, Washington Avenue on the east and above 4th Street on the west

Style:
Double deck 6-span welded steel girder

Length:
Channel span - 228 feet total
             - 251 feet clear
Total length - 1,130 feet

Width:
4 lanes for cars below, and both enclosed and open walkways for pedestrians above

Clearance:
70 feet MLW

Date completed:
October 1965; replaced 1886 iron truss

Designed by:
Sverdrup & Parcel, St. Louis

Bridge:
#9360 Minnesota

Owner:
Minnesota DOT

Unique feat:
Only highway bridge on the Mississippi with enclosed decks

Washington Avenue Highway/Pedestrian Bridge, Minneapolis   *Mary C. Costello*

*A*long with railroad lines, railroad bridges often change owners. As with all name changes, human or otherwise, we are creatures of habit and tend to hold onto an old title. The Northern Pacific Railroad built this span in Minneapolis, merged to become the Burlington Northern, but in 1999 was converted to a recreation path by the city of Minneapolis.

This railroad bridge is also recognized in Minneapolis because of the area's well-known designer/engineer, Frederick Wm. Cappelen.(See Bridge #34). The span was the first bridge he designed after immigrating to the U.S. (Cappelen originated the series of local open spandrel concrete-arch bridges that dominate the Minneapolis/St.Paul area, though this railroad structure reflects none of that design.).

Minneapolis' Bike and Pedestrian Bridge is a two-span deck-truss bridge with deep girder approaches across the river valley. The Baltimore-truss bridge looks very much like a through-truss, but it has the train tracks on top instead of inside the trusses. It was built in 1885 with a double track. Around 1917, just before the U.S. entrance in World War I, the bridge was rehabilitated to carry heavier trains and a center row of trusses was added. By 1924 the bridge was relocated off the University of Minnesota campus, and thoroughly remodeled. It was repaired in 1955 and again in 1963.

My initial view of this bridge was from behind apartments southwest of the span. A person was crossing on top of the 100-foot high bridge at the time, which seemed dangerous though there was metal fencing on the sides of the tracks. The view must have been spectacular from that height if the person had time and courage to appreciate it.

Stone piers support the truss spans on both ends and the center of the structure. Those supporting the end girders are taller and slightly thinner piers of the same material--tan in color--capped with concrete.

The new 24-foot-wide deck has separate paths for both bikes and pedestrians. Topsoil and sod replace the train tracks and rails between 54-inch structural tube railings, and eight-foot tall gooseneck-like lamps with flared shades which shine inverted to light the two bicycle lanes and pedestrian walkway. An historic marker gives the interesting history of the bridge.

Trees completely engulfed the bottom third of the historic bridge, the river and anything else that I might have seen below. Besides the bridge, only the tall University buildings penetrated the clouds of green trees.

Use:
For bicycles and pedestrians only, started in summer 1999

Located:
From 20th Avenue South to near the East River Road in Minneapolis; below the Falls of St. Anthony, originally on the University of Minnesota campus

Style:
2-spans of deck-trusses and 5 spans of steel girders

Length:
Channel span - 160 feet clear
            - 245 feet total
Total length   - 952 feet

Width:
24 feet, with two 7-foot bike lanes in center (one for each way) and 5-foot pedestrian paths on each side

Clearance:
39 feet MLW

Date completed:
1885 in middle of the University of Minnesota grounds; rehabilitated to carry heavier traffic in about 1917; in 1922 till 1924 Northern Pacific Railroad relocated bridge here; repaired in 1955; out of use as a railroad bridge in 1981; converted to recreational use in 1999

Designed by:
F.W.Cappelen; MNDOT designed pedestrian/bike paths

Bridge:
#94246, former railroad bridge #9

Owner:
City of Minneapolis since 1987; before that Burlington Northern Railroad; originally the Northern Pacific Railroad

Unique feat:
Designed and engineered by Frederick Wm. Cappelen; one of the first steel spans in the Northwest; recreationial path has an historic marker on it.

Pedestrian/Bike, Former Railroad Bridge, Minneapolis   *Mary C. Costello*

81

Tenth Avenue Highway Bridge, Minneapolis, SR 36

*T*his elegant open-spandrel concrete rib-arch bridge, originally called the Cedar Avenue Bridge, was completed and dedicated on 20 September 1929, a month before the stock market crash that began the Great Depression. The original bridge was 40 feet wide with eight-foot sidewalks. In 1976, the 47-year-old bridge was rehabilitated owing to potholes and crumbling curbs, sidewalks and weakened spandrel walls. During this reconstruction period, the bridge was widened and the south approach shortened by 700 feet. No change was made in the modified S-curve configuration but the south end was changed to go straight to Washington Avenue. The total structure cost only $1,100,000 to build in 1929, but its renovation cost $4.6 million.

The Tenth Avenue Bridge consists of two 266-foot arches anchored in giant-sized piers and five small arches on gradually rising land. Only one pier is in the water and its only difference from the others is a triangular addition near the bottom on the upstream side. Its purpose is to deflect the water and ice--unglamorously similar to a cow-catcher on a train--preventing disaster. With the other piers placed on shore, the river is more open for traffic. Three smaller arches carry the northeast side of the bridge, and the two on the southwest cross train tracks. For decoration these gigantic concrete columns have two grooves cut just short of full length. At the top they turn and almost meet, thus creating an interesting sculptured look.

Between the arches and the bridge roadway are spaces called "spandrels." In this area are flat white columns looking very much like the louvers in a vertical blind. Where these spandrels meet the deck, brackets of equal thickness project out to support the outer deck. The concrete deck-arch bridge design is popular in the Twin City area--the Third Avenue, Ford Bridge, I-94, Franklin and this Tenth Avenue Bridge. All are beautiful bridges, especially when appearing pure white.

The original "Cedar Avenue Bridge" was built in 1872, closer to and contemporary with the first Hennepin Suspension Bridge (1855 to 1876).It was a horse and buggy bridge that became known as "the suicide bridge." The Parker truss iron structure had a 17-foot roadway and sidewalks on each side. There is a story about a census fight" between Minneapolis and St. Paul in 1890. The judge from Minneapolis was headed for the courtroom at the State Capitol when some St. Paul men followed and tried to stop him. Both carriages crossed the old Cedar Avenue Bridge with their horses at a furious pace but, with the help of some of the judge's friends, the second carriage was halted at the far end for violating the city ordinance concerning speeding on the bridge. The judge reached St. Paul and carried out his mission.

The old Cedar Avenue Bridge was not taken down when the new one was built but was condemned in about 1934 and the walks removed. It was used, however, as a footbridge until 1942, when its 400-plus tons of metal became scrap and were used for the World War II war effort.

Use:
State Highway 36, MSAS 328 and local traffic

Location:
Between 10th Avenue on north side of the river and Cedar Avenue on the south

Style:
7-span concrete rib deck-arch and 13 girders

Length:
Channel span - 137 feet clear
- 266 feet total
Total length - 2,174.9 feet

Width:
2 lanes, 68 feet including two sidewalks

Clearance:
101 feet MLW

Date completed:
September 1929; rehabilitated with widened roadway, shortened approach, straightened the south end directly to Washington Avenue in 1976; replaced 1872 truss span which remained in place until 1942 as a footbridge; a wooden bridge was built here originally while a ferry still ran.

Designed by:
City of Minneapolis

Bridge:
#2796 Hennepin County

Owner:
Minnesota DOT

Unique feat:
Built on the day-labor system

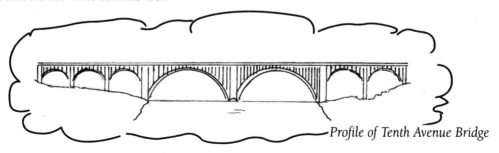
Profile of Tenth Avenue Bridge

Tenth Avenue Bridge, Minneapolis

Mary C. Costello

83

Interstate 35W Highway Bridge, Minneapolis

*T*was a good spot. The side of the I-35W Bridge was in plain view. I had found my way down to a fence on the southwest side of the river behind some apartments and close to a dumpster. Along here I could see the undersides of a number of bridges--Burlington Northern Santa Fe Railroad Bridge (former Northern Pacific Bridge), Tenth Avenue Bridge and the I-35W. After I took pictures of the others through the fence, I moved to a shaded area under the Interstate Bridge. Another car was parked there and the driver was fishing below. We were near a dam, in a secluded spot, and had a cool, free place to park--a fisherman's paradise. It was around noon and getting hot, but it was enjoyable in the cool of the bridge, so I parked there, too. Under a concrete arch of the Tenth Avenue Bridge I found my best view of I-35. Behind me, up a cemented slope near the abutment, was a teenager breaking up some junk he had found. He didn't pay any attention as I photographed the interstate bridge and started my sketch.

The dark green steel deck-truss bridge in front of me was definitely not the most attractive bridge on the river. Riverboat people must like it, though, because it leaps with a single arch 458 feet across the water without touching down --the only span in the Twin Cities to make that claim. However, the bridges are very close here and angled so that it is impossible on land to appreciate the sight. From a boat in the river, one could see its profile, but a person would need to take a fast glance upward before the bridge would be overhead.

The two main supporting piers of the I-35W consist of tubular-shaped concrete pillars one on each side of the bridge. On these piers rest the deepest points of the deck arch truss. The heavy vertical steel attaches to each pier directly. All piers are on land.

Built in 1967, by the State of Minnesota for $5 million, the first bridge on the spot, the I-35W Highway Bridge is just below the St. Anthony Falls and the lock and dam that allow boats to travel further north. Before 1963 this was not possible because of the impassable falls. Though the towering I-35W span is close to the historic St. Anthony Falls, it takes on no airs. The widest bridge in the Twin-City area, it provides shade, a non-interfering crossing and stays out of the limelight.

Use:
Interstate traffic

Location:
Just north of Tenth Avenue Bridge in Minneapolis; from Washington Avenue to University Avenue

Style:
3 spans of deck-arch trusses plus 11 girder approach spans

Length:
Channel span - 390 feet clear
          - 458 feet total
Total length   - 1907 feet

Width:
4 lanes, 108 feet between curbs

Clearance:
64 feet MLW

Date completed:
November 1967

Designed by:
Minnesota DOT, Bridge Section

Bridge:
#9340 Hennepin County

Owner:
Minnesota DOT

Interstate 35 W Highway Bridge, Minneapolis

Mary C. Costello

85

James J. Hill Stone Arch Bridge, Minneapolis, Formerly Railroad, Now Pedestrian

Just as St.Louis has its steel arch, Minneapolis has 21 stone arches originally joined together in a curved railroad bridge that some claimed "it couldn't be done." Jim Hill's Stone Arch Railroad Bridge in downtown Minneapolis was "The hardest thing I ever had to do or the hardest undertaking I ever had to face," said James J. Hill, railroad promoter. Built to accommodate the St. Paul, Minneapolis and Manitoba Railway (later the Great Northern), the bridge would be the"finest of its kind on the continent," Hill predicted.

Constructed over 100 years ago, the Stone Arch Bridge remains as solid as any Roman antiquity. Now owned by the Minnesota Department of Transportation, the bridge was built before sophisticated engineering was available, by manpower refusing to believe "it couldn't be done." It has a six-degree reverse curve that many thought impossible to construct over rushing waters. Made of St. Cloud granite, concrete and limestone, it is as sturdy today as the day it was built.

Nothing had been changed on or done to the Jim Hill Bridge until 1963, when two arches and one pier were removed (there were 23 arches) to allow river barges and other traffic to go further north to assist industry there. A steel truss, 198 feet long, was added to support the tracks and trains in place of the missing arches. Work on the bridge was carried out between the guide walls (built by the Corps of Engineers after the 1952 flood) leading to the St. Anthony Falls Upper Locks, about the same time as the locks were added.

Work had to be accomplished without delaying some 32 daily passenger trains from six rail lines. The longest interval between trains was from 11 p.m. to 6 a.m., so most of the work was done at night. It was completed in the summer of 1963 with rail service discontinued only long enough for the railway to remove temporary fill and lower the tracks from temporary elevation.

On 18 April 1965, a Great Northern switch crew taking empty equipment over the railway's old Stone Arch Bridge felt a sharp jolt. It was during the great flood, and the cause was quickly found to be a sag in the surface of the bridge, a third of the way across from the east. It was temporarily closed due to emergency damage for the first time in its 82-year history.

Some facts about the bridge are worth noting. Sixteen of the spans are perfect semi-circles but the rest are different arch lengths. Because the train tracks were recessed between the stone walls, no railing was needed, making the bridge look more like a Roman Aqueduct. The bridge is one of the most difficult to photograph because of the trees and other bridges, as well as the curve that takes it behind several buildings. The masonry bridge cost $750,000 in 1883.

In the beginning the Romanesque Arch Bridge was called by the media and others "Jim Hill's Folly." Hill's men built it stone by stone, fighting nature all the time and the rushing waters of the St. Anthony Falls. When the bridge was complete, 76 feet above the Mississippi River, the stories changed. It was called a "magnificent structure" and a "fitting monument to the liberality, sagacity and enterprise of President Hill."

In the early 70's passenger traffic gradually declined until 1978 when the historic span was closed. By 1992 new owners, MNDOT engaged A.G. Lichtenstein and Associates Rehabilitation Incorporation from New York, to update its exterior and roadway and convert the bridge to a twelve-foot-wide trolley and bike path with two six-foot concrete walkways. Today 13,000 runners, cyclists, walkers, and skaters enjoy the Stone Arch Bridge each week. James Hill, if alive, would be shocked at the turnabout, but pleased at the bridge's restored beauty after well over 100 years of service.

Use:
Closed to trains in 1978; used for trolleys, walkers and bikers since 1994

Location:
Below the St. Anthony Falls; curves from the east bank near Tenth Avenue Bridge to the west bank and Third Avenue Bridge

Style:
21-span stone-arch pedestrian bridge (originally 23 spans), plus one steel deck-truss span

Length:
Channel span - 56 feet clear
- 197.5 feet total
Total length - 2100 feet

Width:
25 feet useable, 28 feet total

Clearance: 24.4 feet MLW

Date completed:
1883; in 1963 2 arches and a pier removed to allow barge traffic through to the Upper Harbor; in 1910 strengthened for heavier trains with two feet thick concrete over arches; in 1965 a one-foot sag in the bridge surface was repaired; in 1994 cracks injected with epoxy gel with epoxy gel for walkway

Designed by:
Colonel Charles C. Smith, chief engineer of the Minneapolis Union Railway Company [3]

Bridge:
#27004; #U9.9 was BN railroad number

Owner:
Minnesota DOT (1988); today MNDOT owns the lower part of bridge and the Minneapolis Park Board the upper part; reverse lineage: City of Minneapolis; BN, GN and originally StPM&M Railway

Unique feat:
Only stone arch bridge and second oldest bridge on the Mississippi River, (Eads is oldest); in 1995 designated a National Historic Civil Engineering Landmark

Stone Arch Pedestrian/Bike Bridge, Minneapolis

Mary C. Costello

87

Third Avenue Highway Bridge, Minneapolis SR 65

*F*rom over the water I could hear "America, the Beautiful" being sung. It was coming from the St. Anthony Main, an attractive mall area a half-mile away on Minneapolis' riverfront. While I admired the Third Avenue Bridge from its neighboring Hennepin Bridge, the sound carried. The tune, always inspiring for me, was more so in this setting.

Both God and man have worked together to create what I saw--the solidly puffed white clouds reflected in the yawning water below me. Trees on my left were a greenish black, and on my right the bank was the same dark color. Through the middle of this God-made setting was the open spandrel deck-arch bridge with the St. Anthony Falls below and the Minneapolis skyline behind. Everything was in values of grey--from the white concrete bridge which at the time took on the color of the light grey water, to the dark grey recesses in the spandrels and the multi-toned grey buildings behind. The liveliest color in the scene was tan shared by both the right bank and a row of circular protection-cells in the river, identifying the boat channel. The white in the sky and the water added that needed sparkle. I was impressed and inspired both by what I saw and what I heard. It was truly beautiful America!

The Third Avenue Bridge, originally called the St. Anthony Falls Bridge, is seven arches of reinforced concrete with girder approaches--steel girders on the east and concrete on the west over railroad tracks. This was the last major use of Melan rib arches in reinforced concrete bridge construction in Minneapolis. Five spans are 211 feet long and two are 132 feet. Opened originally on 13 June 1918, the span was designed with a shallow reverse S-curve to avoid four breaks in the limestone strata on which it rests. The bridge is unique and attractive both because of its location over St. Anthony Falls, the largest cataract on the river, and because of its graceful curve.

Originally this central downtown bridge had a cement railing, streetcar tracks, old decorative lights and a spiral stair between the deck and Main Street. Along the way these features have been covered, replaced or removed entirely. Even without them, however, the bridge was thought by Arun M. Shirole, engineer, to be aesthetically "the best of the city's bridges."

In 1980 the Third Avenue Bridge was completely renovated with new spandrels, deck and approaches. The beautiful 1939 art-deco style metal railing was repaired, repainted and returned to the bridge. This downtown span has the restored the curved viewing platforms for observing the river and the falls--a feature that is unique on the Mississippi River to the Twin City area. The bridge lights are fluorescent with modern, black, steel poles set in the concrete barricade that protects the wide walkway. The light is flat-topped, boxy and attached to the pole at right angles. Since the decorative railing would not keep a car on the bridge, there is a concrete inner wall with a black pipe supported on short legs.

The square piers of the Third Avenue Bridge are massive concrete pourings, becoming round at the bottom quarter for decoration, to stop eddies and help break up ice. The round areas have concrete caps on top. At each end and on each side of the bridge are abutments that project out from the line of the bridge and hold the observation platforms.

"O beautiful, for patriot dream that sees beyond the years." The words were appropriate.

Use:
US 8, SR 65 & local traffic

Location:
Between Third Avenue on west bank and Central Avenue on east; across the upper St. Anthony Falls dam

Style:
7-span open-spandrel concrete deck-arch bridge on a reverse S-curve, with both steel and prestressed concrete girder approaches

Length:
Channel span - 150 feet clear
              - 211 feet total
Total length - 2,223 feet

Width:
4 lanes, 54 feet total, plus two 12-foot walkways

Clearance:
42 feet MLW

Date completed:
13 June 1918; Art Deco metal railing added in 1939; November 1980 completion of major renovation, including the curved viewing platforms and restoration of the spiral stairs

Designed by:
Concrete Steel Engineering Company of NewYork; Frederick Wm. Cappelen redesigned the approaches

Bridge:
#2440 Hennepin County

Owner:
Minnesota DOT

Unique feat:
Built over a dam; awarded National Register of Historic Places in 1971; and National Design Award for Historic Preservation in 1980; largest concrete arch bridge on a reverse curve...a unique engineering feat, 1918

Third Avenue Bridge, Minneapolis

Mary C. Costello

89

Nicollet Island Ornamental Pedestrian Bridge, Minneapolis

*T*here is a warm charm about the Nicollet Island Bridge--an ornamental,1887 span over Minneapolis's quiet Mississippi back-water. The lantern lights and immaculate tip-to-toe wrought iron restoration work in a rich brown color add a 19th century enchantment.

This single truss span was a part of the old Broadway Avenue Bridge a mile upstream and was moved to this picturesque location in 1987 to preserve the century old structure for future generations. This was and is the fanciest of bridges over the Mississippi River, a pin-connected Pratt through-truss. In its new location it is only decorative, supported on a beam from underneath.

The bridge over the Mississippi east channel allows residents and visitors alike to walk from Southeast Main, where brick paving and old-fashioned decor prevail, to Nicollet Island, recently made into a part of the public park system. Cars, trams and other light vehicles may use it.

Diamond shapes are the main decorative feature of the old Broadway Avenue span. All the struts, the railings, the portals and an unusual center, "wind-and-sway-bracing", use this motif. The coarser metal railing and portal struts have the same geometric-shaped intersections reinforced with small metal gussets and vertical and horizontal rods.

Paying attention to details, the original designer of the Nicollet Island Bridge (then the Broadway Avenue Bridge) placed hexagonal embossed plates centered high on both ends of the span. These cast iron plaques carry the date (1887) and the name of the bridge company that designed and built the bridge. Someone tried to steal one of them when the bridge was being moved but dropped and broke it, so the city had to have a new one made. Above the four corners of the span is a "finial," a pointed ornament forming the pinnacle. Between these topmost decorations, but only on the ends of the bridge, are a band of fancy crosses side by side, though not touching. Treated-timber sidewalks run outside the superstructure trusses. Finally the elegant lights are mounted on the bridge's vertical members. One style lights the sidewalk and another the two-lane road that carries trolleys or other small vehicles across the Mississippi back channel.

The two piers on the ends of the single span are low, rectangular and notched to allow the bridge roadway to sit level with the banks on either side. Since the bridge didn't quite fill the space, there is a short, steel beam span from the pier to the abutment on both ends. It took imagination and foresight to have achieved this beautiful crossing. My hat's off to Minneapolis!

Use:
Pedestrian and light vehicular traffic

Location:
Across the back channel in Minneapolis between Nicollet Island and the mainland, or Main and Merriam Streets

Style:
Single-span pin-connected through-truss supported on steel beams with 2 short I-beam approach spans

Length:
Channel span - 147 feet
Total length - 256.7 feet

Width:
2 lanes plus 2 walkways

Clearance:
14 feet MLW

Date completed:
1887 as part of Broadway Avenue Bridge; July 1987 one span placed in this location

Designed by:
King Iron and Bridge Company, Cleveland in 1887, (present setting VanDoren, Hazard and Stalling)

Bridge:
#27664 Hennepin County

Owner:
City of Minneapolis

Unique Feat:
Only decorative truss pedestrian span on the Mississippi

Nicollet Island Pedestrian Bridge, Minneapolis

Mary C. Costello

91

East Channel Hennepin Avenue Bridges, Minneapolis

*T*hese East Channel Bridges are not glamorous, picturesque or exciting as they stand today...both are small girder spans. Their history, on the other hand, is long and interesting. They go back farther than the first bridge to cross the mighty main channel.

In the 1840's Franklin Steele had built a dam from St. Anthony, the little village on the east bank, to Hennepin Island and then to Nicollet Island (see diagram). Pedestrians crossed the east channel on this dam but had to take a boat the rest of the way across the river to the tiny community that was to become Minneapolis. It was at this time that a Dakota Indian squaw ferried foot passengers across to augment her fishing income. Whether hers or others, often boats would turn over at the slightest provocation. In winter, it was easy to walk or take a sleigh on the ice, but otherwise it was often a hazardous under-taking. In 1847, Steele began a rope-tow ferry service across the wider channel from his St. Anthony mill to the government mills on the west bank. By 1851 he had built a crude bridge over the shorter east channel. Therefore, before 1855 the back channel had two "bridges" or means of crossing.

In the year 1855, when the main channel suspension was built, people may have used Steele's temporary wooden bridge to get to it. A new bridge was probably constructed for the increased traffic. As time passed there may have been other bridges across this back channel, but the next record I have is of a stone-arch bridge built in 1878. This span was so well built that when they were removing it in 1973 to build the present east-west bridges, one of the workmen said, "That's the toughest, solidest 'falling down' bridge I ever hope to see."

Today's "almost twin" bridges going across the back channel are one-way spans. Painted to go with the new Hennepin suspension bridge, the steel beam bridges differ only in length. For a parapet the two spans have a simple square steel post that wraps around the long pipe rail with metal balustrades below.

Though little attention is paid to these small bridges, without the east channel crossings the first bridge would have been incomplete. Without the "twins" today no one could cross at Hennepin Avenue.

Map of area

Use:
Twin approaches to and from the Hennepin Avenue Bridge, CSAH 52

Location:
Between Nicollet Avenue and Hennepin East, or First Avenue

Style:
3-span bolted steel continuous beam

Length:
Channel span - 97 feet
Total length   - 383 feet south
                     - 413 feet north

Width:
2 lanes plus sidewalks on one side of each span

Clearance:
22 feet MLW south bridge 27 feet MLW north bridge

Date completed:
1972 north span, 1973 south; painted in 1989; originally in 1840 a dam on which people often crossed; 1851, a crude bridge; 1878, a stone arch bridge, in 1899 bridge was widened

Designed by:
Van Doren-Hazard-Stallings-Schnacke

Bridge:
#27538 & #27537 Hennepin County

Owner:
Hennepin County

East Channel Hennepin Avenue Bridges, Minneapolis   *Mary C. Costello*

93

Hennepin Avenue Bridge, Minneapolis, County Highway 52

*T*he Hennepin Avenue Bridge is the location of the first bridge across the Mississippi River,* appropriately called in 1855 "A Highway In the Wilderness." Minnesota was still a territory, the village of St. Anthony was just incorporated that year and Minneapolis took that step the following year.

The first bridge was a wire suspension bridge designed by Thomas M. Griffith of New York, an experienced engineer. It was 620 feet long overall with a 17-foot-wide roadway and 3.75-inch-diameter cables. The bridge cost $36,000. The wooden towers--two per end--were connected by a walkway and housed the toll booth which charged:

> Foot passenger - 10 cents
> Horse or mule - 15 cents
> Two horses, two mules, ox teams,
> with driver - 25 cents
> Single horse carriage -25 cents
> Swine or sheep - 2 cents

The span was used so much that it brought in over $1000 a month but the sight must have been chaos with sheep, pigs, women, children, horses and carriages all mixed up on the roadway as there were no sidewalks.

The grand opening on 23 January 1855 was a formal and elaborate "top hat" affair. Sixty-one sleighs crossed the bridge from St.Anthony into Minneapolis and back again, where a banquet was held for 300. There was a brass band and a cannon salute. The legislature recessed and attended the festivities along with the governor.

As mentioned in the East Channel Bridges story, the river here is divided into two channels by Nicollet Island. The back channel already had a bridge, privately built by Franklin Steele, so the "Mississippi Bridge Company" had only to span the west channel from Nicollet Island to the Minneapolis-to-be shore. The resulting bridge was "spider-like" with its cables and many wire hangers, but beautiful nonetheless.

In March of 1855, a high wind tore the deck from the suspension bridge and broke the castings to which the cables were attached. It was soon repaired, and the bridge survived until 1875 when Griffith designed a higher crenellated stone suspension bridge with 10-inch-diameter cables to replace it.

Between 1888 and 1891, a plate-girder deck-arch bridge was built, consisting of two solid web metal arches with open spandrels. This bridge had a grid deck added in 1964, viewing platforms and one-of-a-kind decorative iron railings.

By 1990 this bridge also disappeared and another suspension has taken its place on the approximate site of the "original bridge" across the Father of Waters. It is a six-lane, concrete deck suspension span having three connected towers at the ends. Appropriately this span continues the historic past of suspensions on the spot. It continues also the fancy wrought iron parapet, the projected lookout spaces with steps to the ground. It might well be called "A Superhighway in a Metropolis."

Use:
Local traffic and CSAH 52

Location:
Downtown Minneapolis on Hennepin Avenue

Style:
Five-span suspension with three towers per end

Length:
Channel span - 625 feet
Total length   - 1,037 feet

Width:
6 lanes, 134 feet with two lanes for public transportation and two 14-foot walkways

Clearance:
37 feet MLW

Date completed:
1990; originally a ferry operated by an Indian squaw; then in 1855 a wire suspension; in 1876 a stone tower suspension; in 1888 a two-span solid web iron deck arch; in 1891 widened to a 6-rib arch from a 3-rib arch

Designed by:
Howard, Needles, Tammen and Bergendoff

Bridge:
#27636

Owner:
Hennepin County

Toll:
Until 1872

Unique Feat:
Location of the first bridge across the Mississippi*

---

*This is a much sought after glory. We thought we had the first bridge in the Davenport/Rock Island area, until we found ours is the first railroad bridge, 1856. Some St. Louis citizens think they have the first bridge, but theirs is the oldest existing bridge, the Eads, 1874.

Hennepin Avenue Bridge, Minneapolis

Mary C. Costello

Second Avenue North (East Channel) Railroad Bridge, Minneapolis

*I*t looked like a miniature railroad layout as I viewed the Second Avenue North Railroad Bridge from the street overpass above. I could see the double tracks and long wooden plank between. There was a high pedestrian viaduct crossing the tracks ahead, and beyond that was the end of the through-truss of the train bridge over the main Mississippi channel. I could see a little of the back channel water, enough to know where the foreground bridge began and ended. Telephone poles without any cross bars or visible insulators lined up on the left side of the track. To the right on this "Minneapolis spread" was a trackless spur, curving north under the trees. [4]

Down on the bridge level, I could see the side of the black steel girder structure on which was printed "GREAT NORTHERN RAILWAY" in all caps between the protruding metal plates. The bridge has no railing or fence. I wanted to cross on the tracks, but it seemed more dangerous without anything on the sides, so I didn't. My excuse was the "No Trespassing" sign on a post.

Shortly after I arrived, a short freight approached from the east. I could see its bright headlamp coming very slowly. It may have just picked up or left off freight, or perhaps its tortoise speed was due to being in the heart of Minneapolis. To my delight the engineer waved as he passed. I was quite close and trains are exciting to me, though diesels have taken some of the thrill out of the viewing. It brought memories of the steam engine days, when my heart would have really been pounding.

Standing on the east bank this cold May morning, I peered down the stone-stepped embankment to the soot-blackened stone piers. There was but one pier in the center of the water; the others were against the banks. This middle support grew both thicker and longer the closer it got to water level.

This bridge has a history of mostly mergers. In G.K. Warren's "Diagram 4," a bridge on this spot (1878) is indicated with the St. Paul and Pacific Railway as owners. The Great Northern Railway were the next owners in 1893, and with their merger (1971) Burlington Northern became the owner's title. But since 1995, Burlington Northern Santa Fe has its name on the railroad.

There were many softly rounded trees in the setting to contrast with the linear rails and girders. Now the area was comparatively quiet, but in its history, with the spur line active, I can imagine it was a very busy spot. The day was too cold to spend time here dreaming though--I needed to warm my hands.

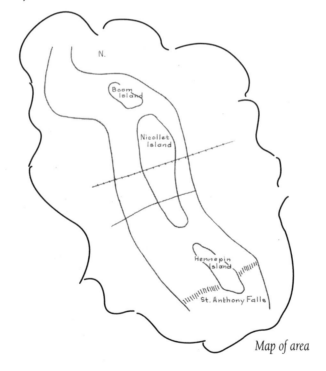

Map of area

Use:
Burlington Northern Santa Fe trains

Location:
East channel at 2nd Avenue North, Minneapolis

Style:
3-span steel deck plate-girder

Length:
Channel span - 67 feet
Total length   - 227 feet

Width:
2 tracks

Clearance:
14 feet MLW

Date completed:
1893 by Great Northern Railroad; August 1925 remodeled; shown in 1878 diagram by G.K. Warren as a St. Paul & Pacific Railway Bridge

Designed by:
Great Northern Railroad

Bridge:
#A1.1

Owner:
Burlington Northern Santa Fe Railroad

Burlington Northern Santa Fe East Channel Railroad Bridge, Minneapolis   *Mary C. Costello*

97

Main Channel, Second Avenue North Railroad Bridge, Minneapolis

*I*n the morning sunlight I saw a silver truck cross the Second Avenue Railroad Bridge and was confused. As I stood on the Hennepin Avenue Bridge across from it, I puzzled how a vehicle could be using a railroad bridge. Two bikers stopped to enjoy the river view and informed me that the caretaker had special wheels on a truck so he could ride the tracks to inspect them.

This is a combination bridge. It has girders on six spans and one through-truss span over the main channel. The solid stone piers are pointed upstream and square on the downstream end. The main or west channel piers are well-protected from boat damage by guide fences.

Four of the silver girders are different depths. The deeper one is near the center of the river where the greater strength is needed. At the time I couldn't understand an angled section of the bridge, but the Coast Guard diagram informed me that it is a spur-line track. It starts to veer off from the main track at the second-from-the-end pier on the west end of the structure or left in the picture.

Built in 1893 as a girder bridge, it was remodeled in 1926. A pier and two girder spans were removed in 1963, and a through-truss was added in their place. This last remodeling made the navigation channel wider and higher for boats going upstream. The truss on this renovation is called Petit, not an ordinary design on the Mississippi. Just as I noted on the East Channel span, there was a bridge in this location in 1878 built by the St. Paul and Pacific Railroad.

Trees hid most of the urban life surrounding the bridge, though some buildings and towers were visible above. The unusually bright-colored railroad bridge glinted in the sun's rays showing the metal railing along the sides. Though I saw no trains cross the bridge, the caretaker made sure that the tracks were ready.

Use:
Trains of Burlington Northern Santa Fe (originally Upper Great Northern)

Location:
Second Avenue north of Hennepin Avenue Bridge across the main channel

Style:
7-spans, one through-truss, three plate-girder and three beam spans

Length:
Channel span - 121 feet clear
               - 171 feet total
Total length   - 550 feet

Width:
2 tracks, 33 feet 6 inches; with a single-track spur

Clearance:
24 feet MLW

Date completed:
1893; 1926 thoroughly remodeled; June 1963 one pier removed and truss added; 1987 modified; original bridge here 1878

Designed by:
Upper Great Northern Railroad

Bridge:
#A1.3

Owner:
Burlington Northern Santa Fe Railroad

Burlington Northern Santa Fe Main Channel Railroad Bridge, Minneapolis   *Mary C. Costello*

Pedestrian/Bike (Former Railroad) Bridge, Boom Island, Minneapolis

Just thinking about a Chicago & Northwestern train crossing this backwoodsy bridge in the past is thrilling to me. The bridge is over the east channel of the Mississippi, north of Nicollet Island, and is a part of the spur which started at Second Avenue. It is a single span Pratt truss bridge--a tall superstructure with trees at either end. The train tracks were removed and the bridge converted to a pedestrian bikepath and walkway. Only park board and city motorized vehicles are allowed on it. Conveniently the dirt path to and from it are level and reasonably straight. Not so, when I first visited the span.

It was a cool May morning and I had on a spring jacket, but my hands were cold. There was a wind and it looked like rain. I knew from the map that there was another railroad bridge across the river. I sought information from a woman who was taking her garbage out a little before 8 a.m. She didn't know. "I don't drive," she said. We had a little conversation, and then I crossed the street and asked a city employee who directed me over an open field. At the edge of the not-too-level open area was a thicket and a path down to the river. The rugged footpath was steep in places. But the narrow waterway was picturesque even on a day like this with a variety of trees surrounding it. I could see the bridge truss a little farther north surrounded by elm, poplar, maple and oak trees. Although the end of the bridge had a chain-link fence across, people had made an opening to go through.

The bridge looked sad with the rails gone and only the ties remaining. A single plank had been added in a position out over the water from which some venturesome souls must dive when it is warmer. As I crossed the bridge on the boardwalk which lined both sides of what had been track, an eerie feeling crept over me. I thought about the past--trains coming out of the forested area, smoke rising from the stack and the clickety clack sound of the wheels riding the steel track.

On the other side of the bridge were steps going up and out of the underbrush--to what, I didn't know. I followed just

far enough to see ties, partially buried, used as a walk. Extensive research revealed that Boom Island formerly housed a railroad yard, and before that was home to a log-booming industry (from which it got its name).

As I started back, a middle-aged man came through the fence as I had done, and walked on the other side of the bridge hardly paying attention to me. A while later as I was sketching, a boy on his way to school walked past and commented on what I was doing. Then a happy, whistling person and next a career woman crossed the span. It was a much used shortcut. A little above and to the left of where I stood was a hobo camp under a circle of trees. When the trains ran, this must have been heaven for them hopping freight trains coming from the railyard.

Almost finished, I noticed a beaver swim past with his head above the water and his back legs paddling hard. When the bridge is incorporated into the city park plans, I thought, I hope they keep it rustic so wild animals stay.

Well, all has not changed. There are still the trees and undergrowth for Mother Nature's animals. On the other hand, it is not nearly so secluded a spot today--that is better for safety reasons. The bridge now has a solid, wooden-deck path for bikers and walkers with a chain-link fence on the bridge sides.

My mind romanticises, when I see this span, that my grandfather, as a CNW engineer, may have driven his train across this bridge--across the very spot where I have stood, though years later.

Use:
Pedestrian path and city worker vehicles

Location:
North end of Nicollet Island to Boom Island; off spur north of 1st Avenue North

Style:
Single span, iron through-truss

Length:
Channel span - 67 feet clear
            - 172 feet total
Total length - 176 feet

Width:
19 feet

Clearance:
6 feet MLW

Date completed:
1890; Chicago & Northwestern bought about 1965 and abandoned in 1971; Carl Bowlander owned until 1981 when the Park Board bought it; converted for recreation in 1987

Designed by:
Unknown, possibly the Great Northern Railroad

Bridge:
No number

Owner:
Minneapolis Park and Recreation Board
Minneapolis

Boom Island Pedestrian/Bike Bridge, Minneapolis

Mary C. Costello

101

Plymouth Avenue Bridge, Minneapolis, Minnesota

*T*he Plymouth or Eighth Avenue Bridge, when seen from the riverside, appears to be a normal concrete girder bridge with a slight arch in the center span. Looks can be deceiving, however. This bridge is not like older girder bridges. It was constructed with a design and technique not used before in Minnesota or in most of the Midwest at the time.

Built with utopian technology in 1983, this Plymouth Avenue Bridge has post-tensioned, segmental box girders cantilevered out over the water. At one point, 2.5 million pounds of bridge hung over the river without support from below. A "form traveler", which looks like "Tinker Toy" pieces at the edge of the bridge, shaped the concrete. The planning firm said it was similar to the "slip form" used in skyscrapers only here it was horizontal instead of vertical. Two concrete boxes run beneath the deck, big enough for people to walk through--10 by 18 feet. These support the span and house the wires for cables and traffic signals.

Another utopian feature of the four-lane bridge is the concrete itself. It is salt-resistant, theoretically. Tubes run through the concrete containing strands of cable. "We put tension on the strands which compress the structure and are supposed to resist salt." says George Handy from the designing firm. (Further explanation from Harold Sandberg says, "It prevents cracks and hence hinders the ingress of salt water.") The bridge has 110 miles of this cable. Unlike the concrete arch bridges, such as the Third and Tenth Avenue spans, where tons of wooden falsework was used, no falsework was needed in constructing this bridge, and river traffic was not impeded. In fact, the reason this style construction started is that after World War II in Europe, engineers did not have the materials needed to build temporary supports and began using the cantilever method.

To tie in with the bridge's simple lines the piers are the simplest possible--two rectangular slabs held together at the bottom only with a flat base, rounded front and back.

The previous Plymouth Bridge was built in 1882, when "The heaviest thing it was designed to carry was a horse-drawn cart" Wrong! It was designed so well that it lasted almost 100 years bearing much heavier weights. The through-truss bridge was raised 16 feet in 1953 for additional navigation clearance. In 1981 it was closed because it was found "the floor beams that made it work were so decayed that you could push a pencil through the steel," ··all due to salt that couldn't escape.

Before that bridge, in about 1870, a long low wooden bridge was located at the site, built about the same time as the first 10th Avenue Bridge.

I saw the bridge from a distance. It was attractive viewing, with downtown buildings behind and cumulus clouds above--like a calendar picture.

Use:
Vehicular traffic, bicycles and pedestrians

Location:
Between Plymouth Avenue N. and 8th Avenue, N.E.

Style:
4-span segmental concrete box girder

Date completed:
1983; replaced 1882 through-truss; raised in 1953 for more clearance; original was wooden bridge 1870

Length:
Channel span - 140 feet
Total length   - 943 feet

Width:
4 lanes, 55 feet, plus 9-foot bicycle and 6-foot pedestrian paths

Clearance:
25 feet MLW

Designed by:
VanDoren-Hazard-Stallings

Bridge:
#27611 Hennepin County

Owner:
City of Minneapolis

Unique feat:
Only bridge of this style in Minnesota (1983)

Plymouth Avenue Bridge, Minneapolis

Mary C. Costello

103

Broadway Avenue Bridge, County Highway 66, Minneapolis

*B*roadway Avenue has been the sight of three bridges. The first had a short history. Built according to a 1857 charter, it was swept away in a June 1859 flood, and the debris from it threatened the survival of the suspension bridge downstream at Hennepin Avenue. "It was a long structure of wood on log piers placed on a sandy bottom." The Broadway Avenue Bridge charged a toll--the same rate as the suspension span, a mile and a quarter downstream.

The next two bridges on this spot were built 100 years apart, but were complete opposites-one fancy and one plain.

In 1887 a four-span Pratt through-truss bridge united the northern new industrial district that was developing on both sides of the river. It was an ornate bridge, the fanciest of all in Minneapolis. Between the finials on the top of each corner of the bridge ends was a band of scrolls, crosses and holes. In addition,the horizontal struts and guard-railing used X's or diamond shapes for a pattern, depending on how a person views them. An unusual feature was a high lengthwise wind-stablizer for the otherwise frail horizontal struts. The l9th century wrought iron structure had stone piers and a cedar-block surfaced deck "which didn't make for smooth riding", recalls Joe Justad who was then a small boy. It didn't matter much because the wagons and buggies had big springs, he stated. Since the bridge was only 12.6 feet above water, it was raised nearly 20 feet to allow barges and larger boats to go under. Starting in 1950 hydraulic jacks raised it 6 inches at a time,taking 16 months to accomplish. At that time open steel grating replaced the wood block flooring. The year 1985 saw the demise of the old bridge--that is, all but a single span which has been preserved for ages to come in a park setting on Nicollet Island. (#42)

In July of 1987, a new four-span Broadway Avenue Bridge was completed. Designed as a steel girder structure, it is a streamlined bridge with the most ornate part being its piers. Their design consists of two flat columns that taper together, but the base extends out again to the full width of the bridge. It is unusual because the pier center is filled instead of open. The center is grooved concrete giving a coarse texture lending interest and contrast. The brown color of the girder has been repeated in the tall, tapered light pole and square light fixture. The railing consists of pipe posts and double horizontal bars.

Several days after its grand opening, I crossed the new bridge,thinking about its predecessors. The one thing I was sure of was I'd much rather be crossing this one in my little Datsun than the 1857 bridge in a horse and carriage. We have come a long way.

Use:
CSAH 66 and local traffic

Location:
Joins East and West Broadway Avenue in north Minneapolis

Style:
4-span steel girder bridge

Length:
Channel span - 186 feet
Total length   - 857 feet

Width:
4 lanes, 52 feet, plus two 8-foot sidewalks

Clearance:
22.6 feet MLW

Date completed:
July 1987, replaces the 1887 through-truss, original 1857 span washed out in flood

Designed by:
Van Doren-Hazard-Stallings

Bridge:
#27608 Hennepin County

Owner:
City of Minneapolis

Broadway Avenue Bridge, Minneapolis

Mary C. Costello

105

Burlington Northern Santa Fe Railroad Bridge, Minneapolis

*T*his bridge was originally constructed for the Upper Northern Pacific Railroad with five through-trusses. Later, in 1927, after renovation, the bridge had nine deck plate-girder spans with trains riding on top. In 1963, however, the bridge was completely remodeled. It received new, heavier center piers while two girder spans and three regular piers were removed to make room for a l92-foot Warren through-truss span over the main channel. In addition the whole bridge was raised--all to make the navigation channel accessible to larger boats. The work took almost two years.

The BNSF Railroad now owns the black-painted bridge. It is not very high because the river banks are not. In fact, the plain piers, pointed at each end, appeared to be little higher above the water than the girders are deep. Though everything else was dark, I noticed a silver railing beside the open track glistening in the sun. To protect the piers, a sheer fence has been installed.

This was a gala Sunday in Minneapolis--the day of the river festival. Crowds of people had come and were watching from the grassy banks. As I arrived, the "raft regalia" was in progress and I caught a picture of ten people and a shed on a raft. It looked crowded. Crazy homemade rafts turned over and people jumped or fell into the river with no apparent worry. This was difficult for me, since in my hometown we respect the river for its treacherous ways and would avoid such activity. Here there is no current, the river bottom is at least partially sandy and the river depth varies from 9 to 18 feet. I am told it is relatively safe though most people wouldn't swim in it.

If the BNSF Bridge had had a passenger train cross at this time, the crew and passengers would have had a distant view of the activities six blocks away.

Use:
Burlington Northern Santa Fe trains

Location:
24th Avenue North, in Minneapolis

Style:
Seven plate-girder spans and one through-truss span

Length:
Channel span - 150 feet clear
- 192 feet total
Total length - 821 feet

Width:
Two tracks

Clearance:
27 feet MLW

Date completed:
Built in 1884; remodeled in 1927; in July 1963, bridge was raised and one through-truss replaced two girder spans

Designed by:
Northern Pacific Railroad

Bridge:
#12.1

Owner:
BNSF Railroad since 1971

Burlington Northern Santa Fe Railroad Bridge, North Minneapolis   *Mary C. Costello*

107

Lowry Avenue Bridge, Minneapolis, County Highway 153

Called the "20-Ton Bridge", the Lowry Avenue Structure is certainly strong enough to carry the regular highway load. The original riveted bridge was a metal truss built in 1887 with Kristoffer Olsen Oustad, Norwegian designer/engineer with the city. In 1905, a new bridge was built of the same style. This one lasted 51 years, until it became too weak to carry the traffic.

Today's 1958 design is a riveted five-span truss, raised 20 feet above what the bridge had been and completely remodeled so navigation could be extended farther north on the Great River.

Although the Lowry Bridge is a camelback superstructure, it has a modern look because it has hole-free beams for verticals and diagonals. The only beams with openings are in the overhead struts; the holes make them lighter while maintaining strength. This blue-green Pratt truss bridge is twice the width of most old truss bridges therefore it looks low and wide, features characteristic of today's designs.

There are two unusual features about this Mississippi river bridge. One concerns the piers and the other the outer edge of the bridge deck. The four piers in the river are hexagonal shaped columns, which are not common. Even more uncommon is the platform visible at the base of the closest pier. Logs get caught on this floor, though I don't believe that was its intention. Could it be for fishermen? On the upstream side of the piers is an angle to help break up ice, according to the Minnesota DOT.

The other unique feature about the bridge is that the space below the deck is open at the sides. On the whole river I have not noticed such a thing. This space is usually covered with steel. In the dark shadow of the protruding sidewalks I could see some shapes but they were hard to decipher. I wondered if they were working on it, but there was no sign of that.

Later Harold Sandberg, Chairman of the Board of Alfred Benesch and Company, Chicago, Illinois, informed me that what I saw were stringers, or their ends, and that the space is left open to facilitate maintenance. It's great to get answers.

A large tree provided shade but blocked most of the first span from my view. A tall rusty colored wildflower, remains of last fall, and varied bushes lined the bank near me. The opposite shore looked more commercial. As I drove over the bridge, I noticed the sidewalks on the outside of the trusses. I only wished I had had time to go for a walk on them.

The first Lowry Bridge was one of at least eight spans built across the Mississippi in Minneapolis in the 1880's-- some railroad but mostly wagon bridges. In 1882, the Tenth Street Bridge, (second bridge on this spot); in 1883, Hill's Stone Arch; in 1884, the Upper Northern Pacific Railroad at 24th Avenue North; in 1885, the Northern Pacific Railroad on University grounds; in 1886, Washington Avenue Bridge; in 1887 Broadway and Lowry Avenue Bridges; and finally in 1888, the third Hennepin Avenue Bridge was completed. What a busy time for the young town of Minneapolis! It must have been exciting along the river in those days and have set some kind of record!

Use:
CSAH 153 & local traffic

Location:
Between 2nd Street North on the west and Northeast Marshall on the east

Style:
5-span camelback steel through-truss

Length:
Channel span - 143 feet
Total length   - 889 feet

Width:
4 lanes, 40 feet, plus 2 walkways outside trusses; total 57.2 feet

Clearance:
33 feet MLW

Date completed:
1905 piers and abutment, but July 1958 new trusses were added; original bridge built in 1887

Designed by:
The 1905 portion is unknown; the City of Minneapolis designed the 1958 portion.

Bridge:
#2723 Hennepin County

Owner:
Hennepin County DOT since 1950's

Lowry Avenue, Bridge, Minneapolis

Mary C. Costello

109

North Minneapolis, Canadian Pacific Railroad, "Camden" Bridge

*T*his Old Milwaukee Railroad Bridge now the Canadian Pacific, has always been considered the "head of navigation" for barges and larger boats. The title still remains even though changes have been made to allow larger boats to go farther north. Clearance below this railroad bridge, for example, has been raised ten feet by changing the center span from a deep deck-truss to a shallower girder span. Taller boats can now navigate under it but the 9-foot channel depth, maintained by the Corps of Engineers, still starts with this railroad bridge. "Squat" tugboats navigate above for companies located there and form barges that merge below St.Anthony Falls locks.

The northern Minneapolis Canadian Pacific Railroad Bridge was built in 1905 for the Minneapolis, St.Paul and Sault Ste.Marie Railway Company. The often-called "Camden Railway Bridge"(because the area in northern Minneapolis in which it is located was known as Camden) is a Warren style deck truss structure. It previously had only an 18-foot vertical clearance, preventing all but small boats to navigate it.

To me, the most unusual features of the railroad bridge today are the angle at which the piers are set and the slanted base on which they rest. Instead of the normal 90-degree angle to the roadway, these piers are at 60 degrees. The river curves southeast under the bridge, and so the piers are set in line with the river current to prevent trouble.

I could see only five piers because of the surrounding trees, but there are seven. They looked very white next to the black bridge trusses and the darkness of the green trees; the late afternoon sun helped also to bleach the piers. Not very tall, the pylons are rectangular, pointed on the northern end. In 1977, the bridge piers were modified with a wide base that is convex in shape and has a scalloped edge of concrete. Only piers 3, 4, 5, and 6, which are in the mainstream of the river, have the larger bottom. I am sure this design is meant to ward off boats, logs and ice that might damage the pier.

I was standing in what I think was a boat launching area that had a variety of surfaces--cinders, gravel and some residual concrete poured in one spot. There were scattered chunks of stone or concrete, some timbers, a rusty pipe and quite a few pieces of weathered logs. The housekeeping was a little messy--a mess no one cares about when putting a boat in or out of water. About 10 feet out were wooden pilings sticking 2 feet out of the water for boats to tie onto. I was wondering how you get to land without getting into the water until I noticed a twisted silver post on land. Maybe the others are for bigger boats.

The ground was several feet higher closer to the bridge and had some grass before a thicket of trees and bushes. Since this span is close to the city limits of Minneapolis, there are no buildings to be seen above or around the bridge. From where I stood, I could see only trees.

Use:
Canadian Pacific Railroad

Location:
41st Avenue North, Minneapolis

Style:
5 spans cantilever truss with a suspended girder span

Length:
Channel span - 83 feet clear
             - 89.75 feet total
Total length - 904 feet

Width:
One track

Clearance:
28 feet MLW

Date completed:
May 1905; July 1977 piers were modified and girder added.

Designed by:
Soo Line Railroad Company

Bridge:
#D1.00 called "Camden Bridge" or "Upper Harbor"

Owner:
Canadian Pacific Railroad

Unique feat:
End of navigation officially

Canadian Pacific "Camden" Railroad Bridge, Minneapolis

Mary C. Costello

111

This is the most vivid royal blue bridge I remember seeing on the river. It is a steel plate-girder that is haunched above each pier and has a ridge the length of the span about a foot from the bottom. This groove is a longitudinal stiffener on the girder to permit the use of a thinner one. The only other decoration is another shorter ridge in the girder over the piers, no doubt for the same purpose.

Both this bridge and the previously discussed Canadian Pacific Railroad Bridge have been given the title of "Camden Bridges" (see explanation on previous bridge) in old newspaper articles, but officially they are identified as the "41st and 42nd Avenue North Bridges". Though the location of the two bridges is close, the navigation span width is very different. The railroad bridge's horizontal clearance is only 83 feet and the highway bridge has 244 feet between the main piers.

This 1977 bridge replaced an old, 4-span steel bow-truss span found to be unsafe on August of 1973. Originally built at the start of World War I for traffic including horse-drawn wagons, it was 36 feet wide and was flanked by two sidewalks. The west approach was supported by concrete columns that formed a viaduct for what was then the Soo Lines Railroad tracks. When the old bridge was dynamited in the summer of 1974, pedestrians were left for three years without a place to cross on foot from Lowry Avenue south to Anoka farther north. Only cars could cross the river on I-694 or Lowry Avenue.

When I approached from I-94, which goes under the western approach to the bridge, I saw a little road to the right with a sign saying "Mississippi River Access". This two-lane street took me a short distance to the bridge area. The clearing to the right of the bridge was partially cemented. It had a high, square, red canvas lifeguard canopy over an empty lifeguard seat. No one was around when I arrived, but a couple of fishermen came as I prepared to draw. They backed their silver-colored outboard motorboat into the river and headed upstream. Next a young couple came with three children between 5 and 10 years old. They went for a walk in the woods which was to my back. According to the map it is a part of Webber Park, most of which is farther north.

The shiny blue of the bridge structure was striking with the white of the concrete roadway and the four concrete double-T piers in contrast. It was a colorful spot with the greens of the trees in the background and, with the center bridge span as a frame, a solitary red brick building nestled into the bank on the opposite shore. It was a joy to behold.

Use:
City traffic, MSAS 262

Location:
Between 42nd Avenue North and 37th Avenue Northeast in Minneapolis, the Webber Parkway Area

Style:
5-span steel deck-girder

Length:
Channel span - 244 feet
Total length   - 1686 feet

Width:
4 lanes, two 9-foot walkways for a total of 70 feet

Height:
31 feet MLW

Date completed:
July 1977; original 1913 bridge was a 4-span bow truss

Designed by:
Jacus Associates Incorporated

Bridge:
#27549 Hennepin County

Owner:
City of Minneapolis

Unique feat:
Last bridge in city limits

"Camden" Highway Bridge, Minneapolis

Mary C. Costello

Brooklyn Center, I-694 Eastbound, Highway Bridge, Minnesota

What could an old secret pathway possibly have to do with a bridge? Usually nothing, but when it came to these Brooklyn Center Bridges, everything. The area beside the spans and the bridges themselves were SO busy, that I didn't see how I could find a safe spot from which to sketch them. It was scary just crossing the street nearby. So I asked a young waitress at the restaurant/gas station for help. She told me her secret way to the highway as a student. After eating a sandwich from the cool restaurant, I followed her directions to cross a field, go down a side street to a path beside a fence, and onto a bike path going under the bridges. From here I had several views of the twin Brooklyn Center Bridges. Wonderful!

These two bridges were not always together like this. They were originally designed and built at different times and locations, with different piers, girders and even heights. The southern-most I-694 Bridge was the older of the two. It was built in 1945 (during World War II) a short distance downstream. The narrow grey girder or beam span, then called Highway 100, carried traffic both directions for seventeen years. That bridge had eight tall double "T" piers, five of which were alike and in the water. The two end piers on land were sturdier with a triple "T" design. In 1961, the newer bridge was widened at a cost of $300,000 and the next year the second span was built for twice that amount. By 1988 the old eastbound bridge was showing its age and was torn down and a new bridge was built to match the west-bound span.

The two bridges have different numbers and histories. they are independent structures on adjacent spots, therefore, are treated as such by the Minnesota DOT, as well as, by me.

On the shoreline almost level with the river, there was a man fishing. Though the Mississippi is a favorite fishing hole for many, I believe this is one of the few people I've seen fishing on my trip.

Use:
I-694 traffic eastbound

Location:
Between Brooklyn Center and Fridley, north Minneapolis

Style:
5-span steel continuous beam span

Length:
Channel span - 200 feet total
Total length   - 776 feet

Width:
84-foot deck width

Clearance:
43 feet MLW

Date completed:
1988; previous bridge built 1945; widened in 1962 and destroyed in 1988

Designed by:
Minnesota DOT

Bridge:
#27801 Hennepin County

Owner:
Minnesota DOT

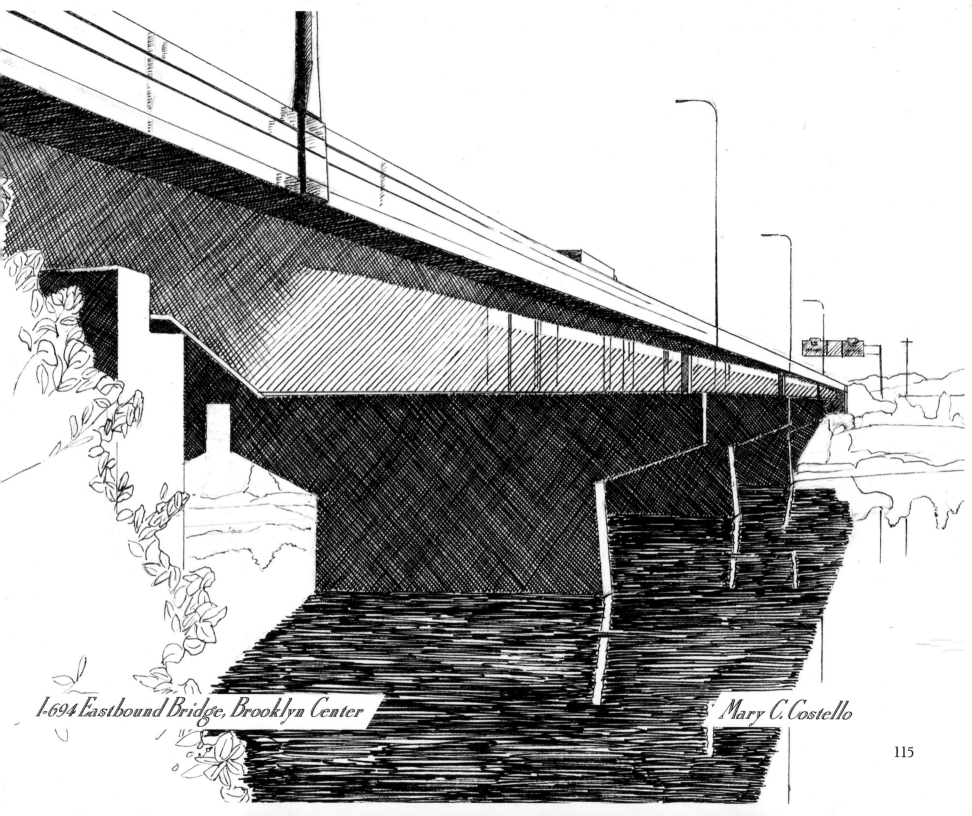

I-694 Eastbound Bridge, Brooklyn Center

Mary C. Costello

115

Brooklyn Center, I-694 Westbound, Highway Bridge, Minnesota

*T*he second I-694 Bridge carries vehicular traffic westward and is located just north of the twin span. They are two separate bridges though they are side by side like one span.

Built in 1963, this second Brooklyn Center Bridge has "he man" piers. I call them that because they remind me of a giant weight-lifter. They are short-appearing and broad with arms that angle up. There are only five piers now for each of the bridges. Three of those piers are in the water 200 feet apart allowing more room for navigation than did the old eastbound span with five piers in the Mississippi and only 94 feet between. Perhaps the only difference in the bridges today are the widths--this westbound span is ten feet narrower and has a walk, while the eastbound one does not.

The plain brown continuous girder is different from the grey plate-girder on the earlier westbound Brooklyn Center Bridge. It was 1988 that saw the big change-removing the eastbound bridge, located slightly to the south, and building it as a twin, while widening and redoing the upper part of the westbound span.

On my first visit here my daughter picked wildflowers on the hillside near the bridge. This trip bicycle path and park were added, but I didn't see the goldenrod and vervain.

The views pictured here are the earlier Brooklyn Center Bridges showing the differences between them. For a picture of the appearance of today's westbound span see #54. They are next to each other and appear identical.

Use:
I-694 traffic westbound

Location:
Between Brooklyn Center and Fridley, Minnesota

Style:
5-span steel continuous beam bridge

Length:
Channel span - 200 feet total
Total Length - 776 feet

Width:
74-foot deck with a 10-foot walk on the right

Clearance:
43 feet MLW

Date completed:
November 1963; widened and new structure above the piers added in 1987

Designed by:
Minnesota DOT

Bridge:
#9321 Hennepin County

Owner:
Minnesota DOT

Brooklyn Center, Previous Bridges

Mary C. Costello

PART THREE

PART THREE
Lower The Decks

Between Coon Rapids and Brainerd, Minnesota, the Mississippi River has 23 bridges and one sees no barges or commercial river traffic. Therefore, with clearance no problem, the bridge decks are built lower. The river direction is mostly northwest as we climb through five counties, elbowing in and out and splitting many islands.

Approximately 830 feet wide and more shallow above Anoka, the river flows past fewer homes as we go north. Sand hills covered with hardwood trees, occasional pines, and some agricultural land abut the river. There are three power plants between Elk River and Clearwater, but from Monticello to St.

Cloud the shores are undeveloped. Unique are the Beaver Islands, just downstream from St. Cloud's dam. They are a group of 30 islands crammed within a two-mile stretch.

In St. Cloud, the banks become quite urban with houses and factories, continuing for two miles to Sartell. The Mississippi passes through four dams on its way to Camp Ripley, becoming noticeably wider above each, with stretches of scenic landscape. Occasional windbreaks of evergreen provide winter cover for deer. Just south of Brainerd is a deciduous forest region with low but steep, variable terrain, where occasional grazing farm animals may be seen.

121

Coon Rapids Bridge, Minnesota, Highway 610

*P*icture a quiet tree-shaded street with oak-shaded low sprawling modern frame and brick homes facing it. One person was sunning herself, several men were talking sports and children were riding bikes. I found myself driving along this street puzzled as to how to get to the Coon Rapids Bridge. Parking my car, I asked a number of these people and was directed down a path behind the houses. But an all-night rain had washed away some of the path so I had to backtrack and take my car (with more directions) to the Coon Rapids Regional Park along the river. From here I drove along the river path to the bridge. The view was worth the $1.50 fee to enter.

The bridge is a very attractive low-to-the-water concrete girder span. The design is the simplest possible. Everything is plain--no grooves, decoration or color to distract. The shadows, however, were striking on this late afternoon. The extended-out roadway cast its long straight silhouette on the girder and the girder did the same on the piers. Mother Nature certainly improves what would otherwise be a stark white appearance.

At the left end of the bridge I was surprised to see an overpass (Highway 252 going to Anoka) over the bridge road. The Coon Rapids Bridge is a direct link to the Anoka County Airport, connecting it to the west side of the Mississippi. The next crossing is I-694 which is about 20 miles south.

There are six piers in the water, wide-stemmed "T's" but thin arms--not the "he man" type. Four different style piers on land were hidden mostly by trees or underbrush. Here some wild-flowers flourished.

Use:
Highway MN 610

Location:
Connects Brooklyn Park with an area near Foley Boulevard in Coon Rapids

Style:
10-span concrete girder

Length:
Channel span - 122 feet
Total length   - 1326 feet

Width:
4 lanes, 68.3 feet

Clearance:
21 feet MLW

Date completed:
November 1987

Designed by:
Gary Wellhauser, MNDOT

Bridge:
#27239 Hennepin County

Owner:
Minnesota DOT

Minnesota Highway 610 Bridge, Coon Rapids

Mary C. Costello

Anoka/Champlin Highway Bridge, Minnesota, US 169

*E*ight beautiful deck arches stretch across the Miss-issippi River to form this charming 1929 bridge at Anoka. When I arrived, it was 5:30 p.m. and the bridge was in shadow making it difficult to see details. I returned later in order to better see the beauty of the Art Deco piers, railing, and lampposts.

I thought it interesting that in building the bridge the engineers had trouble with deadheads--logs lying in the bottom of the river for the last 45, 50 or even 75 years. Some were from the old log drives, and others were in the form of piles driven for the old 1884 bridge. For one pier, 150 logs and 47 piles had to be removed.

Each pier is boat-shaped concrete, rounded in front. A three-ridged pillar having a bracket-top rests on this base and keeps the adjoining ribbed arch rigid. Open spandrels with simple vertical posts provide interesting lights and shadows.

This Anoka/Champlin Bridge has an ornate railing consisting of short, sturdy concrete posts that protrude beyond the slitted, otherwise solid-appearing wall. Above each pier and in line with the railing is a concrete block decorated with relief designs.

Also, unique to this bridge, at each pier there is an old-fashioned lamppost with a naturally formed green patina on the base. The lamps are positioned on top of the parapet with a large oval glass dome for the light.

By 1991 the much traveled 1929 Anoka/Champlin Bridge had deteriorated so that it was closed to traffic. A temporary bridge was built next to the location so that people would be able to cross while renovations were made. The old bridge was torn down to the piers and arches, was widened, a new deck and support system were added and the ornamental concrete railing was duplicated. (That was a real challenge, I'm sure, because all parts must look the same as the original for an historically registered bridge like this.) The temporary span was removed in 1998 when reconstruction was completed.

Before this bridge there was a steel through-truss swingspan built in 1884 slightly north of this spot and was still in use in 1929. During the 1929-30 winter season when the ice would allow, it was lifted off its piers and deposited on the ice. There it was broken into sections and transported to a northern part of the state.

This is a busy, busy bridge--41,000 cars a day and more added each year. Because the traffic was so heavy on and off the bridge, it was difficult to get back into traffic. Anoka is identified as a star town in Minnesota, and the bridge has repeated stars in its decoration and on the bronze plaque at its entrance. It earns a star, in my thinking, for being well used.

Use:
City and US 169 traffic

Location:
Between Anoka and Champlin, about 20 miles north of Minneapolis

Style:
10-spans of open spandrel concrete deck arches, two are smaller arch approaches

Length:
Channel span - 108 feet
Total length - 1038.4 feet

Width:
4 lanes, 56 foot road, and two 8-foot sidewalks

Clearance:
19 feet MLW

Date completed:
1929; remodeled with new deck and restored parapet in 1998; original 1884 5-span through-truss swingspan bridge; ferry started 1855

Designed by:
Possibly Minnesota Bridge Company who built it; HNTB did restoration work

Bridge:
#4380 Anoka County

Owner:
Minnesota DOT

Unique feat:
On the National Register of Historic Places, 1979

US 169 Highway, Anoka/Champlin, Minnesota

Mary C. Costello

125

Northbound Highway 101 Elk River Bridge, Minnesota

*T*he wind was quiet this late August afternoon, contrary to my first visit where the wind caused whitecaps on the Mississippi River under the Highway 101 Bridge near Elk River.

I was able to park next to the structure--always a joy. Shortly after, a young couple wanting a break from their driving followed my suit but pulled up even closer to the bridge in the tall grass. To get a better view, I walked down the rutted twelve-foot embankment to the water's edge.

This bridge had a deep steel girder with a large graffiti sign painted on it when I last visited it. Also the water had trash sticking out: tires, water heater and natural debris. Today both the girder and water were clean except for one interesting log protruding.

Several things stood out as being different about the span. One was the square drainage pipes installed along the outside, from the deck to the bottom of the girder--longer than most and more regular.

Though the piers were plain--solid slabs of concrete, rounded at the ends and capped--the railings were unusual. The short square concrete posts were arranged in a two-then-one pattern all across the span. The post tops, cut at an angle, were secured to a sturdy concrete rail. Above this parapet was a two-pipe steel rail.

By July 2002, there will be another bridge in this very spot. Dave Dahlberg, one of the designers with MNDOT, said that, difficult as it is, they are building the piers over the existing ones so as not to interrupt traffic as much. The new span will be a wider, prestressed-concrete beam bridge. The next 101 northbound span will be almost the exact same length (706 feet) but three of the five spans will be 57 feet wide. The other two spans will be slightly narrower because there will be an east ramp veering off from them to Highway US 10.

This segment of the river has a rich historical background since early explorers including Father Louis Hennepin, Jonathan Carver, Zebulon Pike, J.C.Beltrami and Henry Schoolcraft were fascinated with the area. Steamboats ran regularly in the 1800's between St. Cloud and St. Anthony Falls. First it was trappers who came for the animal furs, then it was lumbering and the sawmills. Passengers and freight went regularly upstream and wheat downstream.

Use:
Minnesota Highway 101, north bound

Location:
North of Elk River

Style:
4-span steel plate-girder

Length:
Channel span - 150 feet
Total length   - 708 feet

Width:
2 lanes, 36.9 feet

Clearance:
15.5 feet MLW

Date completed:
1967 as two-way Highway 101; in 1993 became one-way

Designed by:
Minnesota DOT

Bridge:
#86001 Wright County

Owner:
Minnesota DOT

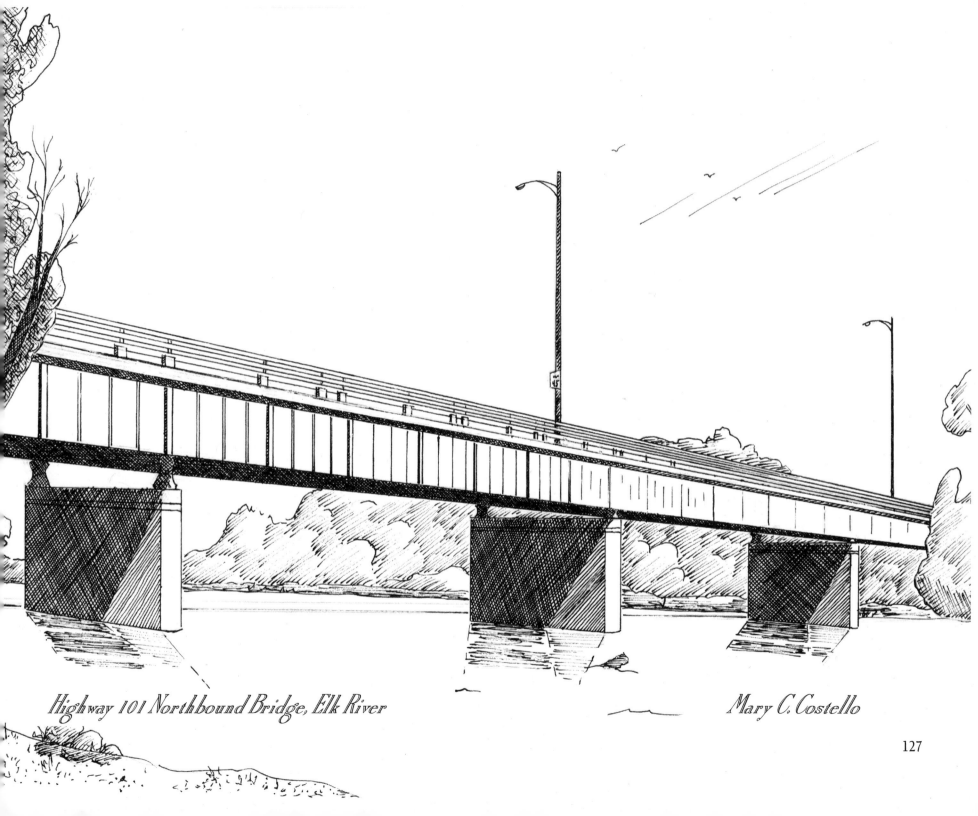

Highway 101 Northbound Bridge, Elk River

Mary C. Costello

127

Southbound Highway 101, Elk River Bridge, Minnesota

*T*his Highway 101 Bridge is outside of Elk River, a modern precast concrete girder span with simple broad "T" piers, squared off, no angles. It carries all traffic going south. Seeing the bridge with tree shadows on its girders and parapet that were on land, I was aesthetically attracted. No longer plain-looking, the span was softened in appearance and more beautiful. However, trees blocked my view of its crossing the Mississippi, so with the magic of my pen, I took down the impediment and show the whole bridge. A lovely view of the opposite bank is framed by one pier from this span's bridge-mate (seen partially behind).

Uniquely this Elk River Bridge has a ramp, which the DOT treats as a separate bridge. Since it barely crosses the river, I am treating it as merely a part of Highway 101, South. Its exit can be seen on the left side of the picture where the roadway overhang appears to be getting wider as it goes south. This ramp has its own number 86005A, and is two spans long for a total length of 293 feet. It is 32 feet wide and carries traffic off onto US 10 south.

Earlier my view had been by the water's edge where there was riprap under both ends of the bridge to protect the embankment from washing and provided a nice texture and color to the scene. I think the rocks would discourage trespassers, also; at least, I found it uncomfortable standing on them.

Use:
Highway 101 southbound traffic only, with a ramp to US 10

Location:
Outside Elk River

Style:
5-span concrete girder bridge

Length:
Channel span - 150 feet
Total length   - 707 feet

Width:
2 lanes going south, 45 feet

Clearance:
32 feet MLW

Date completed:
1993

Designed by:
Strgar, Roscoe, Fausch

Bridge:
#86005 in Wright County

Owner:
Minnesota DOT

Highway 101 Southbound Bridge, Elk River

Mary C. Costello

129

Elk River Highway Bridge, Minnesota, County Road 42

*T*he present downtown Elk River Bridge is a modern precast concrete beam span with striking piers and unusual rests for the lightpoles. Attractive and worry-free as the 1985 span is, the people of Otsego and Elk River have not forgotten the first bridge here, engineered they thought by Claude Allan Porter Turner, a distinguished bridge designer. Since it was C.A.P. Turner's engineering firm, however, instead of him personnally, who did the designing, or could be proven to have done the designing, the old bridge was not saved nor was it included in the National Register of Historic Places.

The old structure had a single Baltimore truss through-span with deck-truss spans at each end. The attractive inner railing was composed of metal rods that had metal circles and four leaf clovers where each rod crossed. Outside the trusses, on one side of the bridge only, people could walk. That first bridge took the place of the ferry that had shuttled people across the Mississippi previously. The horse and buggies and sleighs crossed on the "opening" day in February of 1906, but, though there was a dinner with a steer and fatted calf, people weren't much interested in an outdoor program since it was the coldest day of the year.

The old truss bridge was the sight of some "terrifying tales", of people climbing the trusses, walking on top, doing headstands and even jumping into the Mississippi from there. The narrow, 506-foot long bridge finally deteriorated and concern for people's safety forced its closing and final demolition in 1984. Sketches of the bridge and its image on Christmas decorations have kept its memory alive for the villagers who used and loved the old Turner bridge.

Today's bridge has smooth flat double-T piers whose legs bow to the inside--making an "Omega" shape. The edge of the concrete deck looks split horizontally below the middle and projects into a shelf in two or three places outside the railing. The silver lightpoles are anchored on these made-to-order ledges.

The large round multi-colored riprap under both ends of the bridge protects the high embankment from washing and provides a texture in contrast to the plain solid bridge. I think it would discourage trespassers...at least I found it uncomfortable standing on the rocks.

I saw a fish jump out of the water and curl back down. Too bad I didn't have a pole.

Use:
Local and CSAH 42 traffic

Location:
Between downtown Elk River and Otsego, Minnesota

Style:
4-span concrete girder

Length:
Channel span - 112 feet
Total length   - 450 feet

Width:
4 lanes, 46 feet, one 6-foot walk

Clearance:
13.8 feet MLW

Date completed:
1985; original bridge built in 1906, a single camelback through-truss; ferry before that

Designed by:
Toltz,King,Duval and Anderson

Bridge:
#86515 Wright County

Owner:
Minnesota DOT

Unique feat:
Original bridge was designed by C.A.P. Turner (or his engineering firm)

County Road 42 Bridge, Between Otsego and Elk River

Mary C. Costello

Monticello Highway Bridge, Minnesota 25

The 1930 Monticello Bridge was a delightfully picturesque humpback truss bridge with a fancy wrought iron railing and decorative old-fashioned lampposts covered with a green patina. What a joy to see and sketch!

On my next trip to this "Bedroom Community", I found things had changed. The old bridge was gone and a new concrete girder structure stood in its place. I was disoriented! I could not find the landmarks I had come to associate with the bridge--the restaurant, the houses, and the alley.

My coming to town this time was not to see the bridge, but to find out about the Monticello span that my research indicated had restrooms in it. This bit of information I discovered in the DOT's microfiche files in St. Paul. I asked around town for any knowledge of this bridge that was "ready for human need". No one I spoke to had heard of it, so I went to the Senior Citizen Center for help. The 89-year-old historian, and person most likely to know, was home baking pies for the ice cream social to be held that day. When the director of the Center talked to her on the telephone, she said the bathrooms had to have been in the bridge the city last tore down. (In the 1800's when the preceeding bridge was built, she logically deducted, they would not have had "restrooms".) She didn't remember them, however. At City Hall I found the city engineer remembered that, "After the Sewage Treatment Plant was installed in 1962, the city felt that connecting the bridge restrooms to it would not be feasible, so the restroom entrances were cemented over."

Actually now I have the "proposed toilet rooms" plans--one for men and one for women built under the 1930 Bridge sidewalk in the southwest corner against the bridge abutment. On the plans is a statement saying,"Labor and material to be furnished by the city of Monticello."

Since the town now had a different bridge, I sketched the span from the park. I was not that far from the park restrooms that were installed to replace the ones lost to progress.

A feature not often seen with a bridge across the Mississippi is the planned-path that goes under the span. (There is one in Brooklyn Center.) This provides the park visitor access to both sides of the park without crossing the bridges' busy road.

Of the eight new piers, short "he-man" style with broad shoulders, only three are in the water. The standard tapered lights and two-rung railing are not exciting.There are two wide sidewalks, a median and four lanes for traffic. This latest bridge in Monticello has simple dynamic beauty. It has everything that is needed for a safe and speedy crossing but is lacking in the fancy and elegant detail of the former span. However, lucky are Monticello residents to have the memory and the refurbished railings from the old bridge in their downtown "streetscape"!

Refurbished railing

Use:
Local & Minnesota Highway 25 traffic

Location:
Pine Street, Monticello connecting to Big Lake

Style:
9-span concrete girder

Length:
Channel span - 111 feet
Total length   - 1007 feet

Width:
4 14-foot lanes, and a median or 62-foot roadway plus 2 6-foot sidewalks

Height:
24 feet MLW

Date completed:
September 1988, replaces 1930 through-truss; original span 1891 swingspan one block west

Designed by:
VanDoren Hazard Stallings

Bridge:
#71012 Sherburne County

Owner:
Minnesota DOT

Unique feature:
Bridge with public restrooms from 1930 to 1962

Minnesota Highway 25 Bridge, Monticello

Mary C. Costello

Clearwater Bridge, Minnesota Highway 24

*C*learwater, a small town about 20 miles south of St. Cloud, has one of the best lit bridges on the Mississippi River--seven lightpoles per side for about 1100 feet of span. The bridge is called a steel beam or girder span and crosses a river road and three spans of floodplain before the "Father of Waters". It is longer than any bridge this side of Coon Rapids with two traffic lanes and two narrow walks.

The silver bridge, which replaced a three-span 1930 bridge, is long and straight with a narrow steel girder which deepens over the river. "The deeper the girder the stronger the bridge" is an understood engineer's axiom, but also understood is that more materials mean more expense. Therefore, in the Clearwater Bridge the extra depth is placed where needed. The concrete roadway and walk project out about 24 inches beyond the steel girder, having a low concrete parapet above. Long narrow drainage openings are cut in the bottom of this wall.

Above the concrete parapet is a sturdy guard rail consisting of two 3-inch horizontal pipes supported by curved flanged posts, wider at the bottom and narrower at the top. One pipe rests on top of the supports and the other goes through the middle.

Breaking the long horizontal lines of the girder aresquare drainage spouts from the bottom edge of the road to the bottom of the girder in an unusual or non-pattern fashion.

The white concrete piers are really bright in the evening sun. I noticed that the five piers in the water are solid concrete slabs with a cap on top, but the three on land are flat concrete double "T"s.

In the late 1800's Clearwater was one of the sites of a sawmill. They received for milling white pine and hardwood logs which had been floated down the Mississippi River from St. Cloud and places north. Those were rugged, rough times. Today I saw only this neat, trim bridge that has nothing more rustic than a canoe go under.

Use:
Local, county and Minnesota Highway 24 traffic

Location:
Off Highway 10, between Sherburne and Wright Counties

Style:
9-span steel girder

Length:
Channel span - 148 feet
Total length   - 1144 feet

Width:
2 lanes and 2 3-foot walks; 38-foot total

Clearance:
42 feet MLW

Date completed:
November 1958, original 3-span bridge in 1930; cars ferried in the 40's

Designed by:
Minnesota DOT

Bridge:
#6557 Sherburne County

Owner:
Minnesota DOT

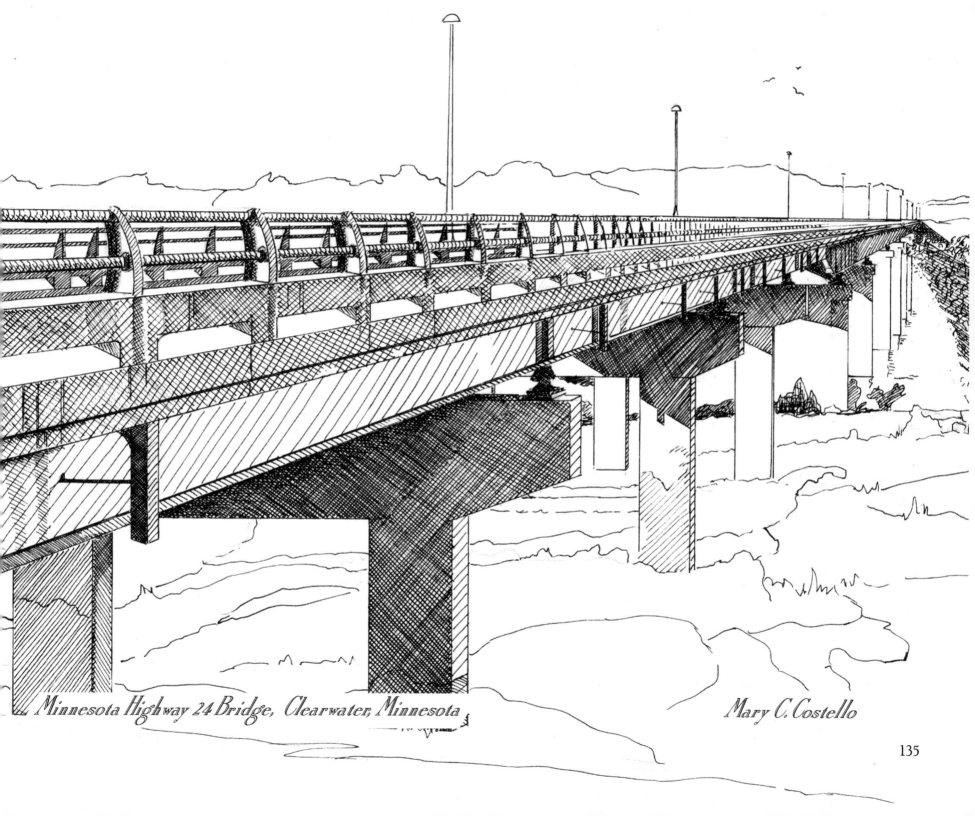

Minnesota Highway 24 Bridge, Clearwater, Minnesota

Mary C. Costello

135

University Bridge, 10th Street, St. Cloud, Minnesota

*T*his is the newest of the bridges in St. Cloud. It is called the University Bridge because of its proximity to the St. Cloud State University. The span has an approach ramp on one side and steps on the other to accommodate both bikers and walkers. From Munsinger Park, a beautiful gardened facility, the ramp rises half the distance and then reverses direction to go the rest of the way to the bridge.

This sloping passage has an interesting pattern on the outer concrete wall. It has vertical cuts 12 to 14 inches apart and deep. Every other line complements the first; instead of repeating it, making a unique pattern. The same cuts are used on the girder sections all across the bridge. Then they are reversed about ten feet away.

Harold Sandberg, with Alfred Benesch and Company in Chicago, tells me that, in the girder section, this "cut-out looking" shape is the flat cap beam of the pier below, cast-in-place. It has a ledge in back on which the precast beams rest. He says the beams are notched to fit the ledge, thereby producing a relatively uncluttered bottom of the deck.

In crossing "Ol' Man River" the bridge angles slightly north adding a curve and a certain charm not found in straight-as-an-arrow bridges.

Another unusual feature of this structure, and most importantly, is the shape of its piers. They are attractive, curved "V" shapes. At the bottom is a "gusset of concrete" decorated vertically with lines, a very graceful base for this park-set bridge. Much of this detail is lost to people, however, because of the shadow under the bridge. These discoveries make my job more enjoyable.

The 5-foot-deep concrete girder is recessed under the thick concrete road. In line with the projecting road's edge is a double-grooved concrete wall and a simple steel guard-railing.

On one of the six lightpoles is the "30 mph" speed sign. This must be an increase over the velocity on the almost one-hundred-year-old span that preceeded this bridge. That earlier bridge was a 4-span through-truss built in 1892.

In an aerial view the St. Cloud Dam, spanning the river below this award-winning bridge, reveals a linked rope (also seen from the ground) designed to keep boats from going over the waterfall. This University Bridge is enchanting from any angle above this wide, slow, clear-looking river today.

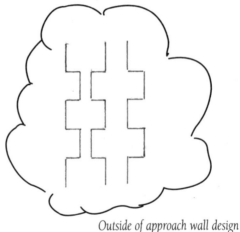

Outside of approach wall design

Use:
City and University traffic

Location:
St. Cloud city bridge between 10th Street South and Michigan Avenue Southeast

Style:
7-span prestressed concrete girder

Length:
Channel span - 169 feet
Total length - 1171 feet

Width:
2 lanes, 53 feet plus two 6-foot sidewalks

Clearance:
20 feet MLW

Date completed:
Fall 1985; in 1892 original through-truss bridge was built

Designed by:
Howard Needles Tammen & Bergendoff

Bridge:
#73540 Sherburne Co.

Owner:
City of St. Cloud

Unique feat:
"Best of 1987" in long-span-bridge category by the Prestressed Concrete Institute

SPEED
LIMIT
30

University Bridge, St. Cloud, Minnesota

Mary C. Costello

137

"DeSoto" Highway Bridge, St. Cloud, Minnesota, SR 23

*S*t. Cloud went formal for the DeSoto Highway Bridge. It is a bridge in black--just one of three in town so painted. The color black can be sad or formal and for the "Majestic River", I think, St. Cloud went formal. Of the central in-town bridges, University Bridge not included, this is the first to be so colored. Although black is typical for railroad bridges (and one of these is included) black is not normally used as a highway bridge color. Here it is elegant, often with white railings.

US 52 and Minnesota 23 cross this span, formerly known as Division Street Bridge. Division is an appropriate title, I found, because the road divides the town almost in half.

The piers for this three-span steel deck-truss are low, long and concrete. The high banks at the main crosstown bridge require deep trusses which arch over the river, making it quite attractive.

The bridge is well-lighted with five lightpoles per side. The plain concrete parapet has on top a two-pipe railing running along the outside of the much-used sidewalk. The bridge plaque at the end states that it was a Federal Aid Project built in 1957.

It was late afternoon, and I parked in a local inn's parking lot while I planned to photograph the bridge. However, in trying to find the approximate length of the bridge by stepping it off," I forgot to take the picture. A year later I came back to capture the image on film. This time my camera malfunctioned. It took a third trip to do the job.

A college-age girl stopped for a minute to see my sketch. I asked her about the location of the St. Cloud Public Library. When I finished my drawing, I went there for more information about the local structures. It was busy, modern and air-conditioned with some beautiful artwork on display. The material I found there never surfaced when I returned home to begin my work. Perhaps it's still on the St. Cloud Library table.

Use:
City, US 52 and MN 23 traffic

Location:
Between 2nd St.South and 3rd St. Southeast in St Cloud, previously called Second Street Bridge

Style:
3-span trussed deck-arch

Length:
Channel span - 280 feet
Total length   - 890 feet

Width:
4 lanes with 2 4.7-foot walks, 70.5 feet total

Clearance:
32 feet MLW

Date completed:
October 1958, only span ever

Designed by:
Minnesota DOT

Bridge:
#6748 Stearns County

Owner:
Minnesota DOT

"De Soto," US 52 Highway Bridge, St. Cloud

Mary C. Costello

St Germain Street or Veteran's Bridge, St. Cloud, Minnesota

*T*his municipal owned bridge is a tall steel beam structure with big "T" piers. The bridge is askew to its banks at St. Germain Street, but the piers are set parallel with the bank and the water flow. An engineer explained that this prevents "scour" and whirlpools from forming at the piers that can circle to the river bottom, dig into the sand at its bed and wear it away. The bridge crosses at a 70 degree angle to the river from high atop tree-lined banks. Looking from the Division Street Bridge, I could see that instead of riprap underneath the bridge, there is a wide permanent sheet of concrete on the east embankment at a steep 45 degree angle.

The guard-rail and its flat metal balusters and heavy support posts resting on steel squares are all painted black-along with the long steel girder. This makes it the second black bridge in St. Cloud. The top railing, however, is white for contrast-"the white tie touch." The whole parapet stands on a curbing of concrete with elongated drain openings below.

To help accommodate the more than 18,400 people daily in St. Cloud, who travel back and forth on St. Germain, there are four traffic lanes on the bridge and a walk on each side. Light comes from tall, silver, tapered poles on each side of the bridge.

The St.Germain Bridge is the oldest bridge in town and has a rich history. Before this 1971 span, there were three other bridges here. The first, built in 1867 by the St. Cloud Bridge Company, was a wooden toll span. In 1887, the city bought the bridge and rebuilt it of iron and of wood. The first deck truss was built in 1894 for streetcars, wagons and pedestrians and survived until the present bridge was constructed.

Use:
Local traffic

Location:
In center of St. Cloud, 200 yards north of Division Street and DeSoto Bridge

Style:
4-span steel girder

Length:
Channel span - 215 feet
Total length   - 767 feet

Width:
4-lanes plus 2 sidewalks; 70 feet total

Clearance:
42 feet MLW

Date completed:
1971; replaces 1894 deck truss; before that 1887 iron and wood bridge; original tall wooden bridge in 1867; ferry service preceeded all

Designed by:
Howard, Needles, Tamen & Bergendoff

Bridge:
#73514 Stearns County

Owner:
City of St. Cloud

St. Germain Street Bridge, St. Cloud

Mary C. Costello

141

Burlington Northern Santa Fe Railroad Bridge, St.Cloud,

*P*eering through a chain link fence may not be the best-way to view a bridge, but sometimes I found it the only way to get what I needed. That was how I saw the St.Cloud BNSF Railroad Bridge, closeup. I could see that the inner bridge beams were trussed beams instead of solid or with holes as they are often built today. It is a high deck-truss structure similar to railroad bridges seen in Minneapolis. I still find them unusual. If a person didn't know better, one might think it was a through-truss. Except for space between the spans being filled at the top, it looks like a Pratt truss super-structure--as if trains could go through below. Not true, trains cross on top.

I was surprised to find on the St.Cloud Bridge what might be seen on street telephone poles--condensers in various quantities. They were on four different horizontal poles one above the other, extending out from the side of the bridge truss. It was a strange sight for me. I don't know if they are in use or left from the past.

There is still another unusual feature on this former Great Northern Railway Bridge. About ten feet below the bottom chord of the deck truss is an extra bracing that hangs between the piers like a hammock. A BNSF employee informs me that to increase the capacity of the bridge, a third truss has been added down the middle. It is the lower section of this middle truss that looks like a hammock. Since large boats do not come this far north, there is no worry about clearance.

Twenty-three trains a day ride 67 feet above land here in St. Cloud with no visible railing. Of the three piers only two are stone. The third is bigger, newer, and of white concrete with a wide flat base extending all around.

With my close behind-the-fence proximity to the bridge and amazement at its bold style there is nothing I would have liked better than to have seen a train cross while I was there. It didn't. I left. So I imagined this one.

Use:
Burlington Northern Santa Fe trains, originally Great Northern Railway trains

Location:
2nd Street North, St. Cloud, Minnesota

Style:
4-span high deck pin-connected truss bridge

Length:
Channel span - 54 feet clear
              - 170 feet total
Total length - 587 feet

Width:
Single track

Clearance:
20 feet MLW

Date completed:
1892; reinforced in 1922

Designed by:
Great Northern Railway, possibly

Bridge:
#10, currently known as #74.2

Owner:
Burlington Northern Santa Fe Railroad

Burlington Northern Santa Fe Railroad Bridge, St. Cloud

Mary C. Costello

Sauk Rapids Highway Bridge, Minnesota, County Road 33

*I*t's a beauty-this Sauk Rapids Bridge! The beauty, I feel, comes as much from the "nature setting" as from the bridge style which is very similar to the DeSoto Street Bridge in St. Cloud. The trussed deck-arch is dramatic located here, and in the morning with the light on it, it would be even more striking. Viewing from below rather than from above, makes a difference in how one can appreciate the structure.

At the town of Sauk Rapids, the Mississippi flows past boulders and rapids, originally descending 20 feet for every fifth of a mile. Since the St.Cloud Dam was built, it is less steep, however. "The Sauk Rapids, formed as the Mississippi tumbles over a broad ledge just below the mouth of the Sauk River, throws large standing waves in high water, which can swamp a canoe." The U.S. Corps of Engineers in 1870 removed large boulders so boats could navigate the river here easier. It is not as challenging to travel as it used to be some have said.

From the bridge, which is less than half a mile below the rapids, the water is still rough and fast flowing. Some rocks create white foam as the river rushes past. Big rocks under the bridge make little falls. I crossed the span and looked down from the bridge upon this rough water. On this hot sunny day, it was very refreshing. After enjoying the view from above, I sat on the ground in the park next to the bridge. Nearby some boys were swimming and jumping off dead tree stumps.

The Sauk River Bridge is a deck truss that gracefully arches from pier to pier. The three stone piers themselves angle to a broad point on both ends. They are the same height as the vertical in the truss above. The bridge on my photo looks dark grey, but my note says it is silver; it must be reflected color from the surrounding trees. The simple railing is made of sturdy, flat steel bars with finer bars between the posts. This is the only bridge in Sauk Rapids and was steadily busy when I was there.

The trusses below the roadway look like a giant web among the trees with a smart spider keeping the color subdued to blend with the surroundings. Like all webs it was beautiful.

Use:
City and CSAH 33

Location:
Below the Sauk River confluence with the Mississippi River

Style:
4-span steel spandrel braced arch

Length:
Channel span - 175 feet
Total length - 565 feet

Width:
2 lanes with wide shoulder and one 6-foot walk; 38 feet total

Height:
12 feet MLW

Date completed:
July 1942; renovated 1985; originally a single camelback through-truss bridge before 1911

Designed by:
Minnesota DOT

Bridge:
#5947 Stearns County

Owner:
Minnesota DOT

County Road 33 Bridge, Sauk Rapids, Minnesota

Mary C. Costello

"Bridge of Hope," Minnesota Highway 15

*H*ow often does one hear of any construction being completed early? Not very often. However, the "Bridge of Hope" was one of those few. The weather was favorable and the work trouble-free between 1993 and 1996 allowing the new bridge, in a first time location, to be completed eight months early.

This Highway 15 Bridge is beautiful in name, concept and design. The name, "Bridge of Hope" was chosen by a group of area high school students. The idea was to memorialize Minnesota's missing children as well as the children who are present. Its design is also special when seen from the side. The double-legged piers create a gothic arch between and are each faced with pressed stone, giving the appearance of a cut-stone surface edged in a plain border. (This is similar to the Wabasha Bridge #26 in downtown St.Paul.) The pointed arch is repeated twice in each opening but only goes halfway where a thin inserted slab connects it to a solid lower half. This general design is very nicely repeated on the outside edge of each pier.

On looking at the plans, I was surprised to find that the bridge crosses a back channel and an island before crossing the Mississippi's main channel. I could never have seen that from where I stood.

How I got here was another story. I received my directions from a boy in the local gas station on Benton Road who advised me to go into the park along the river. (Children know the best ways to get places because they've been there.) Following his instructions, I parked my car next to the gated entrance to the bicycle path. I walked the path a very short distance to the bridge and rock gardens beneath it. What a nice surprise. Shade flowers have been planted inside of rock borders where the ground was high enough between these piers. However between other piers on land were other things like a highway and a train track. However, these flowers, I am sure, are dedicated to the missing children, perhaps kept up by students or some of the mothers. Only two of the 13 piers were in the river as far as I could see. The island blocked some of my view at the distance, however.

On returning to my car, I examined the flower beds more carefully to see what they contained. I found marigolds, petunias, salvia and live-forevers, plus some plants that I didn't recognize, informally arranged in tiers, surrounded by rocks, all adding to the beauty of the spot and the bridge.

Despite what some people think of high school students and the terrible things some have done, this bridge exemplifies that not all teens are self-centered and lacking empathy with others. This is truly a "Bridge of Hope."

Use:
Minnesota Highway 15, connects to U.S. Highway 10

Location:
LeSauk Township or between Sartell and Sauk Rapids, Minnesota

Style:
13-span precast concrete girder

Length:
Channel span - 140 feet
Total length - 1711 feet

Width:
4 lanes or 85 feet

Clearance:
18 feet MLW

Date completed:
November 1995

Designer:
Minnesota DOT, Jim Hill Group

Bridge:
#05011

Owner:
Minnesota DOT

"Bridge of Hope," Highway 15, Between Sartell and Sauk Rapids   *Mary C. Costello*

Sartell, Minnesota "Utility Lines" Bridge

*T*his bridge is unused by human beings but not totally abandoned. It is a full-sized through-truss bridge used for utility lines. Yes, that is what this old highway bridge is doing in the town of Sartell. There is a story behind it.

The span was built as a highway bridge during a six months period in 1914, with William Sartell as the instrumental figure. The bridge served the Model T's of the day and all the cars since until September 1984, when it was finally closed. The Sartell Bridge was a great boon to Stearns County at the time it was built, until its narrow spans gradually became too congested. In addition, traffic was often delayed with trains at the east end where tracks crossed the bridge approach. As early as 1957, heavy vehicles were known to be too much for the span. However, the bridge remained in use twenty-seven more years. Had it remained open longer, trucks would have been banned. When the new bridge was completed several blocks upstream, this senior span retired and took on lighter duties. For a while it was used as a footbridge, but that was not practical for the townspeople with a factory directly at its west end. Now it only carries gas, electric and telephone lines across the river.

From where I stood, the Pratt truss bridge sat low to the water. The top of the last of the three camelback spans was at eye level. The bridge end was below the blacktop on which I stood. As I drew the bridge, the scene became more dramatic looking. The pure white trusses shone even whiter in the afternoon setting sun. The sun caught the thin diagonal rods, otherwise lost to sight for their frailty. The trees in the bridge foreground were dead, and with partially peeled bark, looked naked and scarred. I also noticed gathering fast in the background, as well as overhead, were heavy, draped, lead-colored clouds. In "the quiet before the storm," the river, what little I could see, was smooth and peaceful. Everything reflected perfectly. However, it was too quiet, so I left for my daughter's home before I completed my work to miss the impending storm.

Use:
Carries utility lines only

Location:
In Sartell south of the 1984 bridge in Stearns County

Style:
3-span Pennsylvannia humpback through-truss

Length:
Channel span - 135 feet
Total length   - 587 feet

Width:
2 lanes, 28 feet, 1 sidewalk

Height:
18 feet MLW

Date completed:
1914, officially closed to all traffic September 1984

Designed by:
Unknown

Bridge:
No number

Owner:
City of Sartell

"Utility Lines Bridge," Sartell, Minnesota

Mary C. Costello

Benton County Road 29 Bridge, Sartell, Minnesota

*E*ntering Sartell, I saw tree-lined streets which reminded me of the elm-lined streets of my childhood. It was charming. Though I asked directions to the city bridge, I would have come to it had I driven straight ahead.

The river is getting narrower this far north, as most bridge-lengths indicate. The Sartell Highway Bridge, however, is longer because it crosses not only the river but a part of the paper mill land and a road on the west side. I drove over the bridge in search of a good spot from which to photograph and sketch. Private grounds at the other end of the bridge were beautifully landscaped--a real asset to the area. I parked and crossed the road to get a side view of this attractive structure, but the trees and the gentle curve of the span itself made it difficult.

There were seven full piers in view plus the tops of two more. Five of these are in the water, but I knew there must be many more on the other side. From my location below the bridge approach, I could see the upper portion of the two-toned-blue papermill tower/ smokestack behind the bridge. It had a flickering light on top to warn planes. This Sartell Bridge has done a lot for the town--modernizing it, uniting it and serving, at least for me, a vantage point to see the papermill's protected chimney. It is a bridge with many purposes.

The concrete piers are of two styles. The first one on the west side, after the abutment and the road, is a heavy short one with a deep, wavy top band and three pillar-legs. This I call a triple "T" pier. Beyond the first pier the ground drops to almost river level, and the bridge arches to 58 feet above the water so that the next piers are taller with thinner parts and only two legs--double "T"s. The bottoms are held together with concrete.

The plain white prestressed beam or girder across the bridge is about 4 feet deep. It was in shadow from the wide road overhang as I watched. The masonry railing had two grooves outside for decoration and two pipes with posts as a parapet above. Outside the abutment is an unusual double panel of brown-stained concrete, recessed and framed in white concrete, the engineer's special touch for this special bridge. It appears to be waiting for a relief sculpture saying, "Enjoy."

Use:
Benton County 29 traffic and CSAH 78 in Stearns County

Location:
City of Sartell

Style:
11-span concrete girder

Length:
Channel span - 116 feet
Total length   - 1,173 feet

Width:
2 lanes, and a 6-foot walk; 52 feet total

Clearance:
58 feet MLW

Date completed:
September 1984

Designed by:
Robert R. Tomczak, Erickson Engineering

Bridge:
#05525 Stearns & Benton Counties

Owner:
County of Benton

Benton County Road 29 Bridge, Sartell

Mary C. Costello

The Rice Bridge is a beautiful modern structure in a country setting, although the town of Rice is only three miles away from the bridge on Highway 17.

This low, straight bridge is built of weathering steel girders that will rust only to a point, never require paint and retain an attractive brown color. There are square downspouts every 20 feet on the outside of the girder, made of the same steel, draining the deck. These also serve to eliminate the plain look of the beam/girder from the river side.

The three piers are like others we've seen called single "T"s. The two-lane bridge has a double-grooved outer wall with a single silver pipe guard-rail above.

Because of the dry season, the water was low and ground was visible on the other side of the main channel. There were plenty of trees lining the opposite low bank. Wild grasses and small, white wildflowers abounded at my feet and on the approximately 15-foot embankment down to the water.

There were two signs of humanity while I was sketching and taking notes by this fresh-looking bridge. One was the grain silo and long low white building in front of it at a distance. The other was a young bicyclist who crossed the span. Otherwise, the bridge felt very secluded. Also there were no lights on the bridge, an indication that we were away from town.

My research revealed interesting information. There were several other bridges here or near here after a ferry and before this 1978 structure. The first bridge was built in 1900. It was a 3-span metal truss bridge with wooden planks for a roadway. A sign painted on wood was found preserved in the water 70 years later that said, "$10 fine for riding or driving on this bridge faster than a walk." However, this bridge didn't last long. It was completely destroyed by ice jams on the river in 1906. A second bridge was built in 1907 and lasted until the present day structure was built. It was very narrow and a resident Sam Perry said, "Two cars could meet on the bridge, but it would be awfully close."

I had followed my daughter and son-in-law to get here early in the day, but it now was late afternoon and we both had long distances to go. So I was off to my friend's cabin, but first I had a celebration of the day's accomplishments with a Dairy Queen.

Use:
Benton CSAH 2 and Stearns County 17 traffic

Location:
West of Rice, Minnesota

Style:
4-span Corten-like continuous steel girder

Length:
Channel span - 158 feet
Total length   - 574 feet

Width:
2 lanes, 47 feet, no walks

Clearance:
14 feet MLW

Date completed:
1978; replaced 1907 span; original bridge 3-span metal truss in 1900

Designed by:
Robert R. Tomczak, Robert Erickson Engineering Company

Bridge:
#05521 Benton-Stearns Counties

Owner:
Stearns and Benton Counties

Benton County Road 2 Bridge, Rice, Minnesota

Mary C. Costello

153

County Road 26 Bridge near Royalton, Minnesota

*B*ridge designing has changed from the beginning of the 20th century. Instead of using steel that the designer hopes won't rust and deteriorate, today's engineers uses a steel mixture that does rust but stops after reaching an acceptable limit. Instead of using stone piers today's bridge designers produce pier plans of almost any shape using prestressed or reinforced concrete. Both of these innovations are used on this county bridge.

The day was cloudy and warm. Lead-grey clouds hung over the bridge as I photographed the steel girder span. The lower sky was white like the bridge parapet and the outer edge of the three piers which caught the light. The narrow river had taken on the sky's dark color except for one path where the sun was trying to penetrate the film. The two-lane bridge was straight from bank to bank. In the subdued light, the weathered steel was partially hidden under the road edge and concrete railing. Looking hard, one could see the plate girder, but instead of having a narrow projection where each new steel plate is added, this structure has a 4-foot protrusion from the supporting beam to the edge of the road above. These may be extensions of the floor beams that span between the longitudinal girder, I am told. The unusual addition of steel is the same rich brown as the rest of the girder.

A little easier to see, though in deep shadow, were the three white concrete piers. It is these piers that make this bridge so singular. Each is composed of a thick, 6-foot deep slab of concrete cut at an angle wider at the bottom. This top band cradles the bridge deck and girders and rests on two bow legs.

With ripples in the water, reflections were not so perfect. Grasses and silvery green plants lined the bank, rocky ground edged the water. No light poles or guard rails were necessary since this bridge was out of the city. Greens, greys and rusty browns with sharp white concrete and sky-reflections created an unusual color combination.

From US 10, near Royalton, I saw long freight trains with their double and triple diesel engines pulling, among other things, freight cars of lanky logs. When I asked about them at a service station, I was told that there are 21 trains a day that pass here. "Hurrah!!" I thought. Though in 1918, the year of the first Royalton Highway Bridge, there may have been more trains, these numbers are encouraging.

Use:
CSAH 26 traffic

Location:
Near Royalton, Minnesota

Style:
4-span corten-like steel girder

Length:
Channel span - 115 feet
Total length   - 420 feet

Width:
2 lanes, plus wide shoulders, 43 feet total

Clearance:
26 feet MLW

Date completed:
1983

Designed by:
Robert Tomczak, Robert Erickson Engineering Company

Bridge:
#49528 Morrison County

Owner:
Morrison County

Morrison County Road 26 Bridge, Royalton

Mary C. Costello

155

CP Railroad Bridge near Blanchard Dam, Bowlus, Minnesota

*T*he world looked golden on this October afternoon. The warm sun on the fall colored trees made a beautiful setting for the black railroad bridge at Bowlus. It is a five-span high deck-truss bridge next to one of the biggest dams on the upper Mississippi, the Blanchard Dam. The river makes a bend and is much wider above the dam, making the narrower spot below a good location for the bridge.

Next to the surroundings, the piers are the most striking feature of the bridge. There are four, all of cut-stone 18 to 24 inches deep, on a flat pointed base. Each pier is like a high-top boot in profile, with the toe starting flat and rising to a high instep before cutting over to the perpendicular upper boot. Here is where the bridge rests. In contrast, the back or downstream side of each pier is straight with a flat base.

"The odd-shaped pier," Harold Sandberg, engineer, explained, "is probably that way to allow for another train track with trusses to be erected alongside. The pier would then be enlarged to be symmetrical."

Originally, the "Warren" truss-designed bridge was built in 1907 by the Minneapolis, St.Paul & Sault Saint Marie Railroad then became a Soo Lines Railroad Bridge, bought out by the Canadian Pacific in 1992.

Because of all the rushing water from the dam, fish love the spot, and fishing is a favorite pasttime. Though they were far away, I saw fishermen on the rocky bank, on the pier bases and in boats tied to the piers. Four parties of fishermen were on one side of the bridge alone. There was foam on the water in places, and though it was a peaceful scene, the all-encompassing sound was that of rushing water.

It was migration time, and a flock of Canadian geese flew north following the river route. Loud as they were, they could hardly be heard above the river's roar.

Use:
Canadian Pacific Railroad to cross Mississippi

Location:
About 7 miles south of Little Falls

Style:
5-span high deck truss

Length:
Channel span - 103 feet
Total length   - 650 feet

Width:
1 track

Clearance:
30 feet MLW

Date completed:
1907

Designed by:
Unknown

Bridge:
#0-150.43

Owner:
Canadian Pacific Railroad

Canadian Pacific Railroad Bridge, Bowlus

Mary C. Costello

157

BNSF Railroad Bridge, South Little Falls

My view of the 1898 steel railroad bridge and my drawing were very dramatic--heavy black girders diminishing above and decaying piers below. The very thing that made the BNSF want to replace the bridge was what dramatized my sketch.

Gary Strelcheck, BNSF Engineer Structure, informed me that this bridge has been dismantled for a new precast concrete one completed in 1990. The new concrete bridge has twice as many spans as the old one, and piers of large round pillars under a heavy rectangular cap. The piers parade across the Mississippi at a greater angle than before, askew of the banks, to permit greater train speed (25 mph), said Jerry Lochner, Public Affairs, Little Falls. The railing has top and middle pipe rails with strong posts about five feet apart. It is a sturdy parapet, one of the sturdiest, barring concrete ones.

The tracks and bridge are a part of Burlington Northern Santa Fe's mainline route to the West Coast. On my first trip I missed the bridge. On the second I was close, but I only found it after asking a woman waiting in line at a Dairy Queen store for directions. However, drizzling rain coupled with my determination to drive the great distance to a friend's cabin before nightfall shortened my stay. But a stuck camera meant no pictures and required a third visit on my part.

The 5-span railroad bridge had four stone piers in the water and deep steel girders to support the track bed. The fence on the bridge was composed of sturdy posts with a railing that looked like fine wire. Obviously the rail had to have quite a bit of weight to be seen at all from a block's distance-really a taut wire rope. There were diagonal bars in the railing but only above each pier. Could this be to announce to those above that there is a pier below?

This BNSF Railroad Bridge's history is long and colorful. In 1868 the county (Morrison County of which Little Falls is the seat) built a permanent ferry here. The Northern Pacific Railroad constructed a trestle bridge in 1877 with a Little Falls depot on the east side of the Mississippi River, but when the next bridge was needed in 1899, the depot was placed on the west side and was designed by Cass Gilbert. It still stands and is on the National Register of Historic Places since his is a name well-known for designing the Minnesota State Capitol, the Woolworth Skyscraper in New York, and the U.S. Supreme Court in Washington, D.C. This second bridge has been mistakenly thought to be stone, but it was only the piers that were stone. A photo in the Historical Society from a stereopticon slide shows it to be a wooden (perhaps some metal added), two-span through-truss over the river. The next bridge, as indicated above, had four piers and a heavy girder. Today's 1990 span is neat, low and strong with interesting seams in the outer girder above each pier, allowing for expansion and contraction. The BNSF bridge has gone from the dramatic to being safe and secure, ready for the next 75 to 100 years.

Old span

Use:
Burlington Northern Santa Fe mainline railroad trains

Location:
6th Avenue Southwest crossing diagonally southeast in Little Falls

Style:
10-span prestressed concrete

Length:
Channel span   - 62 feet
Total length   - 566 feet

Width:
Single track, 14 feet

Clearance:
17 feet MLW

Date completed:
1990; replaced 1898 5-span deck girder; repairs done in 1980's; replaced a 1900 2-span stone pier, wooden through-truss; first bridge was a trestle bridge in 1877; ferry started 1868

Designed by:
Hazlet and Erdal, Chicago

Bridge:
#105.41

Owner:
Burlington Northern Santa Fe Railroad

Burlington Northern Santa Fe Railroad Bridge, Little Falls

Mary C. Costello

About a block above the "waterfall-built-on-slate" in the town of Little Falls, Minnesota, is this one-and-only, in-town highway bridge. It is very well used by the townspeople as well as highway passers-through. Many visitors do come because this is Charles Lindberg's boyhood home. Each pier is a solid, short, but very wide concrete rectangle the full width of the bridge. The pier ends are undercut so that the bottom of the pier is shorter than the top. The effect is, therefore, that the pier cap is the only support and is floating on the water. We know that is not true.

On top of these white supports are steel beams/girders 36 inches deep the length of the bridge. Between the pier and the girders are ten bearings per pier on which the bridge sits. This creates some interesting light shapes under the bridge. The low, double-grooved concrete parapet wall and road-edge together are deeper than the narrow rust-resistant girder. The railing above consists of sturdy steel posts every ten feet with lighter weight balus-trades and heavier top and bottom connectors.

Interesting to me was a series of buoys secured to posts in the water at an angle from the first pier across the river to the bank. The purpose is to prevent boats from going over the dam, a short distance farther south. These are removed before winter ice sets in and reset again each Spring.

Little Falls has had five different bridges in this Broadway Bridge area. The first, Bruce Mellor, Morrison County Historical Society Archivist, told me was two bridges. One ran the top of the primitive dam on the east side of Mill Island and was in use approximately one-and-a-half years before a flood destroyed the dam in 1859. The other probably a wooden Howe Truss span went on the west side of the island lasting 8 or 9 years before some rotting and then wind took it down. Ferries were used for almost twenty years (until 1884), when an iron truss bridge next spanned the river. (Surprisingly it was dismantled in 1902 and moved to the Fort Ripley area where it survived until 1947 when floods destroyed it.) The fourth 1902 span made of steel and wood, 24 feet wide, had streetcar tracks, but was called a wagon bridge for horses and carriages. A temporary wooden span served for a year before the fifth, 1942 Memorial Bridge, in memory of the men and women in the Armed Forces, was completed. But by 1983 the 41-year old bridge needed renovation and widening, which were completed in 1985 to form the beautiful white concrete deck, low-slung, 4-lane steel girder span of today.

At the time I was there, the bridge was busy--I think the busiest place in town.

Use:
City and Minnesota 27 traffic

Location:
In the heart of Little Falls, on Broadway Avenue

Style:
5-span steel girder, slightly arched

Length:
Channel span - 100 feet
Total length - 545.5 feet

Width:
4 lanes, plus 2 8-foot walks; 52 feet total

Clearance:
8.8 feet MLW

Date completed:
1942; widened and renovated 1985;which replaced 1902 wagon bridge having streetcar tracks; 1884 iron truss bridge; original bridge c.1859, after using top of the dam for a bridge 1 1/2 years

Designed by:
Nolan Brothers, St.Paul

Bridge:
#5907 Morrison County

Owner:
Minnesota DOT

Broadway Avenue Bridge, Little Falls

Mary C. Costello

North Little Falls Railroad Bridge, Minnesota

We saw this tall, narrow railroad bridge, positively "adolescent" looking, set back between trees and a building, as my family and I drove down Little Falls Highway 371. It was Sunday morning with few people around, so we backed up and took a better look. Closer scrutiny revealed that the through-truss bridge was a conglomeration of things. Its two spans were two different lengths and two different truss designs. There was a good reason for this, as I found later. According to a city hall employee, an eyewitness, (and confirmed by the Morrison County archivist) the design differences were the result of an accident. On 10 May 1974, the train's cargo broke loose, swayed and hit the bridge sides a terrible blow taking the east end of the bridge and a number of freight cars to the river. The railroad acquired another truss span from Washington State (and the Columbia River) to replace it. The size was right, though huskier. The 74-year-old replacement span design did not match. (The new span is a Warren Truss and the old is a Pratt--really unimportant to the use of the bridge).

The bridge on a whole is an interesting mismatch. The single pier near the center of the river is rectangular in shape and is made of small stone or brick. The west side abutment is composed of large cut-stone, while the east abutment is concrete. The paint on the trusses is partly mustard yellow, while the rest is black. The portals are arched on the east span and look square on the west.

Outside of the accident, the North Little Falls Railroad Bridge has litttle history that is known. The Little Falls and Dakota Railroad had a railroad bridge near this location earlier (after 1874, exact dates unknown). Then the Northern Pacific Railroad built a bridge in 1891, according to BNSF records, said to be a "masonry bridge". (I believe this refers only to the piers, because people were so used to all-wooden trestle bridges.) The west span of today's bridge is the original 160-foot span and is a pin-connected through-truss. The east span is the replaced one and is a riveted truss, said an engineer in the BNSF office.

As I quickly sketched the two odd spans from the City Boat Dock, a private pontoon plane landed in the water in front of us and taxied to the shore. It was fascinating to see, especially when the pilot tried to secure his craft to land with a rope. The plane was bobbing on the waves it had created. Luckily no boats came by at the time.

After this excitement, a family of ducks swam towards us, and my grandchildren, ages one and three, were delighted. They were sure the ducklings were meant to be their playmates. The ducks may have intended to come onto land but changed their minds. It was just as well.

Use:
Burlington Northern Santa Fe Railroad trains

Location:
6th and a half Avenue Northeast

Style:
2-span through-truss

Length:
Channel span - 165 feet
Total length   - 330 feet

Width:
Single track

Clearance:
6 feet MLW

Date completed:
1891, August 1974 new span added after accident; Little Falls and Dakota Railroad owned earlier span (probably wooden trestle)

Designed by:
Northern Pacific, the west span; but 1974 east span came from Washington State

Bridge:
#105.8

Owner:
BNSF Railroad

Burlington Northern Santa Fe Railroad Bridge, Little Falls — *Mary C. Costello*

US 10 Inlet Bridge at Little Falls, Minnesota

*I*t was raining as I came upon this small inlet bridge this morning. Somehow I had missed it on my first trip north. The small span is on Highway 10 about ten miles from the heart of the town of Little Falls and only a short distance from the main channel span. God was with me, because I saw the "Mississippi River" sign in the rain and in time to stop on this major highway. Through the raindrops, I took several pictures with my new zoom-lens camera.

The bridge is split with a three foot median, is only one span long and is a precast concrete beam design. There are no lights, no extra railing above the double grooved wall and no piers to describe. The span was built the same year as the main bridge. The bridge has concrete wings on the side of the abutments. The riprap underneath the spans is hard to see for the dark shadows, but is of varied colored rocks. Two silver drain-pipes are the only features that break the horizontal line of the bridge.

The Mississippi River inlet stream here (from above on a map) looks like a relaxed, chain handle on a purse.

Use:
US-10 Highway inlet crossing

Location:
North of Little Falls on US-10 east of the main river channel over inlet

Style:
One-span precast beam bridge

Length:
Channel span - 78.5 feet
Total length   - 80 feet

Width:
4 lanes;   2 each way

Clearance:
7 feet

Date completed:
1973

Designed by:
Minnesota DOT

Bridge:
#49020 Morrison County

Owner:
Minnesota DOT

US Highway 10 Inlet Bridge, Little Falls

Mary C. Costello

165

US Highway 10, Main-Channel Bridge, Little Falls, Minnesota

US 10, which skirts Little Falls, has two bridges, one over the main channel and the other over a small inlet. My family and I stopped north of town to photograph the main bridge and found it to be a modern, low-slung span.

Each elongated white concrete pier rises up out of the water to a small square end. From the side they look like six propeller-plane bodies without the propellers. This seems appropriate for Little Falls, the boyhood home of Charles Lindberg,Jr., the first aviator to fly solo across the Atlantic Ocean.

Above these low, ready-for-flight piers is a deep weathering-steel girder. Its horizontal line is broken by deep right-angle projections that end in bridge drain pipes, about four drains between each pier.

From the outside one can also see the edge of the concrete deck and the low parapet with a simple single-pipe railing above. The shore on both sides of the river is low with lots of grasses and wildflowers. Trees do not dominate the scene as in many previous bridges.

This US-10 Bridge is almost 1000 feet long. It is like two bridges, one for each direction. built at the same time, with a median.

We left the scene before the plug was pulled on the dark heavily-laden clouds above the bridge.

Use:
US 10 traffic

Location:
North of Little Falls

Style:
7-span steel girder

Length:
Channel span - 153 feet
Total length   - 999 feet

Width:
4 lanes, 2 each direction

Clearance:
7 feet estimated

Date completed:
1973

Designed by:
Minnesota DOT

Bridge:
#49010 Morrison County

Owner:
Minnesota DOT

US Highway 10 Main Channel Bridge, Little Falls

Mary C. Costello

167

Somehow from first sight one knew this bridge was different. It wasn't the lack of traffic, because others had been as unused. It couldn't have been the green color, because that isn't so unusual. Possibly it was the train tracks on level with the road. I had not seen this arrangement on the Mississippi since Vicksburg (Volume I, page 22). It could have been the stone wall beside the east entrance to the concrete bridge road. Maybe it was the sturdy railing on the bridge or the rigidity of the total package. Whatever the reason, this bridge appeared government owned.

Fort Ripley was built in 1848 a few miles south of the Crow Wing River to watch over the recently arrived Winnebago Indians and to keep peace between the Dakota and Ojibway. It was abandoned in 1877, but in 1930 a National Guard reservation was established near the site. It was at this time that the bridge permit was applied for and within eight months the 5-span bridge was completed.

The Camp Ripley Bridge piers are rather short, since the river banks are only about 17 feet above the Mississippi. They are close double-columns of limestone with rounded corners. Unusual is the "dripping wet look" in places that really are patched areas with dark, sandy-looking concrete. These areas appear almost like the sides of a cake with dripped frosting; only the cake is upside down with larger patches of concrete at the bottom. The tops of the piers have a cap of concrete and above that the plate-girder rests. The road projects out over the girder about 24 to 30 inches, at which point a pipe is seen supported from bank to bank with steel braces. The braces coincide with the railing posts. The pipe probably carries utility lines.

This Minnesota Highway 115's bridge roadway is concrete with a step on each side bearing a sturdy guard-rail. This feature of the bridge is interesting and unique. The steel posts are like small capped I-beams. A three-inch round pipe intersects the post near the top, and two smaller square pipes run horizontally 6 inches down from there and at the bottom. In this lower space thus formed are balustrades every few inches. However, in the upper 6-inch space there are fewer verticals--only every fourth baluster. For beauty a pointed one-inch wide piece of green steel hangs under the rail between each of the latter.

Although the bridge looks very private and passes directly below the National Guard or Military Reservation, Highway 115 accesses Minnesota 371. I'm told that Highway 115 is a "strahnet" route--a part of the defense highway system.

Use:
BNSF track for carrying heavy things to the federal reservation, Minnesota Highway 115 and National Guard traffic

Location:
Off Highway 371 southwest of Brainerd, near Topeka, Minnesota, south of Crow Wing River

Style:
5-span steel plate-girder

Length:
Channel span - 75 feet
Total length   - 413 feet

Width:
2-lane highway and single train track

Clearance:
17 feet MLW

Date completed:
1931; 1971 reconstructed; in 1998 remodeled

Designed by:
Minnesota DOT

Bridge:
#4969 Morrison County

Owner:
Minnesota DOT

Unique feat:
Train track on level with road, same as Vicksburg; a "Strahnet" highway route

Highway/Railroad (BNSF) Bridge, Fort Ripley

Mary C. Costello

169

PART FOUR

PART FOUR
Amid Lakes and Forests

Above Brainerd, the Father of Waters enlarges, presenting the expected image for the Mississippi--greater size and dignity. "White pines towering above a canopy of mixed conifer and hard-woods, islands, and majestic 50-foot bluffs make this an out-standing scenic corridor." On its way to Bemidji, the Mighty River passes through five more counties and many more changes.

When we reach Aitkin County, the river enters the flat, forested area of the glacier-cut Lake Aitkin the river becomes deep, slow and sinuous with many oxbows. The Mississippi flows through forests of jackpine, aspen and balsam fir before reaching the iron range.

From Libby to Deer River the river turns northwest, where pine and hardwood forests give way to marshlands as seen in Grand Rapids with its rice, cattails and reed canes. From Grand Rapids the Mississippi meanders southwest then north to, and west through, two large lakes, Lake Winnibigoshish and Cass Lake. To confuse further those of us who have trouble thinking of "our" river as passing through anything but land, it crosses three smaller lakes before heading northwest again on its own. Above the hydroelectric dam by Highway 12, the Mississippi puts on its last show of size and might before passing through Lake Bemidji, its last large lake.

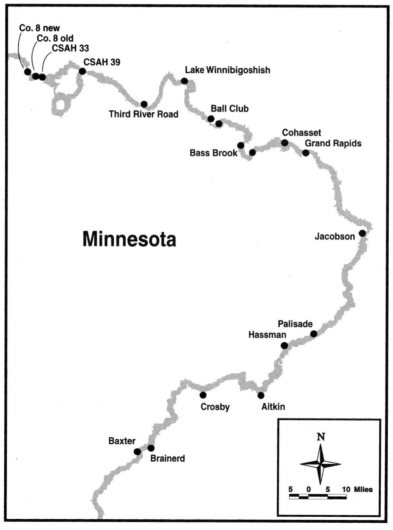

173

State Highway 371 Bridge, Baxter, Minnesota

*F*or the first time, a beautiful bridge has been constructed in Baxter, Minnesota. Instead of the usual plain girder, plain wall and the usual pier selection, this bridge has a scalloped decoration in concrete on the outside of the bridge wall and attractive double "V" piers. In addition, the four corners of the bridge have pillar-like structures with abstract designs of the river valley,--a tree, birch leaves, and a pine cone. The relief forms are of dark-colored concrete mounted on the lighter concrete background fitting the rectangular tower.

Why was this beautiful bridge built here when most bridges today are quite generic? My answer came from MNDOT. This is a six-mile-long new road cut through a pristine woods and the DOT wanted the bridge to be aesthetically pleasing as well as functional. The engineering office even had a contest to determine which of three different pier designs suggested would best fit the span. The bridge and highway by-pass Brainerd traffic.

The parapet on the Baxter Bridge is a short black steel railing with close balustrades, and slightly taller, heavier posts. There is a two-foot median and one almost-12-foot walkway for bicycles and walkers.

I became aware of the span when a friend, who discovered the bridge accidentally, appreciated its striking beauty and took pictures of it. He thought I might not know of its existence. He was correct! I am very grateful.

Use:
Minnesota Trunk Highway 371 traffic

Location:
In Baxter, Minnesota

Style:
4-span concrete beam

Length:
Channel span - 140 feet
Total length   - 532 feet

Width:
100 feet including one 11.8-foot sidewalk

Clearance:
52 feet

Date completed:
July 2000

Designed by:
Kevin Western with MNDOT

Bridge:
#18004 in Crow Wing County

Owner:
Minnesota

Unique feat:
Decorative columns on four bridge corners

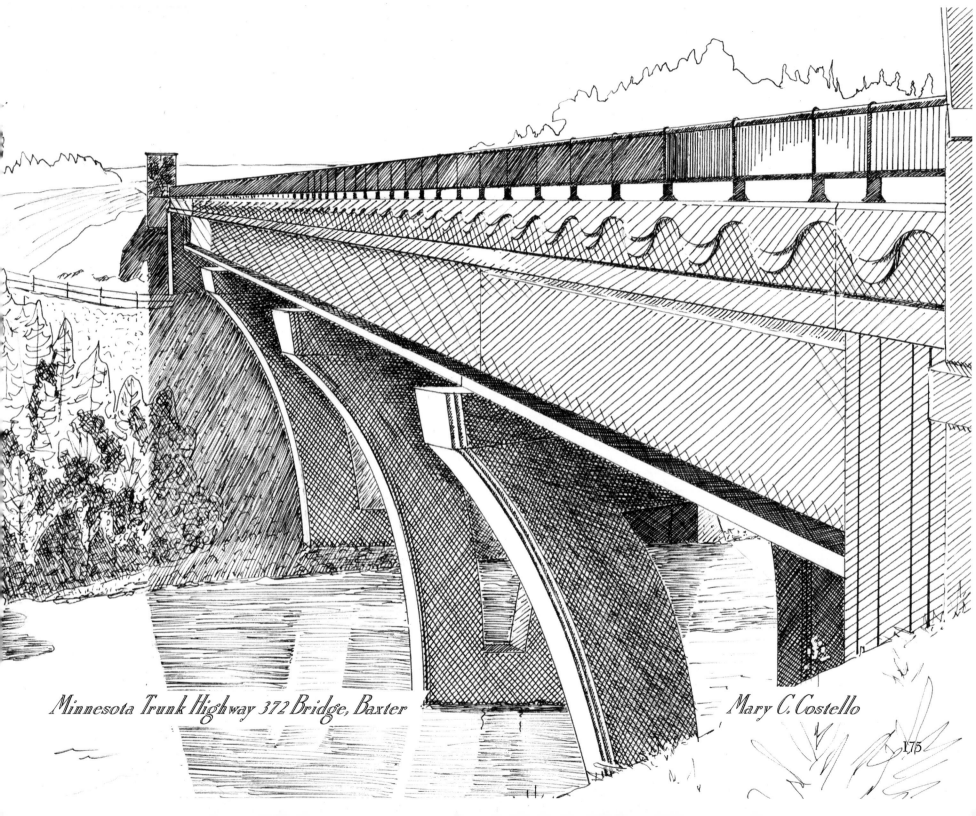

Minnesota Trunk Highway 372 Bridge, Baxter

Mary C. Costello

175

College Drive Bridge In South Brainerd

*T*he day was cloudy and warm and the Mississippi River in Brainerd was like glass. Over it the College Drive Bridge looked like a giant diving board with trees surrounding it. My daughter, son-in-law and children drove along the river road in south Brainerd to get a view of the bridge from the side. The drive was picturesque with shafts of light filtering through a mixture of maple, willow and elm trees overhead. The sun had gone under for a while so the side of the girder and two piers were the lightest shapes visible of the distant span. The rest was in shadow. The river turns on the other side of the modern structure so nothing could be seen underneath, nor could connections to the road be discerned--only trees and one building on the hill behind were visible.

We drove across the attractive bridge; and, after I took notes and did my sketch, we stepped-off its length. From the bridge plaque we found the year it was built and the owner. Close examination revealed that the two piers are solid concrete, with big shoulders and a sturdy trunk. The lights are high pressure sodium lights having been at some point converted from Mercury vapor ones. The railing is above a white concrete wall leaving steel posts with 31 spaces between, from which I could approximate the bridge length. I was 35 feet short.

In speaking to a Brainerd engineer later, I found that the town has 26,000 feet, or 4 4/5 miles, of shoreline and has 5 bridges. That is an impressive figure--one bridge for every mile of shore. I have not compared this to other towns, but the engineer feels it is a record.

The building on the hill behind the bridge is Brainerd High School. It seems there could be a connection there in promoting the school--"the Jumping-Off-Place".

Use:
Highway 126, and local traffic

Location:
West Brainerd on College Drive

Style:
3-span prestressed concrete girder

Length:
Channel span - 83.6 feet
Total length   - 252 feet

Width:
2 lanes plus 2 6-foot walks; 66.4 feet total

Clearance:
20 feet, estimate, MLW

Date completed:
May 1975

Designed by:
Darrell Berkowitz from Toltz, King, Duval, Anderson and Associates

Bridge:
#18505 in Crow Wing County

Owner:
City of Brainerd

Unique feat:
"Brainerd has the greatest number of bridges per mile of river for any town along the Mississippi," said a Brainerd engineer.(Five bridges, one per mile of riverfront)

College Drive Bridge, Brainerd

Mary C. Costello

Laurel Street Bridge in Brainerd, Minn.

Although the Laurel Street Bridge is in the heart of town, a different street enters the bridge than exits it--one end is Laurel Street and the other is Florence. My family and I were immediately confused. Why,? we never found out. We did learn that this is newest of the five bridges in Brainerd. The old Laurel Street bridge was built in 1898 but was torn down 80 years later to make room for today's structure. Inside information has it that the wrong pin was pulled and the old bridge came tumbling down 20 minutes early. Luckily a photographer there had his camera ready and the event was recorded.

Each bridge, I've found, has some claim to fame at the time it is built. The Laurel Street Bridge had the longest and the heaviest concrete girder in the state in 1979--137 feet long and 64 tons in weight. How appropriate that was for a city in Paul Bunyan territory! The girders were delivered by special trailer. I'm sure the sidewalk superintendents must have been very proud.

Mother Nature made building the bridge unusually difficult. The winter of 1978-79 was the coldest on record, so the men could work only half an hour at a time. There were 46 days where the temperature didn't go above zero. Then in the spring the water level on the Mississippi was so high that work stopped. The completion date was postponed from August to December. Then the bridge was dedicated in memory of James Ronald Johnson, a long-time city employee and city engineer, who died about the time the bridge was completed.

This is a unique and beautiful structure with three inverted and truncated "Delta" shaped piers in white concrete, or shaped like a square squeezed at the bottom but open inside. At the top of the pier is a longer rectanglar cap, angled upward at the ends.

Above the concrete girder and extending slightly out over it is the roadway with low guard-walls. The railing consists of two horizontal pipes in posts that are wider at the bottom and curve to the top. The tall, tapered light poles are supported behind the railing and painted silver to match.

Rain, or a heavy drizzle, hampered our visit. Three of us crowded under one large umbrella while gathering information. We must have looked comical to anyone watching. Onward to the Burlington Northern Santa Fe Bridge!

Use:
County Road 48 and city traffic

Location:
Near the center of Brainerd, Minnesota

Style:
4-span prestressed concrete girder

Length:
Channel span - 137 feet
Total length   - 553 feet

Width:
2 wide lanes, plus 6-foot walks; 66 foot total

Clearance:
52 feet MLW

Date completed:
6 December 1979, replaces original 1898 bridge

Designed by:
Darrell Berkowitz of Toltz, King, Duval, Anderson and Associates

Bridge:
#18509 in Crow Wing County

Owner:
City of Brainerd

Laurel Street Bridge, Brainerd

Mary C. Costello

179

Burlington Northern Santa Fe Railroad Bridge in Brainerd

I was impressed with the Brainerd Railroad Bridge's simplicity and well-groomed look. Instead of wooden trestles or steel trusses there are simple plate-girders and four slightly tapered concrete piers. The grey or tan (depending on the weather conditions) of the piers is in contrast to the black of the girders.

The piers are set on a larger base around which sand has collected--visible because of the drought when I was there. Since both riverbanks are high, the piers are tall, two and a half times the depth of the girders. On land the piers appear shorter because of the high inclined bank. At the top of the hill, is a pier of wooden piles in a tepee-like circle capped with flat beams. Under the bridge over land was grass that was as neatly trimmed as any suburban home. It was not the usual weedy, dirty appearance people may associate with railroads.

Brainerd attributes its development as a town to the Northern Pacific Railroad. First, it was the site of Fort Duquesne, part of a chain of posts stretching west from Lake Superior. Then, in 1871, the Northern Pacific built its line through the area and even ran a bureau of immigration, arranging for passenger tickets from Europe to Minnesota. The railroad sold land cheaply to the immigrants and alsobuilt immigrant receiving houses. I have a stereoscope picture of this first bridge in Brainerd. It was a 3-span wooden Howe truss bridge with one through-truss and a deck-truss on either side.

On 27 July 1875, the bridge collapsed and went down with a train. Five people were killed and 22 cars of freight lost. It was the Indians who profited from the accident. They rescued from the river barrels of flour, pork and other commercial goods that might otherwise have been wasted.

In 1909 the Northern Pacific Railroad built a bridge with three spans of deck truss. In January of 1984, Burlington Northern, new owners, completed a three-year $3 million project refurbishing the bridge, reinforcing the piers and replacing a span to accommodate heavier loads. In 1995 the Burlington Northern and Santa Fe merged and became the present day owner.

When the railroad came to town in the 1870's, it gave birth to the town of Brainerd. A town named after the Northern Pacific Railroad president's wife and introduced a special breed of people--firemen, museum people, engineers, secretaries and many more--all kind-hearted and helpful. Thanks Brainerd!

Use:
Burlington Northern Santa Fe mainline trains

Location:
Front Street, Brainerd,Minnesota

Style:
7-span steel plate-girder

Length:
Channel span - 142.5 feet
Total length   - 635 feet

Width:
Single track

Clearance:
45 feet at MLW

Dated completed:
1984 $3 million remodeling to plate-girder; original wooden span 1871; July 1875 bridge collapsed; in 1909 built 3-span truss

Designed by:
BN designed modifications; NP did the original bridge

Bridge:
#119.1

Owner:
Burlington Northern Santa Fe Railroad

Burlington Northern Santa Fe Railroad Bridge, Brainerd

Mary C. Costello

Washington Street Bridge, Brainerd, US 210

*T*his is a beautiful bridge that greets visitors to the bustling town of Brainerd. It has a concrete roadway and four spans of graceful arches below. One must see it from the side to appreciate it.

Mr. Charles Bedore, of rural Brainerd, was a carpenter on the original bridge built in 1934. In The Brainerd Daily Dispatch in 1985 he told that the first bridge was built before the time of unions during the Great Depression. A person couldn't even stop to light a cigarette. Even though he slid 40 feet down the rough concrete archway, he was afraid to tell for fear of being sent home for good. He got up with torn pants and abrasions and continued to work. Payday he got new pants. His pay was only 30 cents an hour but he managed to get a five-cent raise and was delighted. "A dollar bought a lot then," he said.

In 1985 the Washington Street Bridge was completely dismantled down to the arches. New spandrels, floor beams, deck and railing were added. The sidewalks were made narrower to give a wider roadway.

It is the arches that make this bridge special. The simple white concrete spandrels afford a place for light and shadow to play. The pier columns between the arches have "art deco" reliefs, typical of the early thirties. Here is a tastefully done tower-like relief on the otherwise plain rectangular column. The bottom on which the pillar rests is solid concrete the width of the bridge, with capped top and pointed end.

Unadorned 24-inch-deep concrete brackets support the roadway extension and a concrete parapet. Above the low wall is a railing consisting of two horizontal pipes and widely spaced steel posts that taper from a four-inch bottom almost to a point.

The octagonal light poles are of concrete. Like the posts, they taper to the top before arching over the deck with high pressure sodium lights.

The high sloped embankment beside the bridge had some small yellow and white wildflowers. Very colorful large irregular rocks from the area--rust, grey, brown and gold--were lined up in a row at the top of the embankment. The beauty of nature enhances what man has made.

Use:
Local and Minnesota 210 traffic

Location:
Main street in Brainerd

Style:
7-span concrete deck-arch

Length:
Channel span - 124 feet
Total length - 630 feet

Width:
4 lanes,2 6-foot sidewalks; 79 feet total

Clearance:
43 feet MLW

Date completed:
1934; renovated May 1985 with widened road and narrower walks

Designed by:
Minnesota DOT

Bridge:
#5060 in Crow Wing County

Owner:
Minnesota DOT

US210, Washington Street Bridge, Brainerd

Mary C. Costello

Mill Avenue Bridge, North Brainerd, Minnesota Highway 25

BRIDGE 85

*I*t was raining when Barb, Greg, Dan, Kim (my daughter, husband, grandchildren) and I arrived at this northernmost tip of Brainerd. We parked next to the Highway 25 Bridge and took pictures. We knew we were in the rural area as only tree-covered bluffs and farmland were visible. There were not many cars crossing on this Saturday in July, but a fisherman stood on some rocks about ten feet below us.

The last of Brainerd's five bridges is another girder bridge, but it is of steel, painted a light blue. About every three feet the girder has a 3 or 4-inch vertical projection, called stiffeners, giving it an "accordian pleated" look from where I stood. These verticals add beauty as well as strength.

The girder is set 30 inches back under the concrete roadway edge. Above is a two-grooved low parapet wall. On top is a strong steel railing composed of sturdy I-bar posts bolted to the concrete, flat steel bars as balusters and a square top rail. Tall blue, octagonal lightpoles are incorporated into this railing line-up.

There are only two rectangular concrete piers under the bridge. The plain piers have one simple addition--a reinforced slab of concrete about six to twelve inches thick and four feet wide added near the end for design and strength. At the pier ends upstream are special additions of concrete pointed to deflect ice and help prevent eddies from forming

The only other unusual decoration on the Mill Avenue Bridge is on the abutment. It has three layers of tall concrete horizontal steps about a yard apart adding four to six inches of thickness with each step. The abutment becomes thicker as it recedes from the water. Sunlight and shadows make such arrangements interesting. Wildflowers and small trees among the rocks added a softness to the straight lines of the bridge.

Use:
Minnesota Highway 25 traffic

Location:
North of Brainerd on Mill Avenue

Style:
3-span steel plate-girder

Length:
Channel span - 108 feet
Total length   - 373 feet

Width:
2 lanes, 40 feet

Clearance:
11 feet MLW

Date completed:
September 1951; replaced a 1884 trestle; remodeled in 1915 to steel beam span

Designed by:
W.K.Johnson Engineering

Bridge:
#6518 in Crow Wing County

Owner:
Minnesota DOT

184

Minnesosta Highway 25, Mill Avenue Bridge, Brainerd

Mary C. Costello

Minnesota Highway 6 Bridge, North of Crosby

*T*he town of Crosby, Minnesota, recalls different things to me. When I left for the north, Crosby was a landmark to watch for on the way to a friend's cabin. On my first visit with my family, I remember the narrow, twisting, varied-width river near which I found wildflowers called tansies. Going back a second time a year later, I recall the nearby store owners who informed me that I hadn't missed two railroad bridges as I thought from the map; they were power lines.

Highway 6 is simple, almost a generic bridge. It has no sidewalks, light-poles or added railing--just the low concrete parapet wall with the two grooves on the outside. The concrete overhang extends out about thirty inches beyond the concrete girder. Nothing hides the seams or disturbs the horizontal lines. The two piers in the water are of the "adolescent" type. (See glossary) The last thing I noted was that the concrete on the roadway is rough, to help prevent cars slipping from ice or wet pavement.

An interesting sidelight: the city map told me that Crosby has Portsmouth Lake, claiming to be the deepest Lake in Minnesota (about 500 feet deep). Crosby, also, is on the longest river in the United States, the Mississippi River. Pretty impressive stats!

Under the bridge and extending beside it were tons of red, tan, pink and black medium-to-large sized rocks (riprap) to prevent erosion of the banks, very colorful to behold. Beside the span entrance and along the top were yellow and white, both fine and coarse, wildflowers. In the background were Norway pine, and a few white birch among other deciduous trees. This was a pleasant place to be even on a dark day.

Use:
Minnesota Highway 6 traffic

Location:
4 miles north of Crosby

Style:
3-span prestressed concrete girder

Length:
Channel span - 78 feet
Total length   - 237 feet

Width:
2 lanes, 46 feet

Clearance:
25 feet MLW

Date completed:
1984, replaced 1923 high steel span at a different spot

Designed by:
Minnesota DOT, bridge section

Bridge:
#18001 in Crow Wing County

Owner:
Minnesota DOT

Minnesota Highway 6 Bridge, North of Crosby

Mary C. Costello

187

County Road 1 Bridge, Aitkin, Minnesota

The bridge is about 4 blocks north of Aikin hidden among the trees. The river is narrow, running east and west, zigzagging along the way and forming oxbows that look like animal ears or horns if seen from the air.

Aitkin was once a busy port when paddlewheel vessels ran the upper Mississippi between Grand Rapids and here. Some boats were so long as to clip the riverbank when rounding the river's sharp bends.

The prestressed concrete girder bridge is very plain with no additions, but has a guard-rail that is one of my favorites. It consists of low square posts on a concrete curb. Each post top is angled and notched to hold the concrete railing. Then sections are arranged so that there are two posts together, then a single. This two-and-one pattern all across the bridge is very pleasing to the eye.

Looking at the four piers I was surprised at the differences. Rows 1, 2 and 4 are single rows of eight piles. But row 3 has a double row totalling ten piles. While the single rows have columns that are perpendicular or straight down,(except for the outer piles which are battered, or lean out), the different third row has every pile sloping out. The reason "is probably to accommodate a joint in the deck," says Harold Sandberg, Chairman of the Board of Alfred Benesch and Company. "This requires a wider cap. The greater eccentricity of the load (compared to the other piers) is relieved by using two rows of piles." I didn't notice a joint in the deck-- I wasn't looking for it. I did notice a slight arch in the roadway which might have something to do with it.

Minnesota wildflowers and bushes are prevalent here. I found wild mustard and milkweed among others by the bridge entrance. There were trees all around with few house-tops among them.

Interesting is the fact that near Aitkin the Mississippi flows through the Cuyuna Iron Range. It has a high manganese content which may be why I saw so many reddish colored rocks. Cuyler Adams, a surveyor, discovered the ore in 1890 and named the range after himself and his dog "Una." During WWI, 90% of the nation"s manganese came from Cuyuna. These open pit mines are now abandoned and, in most cases, have filled with water.

From here the river will twist and turn and go northeast.

Use:
Local traffic and CSAH 1

Location:
One-third mile north of Aitkin, Minnesota

Style:
5-span precast beam bridge

Length:
Channel span - 70 feet
Total length - 363 feet

Width:
2 lanes, 36-foot roadway

Clearance:
11 feet MLW

Date completed:
1970; replaced the 1898 swingspan;
reconstructed 1934

Designed by:
Erickson Engineering Company

Bridge:
#01506 Aitkin County

Owner:
County of Aitkin

Aitkin County Road 1 Bridge, Aitkin

Mary C. Costello

189

US 169 Highway Bridge, North of Aitkin

The US 169 Bridge has an aura of magic about it. First of all it was listed as being in Waldeck, Minnesota, in the 1935 and 1970 Corps of Engineers "List of Bridges". However, Waldeck was the name of a man, not a town. He owned a farm bordering the Mississippi River on the west about five miles south of Palisade. He would ferry people and their horses across when they rang his bell. This was several miles north of the bridge. The town of Waldeck never existed.

When the Department of Transportation rebuilds a span, I know they are improving and making a safer bridge. However, often the charm of the old bridge is lost. The 1930 bridge here north of Aitkin was one of these spans. This bridge had a single humpback Parker through-truss with pony trusses flanking it (even the titles of the parts are more interesting). Its piers were unusual with a column on each side and two short, but open, arches in the otherwise solid cement center. Complementing the alluring arches was an unusual grove of trees gently sloping down to the water's edge. The cool, green color, the size, and the arrangement of the trees looked like an elf haven.

Now to the present bridge--it is a prestressed concrete beam structure built in 1990, pure white with three "he-man" piers. It has the normal two-grooved concrete parapet and looks very sterile and modern.

The water doesn't look deep here, even in the middle, based on a dead log protruding out of the center of the river. I know that looks can be deceiving, especially with the Mississippi, but perhaps this far north it is not so dangerous. To my surprise, someone was swimming towards me from the opposite shore. Maybe the bridge has not lost all its charm, I thought. If it were St.Patrick's Day, I'd say it was an elf or leprechaun. Since it was July, I don't know,-- maybe a "teenkin".

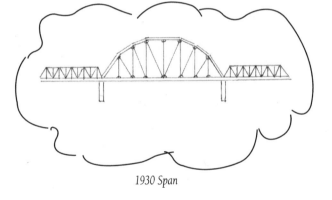

1930 Span

Use:
US Highway 169 traffic

Location:
About halfway between Aitkin and Palisade, Minnesota on US 169

Style:
4-span precast concrete beam span

Length:
Channel span - 94 feet
Total length   - 322 feet

Width:
2 lanes, 46 feet

Clearance:
9 feet MLW

Date completed:
1990; July 1930 a through-truss span; Waldeck ferry preceded several miles north

Designed by:
Minnesota DOT

Bridge:
#01004 Aitkin County

Owner:
Minnesota DOT

US 169 Highway Bridge, North of Aitkin

Mary C. Costello

Pedestrian/Bike Bridge, Former Soo Line, Palisade, Minnesota

*T*he biggest surprise of the day was spotting this Soo Line Railroad Bridge when my family and I thought there were no more. It was west of the highway bridge and cut across the river at a southeastern angle. All but the flat-top truss span was hidden among the trees.

The Palisade pedestrian bridge contained one through-truss plus two deep deck-girder spans. The two piers visible in the water appeared different one from the other. The one to the west was a wooden trestle with a crossed beam for reinforcement. At the pier base was a pointed 5-foot-tall wooden ice-breaker construction to protect it. Below that was concrete in the same pointed shape. The second pier looked round with diagonal lattice protection in wood. Since the plans say they are the same, my viewing angle may be the reason for the apparent differences.

Today the bridge is converted to recreational uses and gravel has been added to the deck instead of train track. All forms of pedestrian trail activities are permitted. Snowmobiles use it in the winter and ATV bikes and walkers in the summer.

Stephen Hill, U.S. Projects Manager for the Canadian Pacific Railroad, told me that the bridge was about 1,066 feet long when it was built in 1910. It had 58 spans which crossed a road as well as the Mississippi River. A deck plate girder was added over the road in 1921 and gradually the trestle spans were filled in, including the road, with clay and sand (almost 21,000 cubic yards of them) thereby shor ening the bridge. In 1964, one end of the bridge was filled up to a single timber span and another timber span was added at the other end. That is the balanced configuration we see today.

The banks of the river are low here and the water shallow. This bridge spot is a secluded place with lots of greenery, maybe ideal for its present usage. I saw the span silhouetted against the grey sky as I stood next to some brush and tall grasses. Beyond to the north the river looked much more open, sunny and bright. But those bridges will have to wait for another day, we're going home.

Use:
Bikers, runners and walkers

Location:
In Palisade, Minnesota, a block from 232 Highway Bridge

Style:
3-span bridge with one through-truss and two deck plate-girder spans

Length:
Channel span - 104 feet
Total length   - 265
                      - 356.6 feet with approaches

Width:
16-foot gravel pathway

Clearance:
34 feet MLW

Date completed:
1910 by M.St.P.& S.Ste.M. Railroad but 1,066 feet long; in 1943 and 1959 spans were land-filled to shorten bridge; in 1964 today's configuration formed; Soo Line owned before abandoning in 1985; county converted for pedestrians in 1988

Designed by:
Minneapolis,St.Paul & Sault Ste. Marie Railway Company possibly; C.A.P. Turner thought possible, but not proven

Bridge:
#P-281.11 as railroad; no number today

Owner:
Aitkin County

Pedestrian/Bike (Former Soo Line) Bridge, Palisade, Minnesota

Mary C. Costello

193

Palisade Highway Bridge, Minnesota 232

At Laverne Sifert's cabin on Cullen Lake, Minnesota, my daughter, her husband and children met me. Laverne, a dear teacher-friend, had given me directions and the key. We used this as homebase for "bridging" in the Little Falls to Aitkin area. After eating a pancake breakfast, we left to find the Palisade Highway Bridge.

From a distance we saw the tall "Dry Idea [2]"-shaped watertower before coming to the highway bridge. We took pictures from across the narrowing river of a three span, half-through truss, a type not common on the Mississippi.

The Warren-style steel trusses and guard rails were painted appletree green. In fact, the whole area was done up in green and white. The sky was clouded over and the shoreline was lush with greenery that was reflected in the river. The only variation was the tan-colored concrete which for the most part was in shadow under the bridge.

The four concrete piers were like legs on a wooden folding table. Each pier had angular columns on the outside with an angular arch inside. The Palisade Highway Bridge piers were taller than those of the railroad bridge (only a block away) because the riverbank was higher here.

Research revealed scouring at the piers had always been a problem for this bridge because the span was built in 1927 for a location in Grand Rapids and was moved here in 1952. The original location was a straight crossing and here it was used at a slightly angled crossing.

The truss span also had been deteriorating from the winter salt used for years until the bridge was declared structurally unsafe in 1999. In order to continue to use it while a new bridge was being built, six steel beams were added to the old span and all reliance on the trusses was removed. Also one lane of traffic and a limit of 50 tons was imposed.

By late summer 2001, the Palisade Bridge described above had a replacement. A three-span precast concrete beam bridge was built next to it and the old pony truss span was destroyed.

At a distance the view of the new Palisade span was very picturesque blending in with surrounding landscape, low and still lush. The river turned slightly and the various evergreen and decideous trees, some at water's edge, made a beautiful bridge setting.

The upper part of the structure is like many others, but not the piers. Don Stanley, construction engineer called them "hourglass shapes" because they resemble an hourglass figure wider under the narrrow arms and tapering down to the water. Two inner lines repeat the contour, are connected near the top with the surface between recessed about six inches. The pier sides gently taper back from a narrow flat end creating interesting shades of gray.

The bright new bridge, built immediately upstream from the original span, is truly beautiful in this location. May it last another seventy-five years.

1927 Span

Use:
Minnesota Trunk Highway 232 traffic

Location:
In Palisade, Minnesota

Style:
3-span concrete beam span

Length:
Channel span - 95 feet
Total length   - 289 feet

Width:
2 lanes, 39 feet

Clearance:
18 feet MLW

Date completed:
August 2001; replaced 1927 pony truss span relocated from Grand Rapids in 1952; in 1979 structural work done

Designed by:
Minnesota DOT

Bridge:
#01012 Aitkin County

Owner:
Minnesota DOT

Minnesota Highway 232 Bridge, Palisade

Mary C. Costello

195

Jacobson, Minnesota Highway Bridge, SR 200

*T*his, the shortest of bridges so far, was one of the most interesting because of the people I met on it. It was late afternoon, cloudy and warm but not rainy.

The bridge was an old single camelback span through-truss painted mostly black. The end near the town was grey spattered with rust. Its narrow, two-lane deck is new timber with no extra room for a walk or shoulder. A unique feature of this bridge is the old concrete "art deco" type wall on either side of the entrances. At its beginning, the parapet on land is curved and then straightens. The top of the wall is a six-inch deep band that is thicker than the rest of the wall plus a middle recessed area about 8 inches high, almost the total length of each section. At one time I'm sure this was a beautiful entrance to the bridge and to Jacobson.

Within a block of the bridge was a corner bar and from the proprietor I got the name of an old couple who were very familiar with the bridge. "John and another man hauled fine gravel in our Chevy truck from Swan River, six miles north on highway 65, for the concrete abutments on the bridge," Mrs. Punkkas, his wife told me. "John also helped clean up the brush where the bridge was to be located," she said proudly, as we sat in their living room. He was in his late seventies listening attentively as she did most of the talking.

From them I learned about early life in Jacobson. Mike and Victor Burquist ran the ferry that took cars across the river before the bridge was built. Harry Riggs brought the mail by motorboat from Aitkin when Mrs. Punkkas was a little girl. On land he had two oxen to provide the postal service to Jacobson. The final and most personal bit of information was that her mother was a cook on a Mississippi River steamboat.

When I went back to the bridge, I found three boys, Dan and Marty Shiek (twins) and Dan Kraft who were with a Lutheran church group headed to New York from Fargo, North Dakota. They were very interested in my book and offered titles and even posed for a picture.

With renewed interest I looked at the quiet pierless bridge John had helped build. It was located at a narrow turn in the river. Beyond the bridge was what looked like a lake because of its shape and size. On this wider part was a park and the bus the teenagers were boarding. I heard a twin say loud and clear over the water's amplifying system, "We're going to be in a book!"

Use:
Minnesota Highway 200 and 34, plus local traffic

Location:
Jacobson, Minnesota

Style:
Single-span steel through-truss

Length:
Channel span - 171 feet
Total length - 175 feet

Width:
2 lanes, 22 feet total

Clearance:
11.5 feet MLW (2 feet at flood)

Date completed:
1927; replaced the ferry

Designed by:
Minnesota DOT

Bridge:
#4516 Aitkin County

Owner:
Minnesota DOT

This 1927 bridge is being replaced as we go to press. It will have temporary abutments built and the bridge will be rolled downstream to them. The truss bridge will be used while the new span is being built. Then the wrecking ball will destroy the old span forever.

Minnesota Highway 200 Bridge, Jacobson, Minnesota

Mary C. Costello

197

Blackberry Township Road Bridge

*I*t was a peaceful spot, this Blackberry Bridge area. Two bicyclists crossed the brush-finished deck. There were plenty of birds chirping and a crow cawing while I drew. I heard a diesel train whistle in the distance; the continued rumble sounded like a long freight train.

On looking down the river, I noticed that the edges were not marshy but rocky with trees close by overhanging the river. Some were dead white, making for an attractive contrast to the greens of the ash and elm.

I went below the bridge to take pictures, sketch and examine the bridge construction. There were three sets of piers, each composed of a top band of concrete about eighteen-inches deep, pointed at the ends. The two outer ones hold ten silver-painted pipe legs, filled with concrete, embedded in the river bottom. All are straight except the first and last, which are battered. The center pier has double legs of six (mostly hidden in sketch). Above the piers was a twenty-four-inch deep concrete girder with small, square, silver drain pipes evenly spaced.

The edge of the roadway extends about a yard over the girder and casts an interesting shadow below. The now almost commonplace wall with two grooves stood above.

Before this bridge, there was a three-span steel beam construction built in June of 1927.

Under the bridge was riprap to hold the bank from washing. Among and beside the rocks I found small, white, nicely scented wildflowers and to my surprise some animal bones. The bony rib cage was as wide as my shoe was long, completely intact, plus a heavy spinal column, about eighteen inches long. At first I thought it might be a deer but decided it was too small. Maybe it was the bones of a dog or red fox or coyote. My finding them at least speaks for the lack of human frequency to the area.

Use:
Township Road traffic

Location:
About 6 miles south of Grand Rapids, 2 miles off Highway 3

Style:
4-span concrete girder

Length:
Channel span - 72 feet
Total length   - 295 feet

Width:
2 lanes plus shoulders; 39.8 feet total

Clearance:
22 feet MLW

Date completed:
1977, replaces 1927 span

Designed by:
Robert R. Tomczak, of Erickson Engineering, St. Paul Park, Minnesota

Bridge:
#31516 Itasca County

Owner:
Itasca Township

Township Road Bridge, Blackberry Township

Mary C. Costello

199

The Robert K. Horn Bridge in Grand Rapids, Minnesota

Named after a former mayor of Grand Rapids, the Robert K. Horn Bridge is located in the southeast part of town and is modern and attractive. It was busy when I visited it, maybe because the bridge is enroute to the airport, the largest fixed base operation in Minnesota.

Ahead I could see the vivid blue Blandin Paper Mill plant. Nearby there were a number of wild flowers--yellow trefoils, plus a sweetly scented little white flower and tall yellow weed-like plants. Rocks and sand border the clean, clear river here, and jack pine, aspen and balsam fir act as sentinels on the east. To add to the pleasantness, crickets were playing their steady hot-weather tune.

This modern bridge has two "stunted big shoulder" piers, a plain concrete girder under a wide projection of the roadway. Outside the low wall and railing is just enough room for the three light poles to rest. These are traditional dark green, slender, steel tapered poles with the added curved arm and mercury-vapor light.

The silver Horn Bridge guard-railing has steel post supports with two pipe railings; the lower pipe is about double the size of the top.

After my bridge visit, I went to the city engineer's office in town. His secretary let me examine the original bridge plans in the city hall meeting room. I felt very special to be so honored, but in reality it was they who were special. Grand Rapids and its bridges I will remember.

Use:
Local and airport traffic

Location:
7th Avenue east, Grand Rapids, Minnesota

Style:
3-span prestressed concrete girder

Length:
Channel span - 86 feet
Total length   - 264 feet

Width:
4 lanes plus 5-foot sidewalks, 66 feet total

Clearance:
10 feet estimated MLW

Date completed:
July 1976

Designed by:
Barton Aschman Associates Incorporated, Minneapolis

Bridge:
#31514 Itasca County

Owner:
City of Grand Rapids

Robert K. Horn Bridge, Grand Rapids, Minnesota

Mary C. Costello

201

Pokegama Avenue Bridge, Grand Rapids, Minnesota, Highway 169

Right in the heart of Grand Rapids is the Pokegama Avenue Bridge near the Blandin Paper Company and a dam. It is a very picturesque arch bridge in a very busy area of town.

My stop coincided with roadwork on the bridge, so I asked some of the workmen for stories. I was told that one time a bear from a local summer fair escaped and came right down to the river, knowing either by smell or sound where the water was. He crossed at the dam and was eventually captured.

This Highway 169 Bridge was built at the site of the Kabikons Rapids. In the days of the rapids, the river dropped nine feet in eighty yards, but today, with the reservoir and dam, there is no problem. I asked how deep the water was and found it to be ten feet at the deepest point. People fish here for muskie and buffalo. The workmen who were repairing the deck at the time would sometimes swim in the clean-looking river to cool off.

Having finished what I could do above, I walked the grassy hill down to the water's edge, taking pictures along the way. What I saw from the side was pretty, but the view from below was spectacular. The single, white deck-arch spans the whole river. Above the arch are spandrels which afford open spaces for light and local colors to interact. The deck is four lanes wide with the outer lanes extending far beyond the arch. Originally, the edge of the two-lane road was directly above the lower arch. It was changed in order to widen the roadway. Now wherever there is a spandrel, there is a sturdy bracket of concrete supporting the extended roadway. The silver railing consists of two pipes resting on, and encased in, the curved metal posts. This is very different from the original fancy, "art deco" concrete parapet which was there until 1977.

I knew the concrete was white, but that is not what my eyes interpreted it to be. They saw the arch as pale green, reflected from the water. The river in turn acquired the color from the ash and elm trees above. While inside, the spandrel space was dark--the color of the black willow tree trunk next to me. In contrast, only the outer edge of the roadway looked white.

Besides the color, there was beauty in the textures of the fine willow branches and leaves hanging between me and the solid lines of the bridge. The sand at my feet was warm and soft and the river glassy smooth. The heavily ridged black tree bark complemented the feathery green tree tops on the opposite bank. All in all, it was a lovely view.

Use:
Highway 169 and local traffic

Location:
Center of Grand Rapids

Style:
One-span concrete deck "barrel" arch

Length:
Channel span - 100 feet
Total length   - 160 feet

Width:
4 lanes plus 2 sidewalks; 79 feet total

Clearance:
l9 feet MLW

Date completed:
September 1932; August 1977 widened and upgraded deck

Designed by:
Minnesota DOT bridge section

Bridge:
#5122 Itasca County

Owner:
Minnesota DOT

US 169 Highway, Pokegama Avenue Bridge, Grand Rapids

Mary C. Costello

203

Sugar Loaf Road Bridge, County Road 63, Grand Rapids, Minnesota

This is a bridge of many names-CSAH 63, Sugar Loaf Road, Paper Mill Road or as I called it "Log Road." Truck after large truck loaded with huge logs crossed over the bridge. going to the paper mill's Wood Products Division. I stopped to sketch the bridge.

County Road 63 is another precast concrete girder bridge with the girder shaped like an I-beam. The concrete parapet is perfectly plain with the roadway extending out below. The silver railing above is one we've seen before, consisting of curved steel flanged posts seven feet apart. On top rests a three-inch pipe railing, and halfway down another such pipe cuts through each vertical support.

The river seems wider here than it was at Brainerd but the Mississippi is so changeable and curvaceous with oxbows and such that one cannot say it is any specific width.

Each of the five piers consist of eight round silver-colored legs anchored in the river bed and held together with a rectangular cap of concrete at the top. They are all straight except the outside ones which angle outward. These pipe-legs have a spiral "wrapped look", like the tube inside a wax-paper roll, but they are steel instead of cardboard, seams welded together and filled with concrete.

Going below, I was surprised to find that the bridge abutment had giant balloon-letter graffiti in brown, orange and white chalk, visible only to those going underneath. Here also is a sandy sloped bank with medium-sized rocks near the water's edge. Next to the bridge there are different flowers--tanzies, a yellow cluster flower, some fine purple ones and a sweet smelling white flower. Startling me, a large mallard duck flew out of the rice stands making a loud noise as it escaped.

A year later I was here again and got a totally different point of view. I found that not only trucks use the road and bridge. It was a sunny morning as I drove over the span to Blandin Park on the other side. I talked to a resident couple retired from the mill. They had eaten their breakfast in the park. Together we watched three men put their canoe into the river to go fishing. The rice stands left only a path for the men to paddle out into the main river stream. The older couple told me a little about wild rice and the work it is to pick and process. For want of harvesting, lots of it goes to waste. Much of it is on Indian property, and no one else is allowed to pick it.

As I drew the bridge from private property on the opposite shore where there were more tall rice stands, I thought of another name for the bridge--"Rice Row."

Use:
CSAH 63 and millworker traffic

Location:
South of US 2, west of Grand Rapids

Style:
6-span precast concrete girder

Length:
Channel span - 67 feet
Total length   - 407 feet

Width:
2 lanes plus shoulder; 44 feet total

Clearance:
11 feet MLW

Date completed:
1970; replacing 1913 bridge

Designed by:
Robert E. Erickson, Erickson Engineering, St. Paul Park, Minnesota

Bridge:
#31509 Itasca County

Owner:
Itasca County

Itasca County Road 63, Sugar Loaf Road Bridge, Grand Rapids ~ Mary C. Costello

Old Trestle Railroad Spur Bridge, Grand Rapids, Minnesota

The Burlington Northern Santa Fe Railroad tracks run beside US Highway 2 almost its total length. However, above Grand Rapids, a spur juts off and crosses the river just above the Pokegama Dam leading to the Tioga Iron Mines. A small park near the entrance to the dam area has parking space and one picnic table. I decided, however, to park under the only shade tree and eat on a low fence post. It was very hot, but the rushing water looked and sounded refreshing. A couple of business women thought the same thing and sat on the grass near the dam. A short distance away a few tourists were looking at an encased display of area plants and trees. There was not a lot of space in the park, but it was grassy and green and used like a beach by local residents.

A couple from the state of Washington arrived, ate at the sunny table, and came to talk to me. She was a librarian there and they were both immediate supporters of my project. They even wrote down my name so they could watch for the book.

Finished eating, I walked down a slight grassy hill to the place closest to the railroad trestle bridge. I found that the bridge, 25 feet high, was composed of three different sections. There are three spans of deck plate-girders, one 26-foot-long beam span and five spans of open deck timber pile trestles. The pile trestles below the girder spans must be over the main channel because they had wooden protection cells at their base, shaped like boats. The rest of the wooden piers had no such protection though they were taller.

An irregular line of trees behind the bridge had only one man-made structure--the Minnesota Power and Light smokestack located in Bass Brook Township. It is the reason for a lot of railroad traffic in coal said a Burlington Northern Santa Fe bridge engineer.

Rice beds stood high along the sides of the river and bent with the summer breezes. It was full grown and ready to be picked. But there are not many pickers because it is a lot of work, and one pound sells for so little. A little river inlet next to me had wooden posts in the water to mark the navigation channel. The rice almost infringes upon that lane.

I was standing still for so long that two chipmunks with their little striped bodies and full tails came to within two feet of me before running back into their hole. The only sounds I could hear were highway traffic and a few birds. The noise of the dam was blocked out by the closer highway.

Use:
Formerly, for Tioga Iron Mines, today, daily switch engine to Blandin Mills pressed-wood subsidiary

Location:
By the Pokegama Dam, west of Grand Rapids

Style:
9-span open deck timber pile trestle

Length:
Channel span - 32 feet
Total length   - 340 feet

Height:
20 feet MLW

Width:
l track wide

Date completed:
December 1953

Designed by:
Great Northern Railroad, standard trestle

Bridge:
#0.2

Owner:
BNSF Railroad

Old Trestle BNSF Railroad Spur Bridge, Grand Rapids

Mary C. Costello

207

County Road 62 Bridge, Cohasset, Minnesota

A silver mist was rising off the water when I arrived at the Cohasset Highway Bridge at about 7 a.m. I parked my car near a crossroad fence and proceeded to the water's edge. There I stood by an eight-trunk willow tree. Five of the trunks were standing, but the birds enjoyed the three that lay in the water. Lots of swallows perching in it made a grand exodus when I arrived.

Cohasset's bridge has a concrete road with a walk on one side only. It has two lanes with wide shoulders. The water was so calm that it carried perfect reflections of the piers--flat-ended square concrete cap holding ten pole-type legs. The center pier only has these supports in pairs, with the effect that it looks like an animal carrying the bridge on its back. Even the "body shape" is slightly different from the other two rows.

The girders on this county bridge are not as deep as some, and the railings are like those on Grand Rapids bridges--curved steel posts with two heavy pipes for horizontals, all standing atop a low concrete wall.

Opposite me near the other shore was a bed of rice obstructing my view of the bank. Riprap was tucked neatly under the bridge down to the water and birds could be heard chirping from where they had moved. By now the mist had long since evaporated and the sun was strong. It was going to be another scorching August day. The bright sunlight exposed two utility pipes nestled under the slightly extended roadway (pipes not shown).

Before this bridge was built, there was a very different kind of span serving the area, known as a "wheel bridge," according to an old postcard. In reality it was a vertical-lift span. The wheel title came from the fact that wheels were visible at the top to raise and lower the center section. There are three liftspan bridges on the Mississippi today--at Hannibal, St. Paul and Hastings. This 1904 Cohasset Bridge had four spans with a 57-foot channel opening, and 17-foot clearance at mean low water. In October 1923, the bridge was reconstructed, then replaced in 1971 by today's span.

Use:
CSAH 62 and local traffic

Location:
One-tenth of a mile south of US 2 in Cohasset

Style:
4-span precast concrete beam

Length:
Channel span - 75 feet
Total length - 303 feet

Width:
2 lanes with wide shoulders and one 4-foot walk

Clearance:
10 feet estimated MLW

Date completed:
1971; replaces 1904 vertical lift bridge;
reconstructed in 1923

Designed by:
Robert E. Erickson, Erickson Engineering

Bridge:
#31510 in Itasca County

Owner:
Itasca County

Itasca County Road 62 Bridge, Cohasset, Minnesota

Mary C. Costello

Minnesota Highway 6 Bridge, Town of Bass Brook

*L*eaving one of the few motels I stayed in on this trip, I found this lovely modern bridge on a mirror-like Mississippi, surrounded by numerous wild flowers, rocks and birds.

I heard the birds chirping under the bridge this 7:30 a.m.--their sounds echoing from that hollow area. All of a sudden, hundreds of brown thrashers flew out, soared into the air and then spread out. Some flew up and seemed to enjoy gliding down toward the river, then repeating the feat. When they left, over the water I could hear a woodpecker in the distance with his "dadadada, dadada" pecking echoing in the quiet.

Beauty abounded on the ground as well. There were white shasta daisies, small yellow trefoils, and tall day-lilies. All of these plants were interspersed with rocks partially buried. It was lovely.

The bridge is chalk-white and very simple. The parapet is solid concrete with the horizontal grooves on the outside. The roadway extends a few inches beyond the wall but the plain girder is recessed probably a foot under the deck edge. The road has a brush finish for better traction in bad weather. Being in the country, there are no lights.

The piers have wide shoulders. The arms that reach up and out, are narrow and rounded on the ends. The body, or trunk of the piers is short. One of the most beautiful assets of my view was the perfect reflection in the water. There was hardly a ripple in this placid Mississippi River. This County Road 6 Bridge would be a treat for anyone's eyes on this sun-free morning.

It wasn't always as peaceful as this. From 1911 until 1983 a through-truss swingspan bridge crossed the river here with a 40-foot channel span 15 feet above low water. A bridge-tender would hardly be on duty in this remote spot around the clock. But when a boat came, there must have been lots of activity.

Use:
Minnesota Highway 6 and local traffic

Location:
Southwest of Deer River

Style:
3-span concrete girder

Length:
Channel span - 74 feet
Total length   - 226 feet

Width:
2 lanes wide with wide shoulders; 46 feet total

Clearance:
6.26 feet MLW

Date completed:
1983; replacing 1911 swingspan

Designed by:
Minnesota DOT

Bridge:
#31030 Itasca County

Owner:
Minnesota DOT``

Minnesota Highway 6 Bridge, Bass Brook, Minnesota

Mary C. Costello

Itasca County Road 18 Bridge, Minnesota

*T*wo friendly people and a spider web stand out in my memory of the Itasca County Highway 18 Bridge.

I finished about 8:15 p.m. with my day's research and knew I didn't have the time or energy to drive back to my friend's cabin, a two-hour jaunt, so I drove to a privately owned small motel on US 2 near Deer River. The person in charge was an English teacher in the local high school. She was most interested in my bridges and even volunteered to proofread the book for me. She had done it for others and enjoyed the task. That evening she was managing the motel for a friend. What fate!

A shower and freshening-up made me feel great. It had been very hot. I found that I was getting a good suntan with the sketch pad reflecting the sun's rays onto my face. I planned my day and went to sleep listening to the sound of trains from across the highway.

I left the motel about 7 a.m. and arrived early at the bridge. A large spider's web, wet with dew, was blowing in a light breeze below the "Mississippi River" sign. The center, where the spider had moved about, looked invisible because the dewdrops were shaken off. It is amazing that this insect can adapt his spinning so well to the situation. The web was anchored to two metal posts, the sign bottom and the grass below. It is also unbelievable that it can create such a thing of beauty and strength with no training. I was intrigued by its plan and delicacy. This was God's work.

Next to it was man's work. The bridge, totally concrete, was not as white as if it were just new. The only contrast comes from silver drainpipes spaced regularly along the girders.

The concrete parapet is very attractive. It is set on a 5-inch-high curb and consists of about 14-inch-high concrete posts with a niche cut for the heavy textured rectangular concrete rail. The post spacing varies 2-1-2-1 for aesthetic purposes, as well as it serves an engineering function. There is a joint between the double posts. This joint allows for change in length due to temperature change plus, engineer Harold Sandberg informed me, it prevents the railing from participating in the live load stresses.

The Itasca County Highway 18 Bridge is low to the water and rests only on two piers. Each one consists of two parts--sets of pole-legs and a wider-than-high concrete top, pointed at each end. The river has no rock along the banks, only grasses.

A man from a house within 100 feet of the bridge noticed my Iowa license and came out to talk. He was from Mason City, Iowa, and had moved here in 1984. He told me about the gaging station. It was a small green metal building on ground near the bridge from which the Corps of Engineers takes tests of river water, checking for depth and purity.

Above the bridge was a telephone wire on which a row of little black birds sat. I don't remember them chattering. It was as though they were waiting for something to happen. It happened; I left.

Use:
CSAH 18 and local traffic

Location:
2.5 miles west of Junction with County Highway 16

Style:
3-span concrete girder

Length:
Channel span - 80 feet
Total length - 246 feet

Width:
Two lanes, 36 feet

Clearance:
8 feet MLW

Date completed:
1974, replaces July 1934 15-span bridge

Designed by:
Robert E. Erickson, Erickson Engineering

Bridge:
#31512 Itasca County

Owner:
Itasca County

Mary C. Costello ℔

Itasca County Road 18 Bridge

County Road 3, Below Ball Club, Minnesota

Approaching the bridge from US Highway 2, I saw and took the river access road to get a profile view of the bridge. Though it was not even mid-August, one would think it was fall with all the leaves on the secluded road. The road was parallel with the river for several blocks before turning toward the water. What I saw was the confluence of two rivers--the Ball Club River going one way and the Mississippi River going another. Because of the trees and the curve in the river, I could see nothing of the bridge from here.

Driving along the tree-lined access path, I parked off Highway 3 close to the bridge. The 3-span, precast beam bridge was not unlike others. Each pier consisted of five pairs of cylindrical, rust-colored metal legs secured in an oval concrete top that extended beyond the girder. A single-bar railing was secured on top of the concrete wall and eight square drain-pipes completed the design. The bridge angled across the Mississippi, therefore the piers were set askew, in line with the river flow.

Riprap under the bridge consisted of large colored rock mingled with wildflowers and grasses. A young willow tree was growing on the bank and a chipmunk popped out of the ground near it. I heard only one bird under the bridge and the gentle rustle of the trees. The water was shallow, and plants were growing in the water at the base of some of the piers.

As I prepared to leave, my new car wouldn't start. Cass County Highway 3 was lightly traveled, with no businesses or gas stations. My anxiety level rose. Eventually a man in a pickup truck, taking his granddaughter to register for school, stopped in response to my "Need Help" sign. His inspection discerned the problem to be a loose connection. I was both grateful and relieved. Bless another helpful Midwesterner.

Use:
CSAH 3 and local traffic

Location:
South of Ball Club, Minnesota

Style:
3-span precast concrete beam

Length:
Channel span - 80 feet
Total length   - 248 feet

Width:
2 lanes, 36 feet

Clearance:
7 feet MLW

Date completed:
1979

Designed by:
Minnesota DOT

Bridge:
#11511 Cass County

Owner:
Cass County

Cass County Road 3 Bridge, Below Ball Club, Minnesota

Mary C. Costello

215

Ball Club Railroad Bridge, Minnesota

*J*ust 100 feet from US Highway 2 was an impressively heavy girder railroad bridge. It was a great surprise because no place had I seen it marked. I should have known that when the highway crossed the Mississippi, the railroad tracks running beside it would also cross. I was close and on eye level with the top of the black steel girder. Only some wild rice and tall brush were between us as I stood next to the highway.

This Burlington Northern Santa Fe Railroad Bridge at Ball Club, Minnesota, has two different piers. One pier is a large, octagonal, 2-toned concrete form. It spans the full bridge width. The other pier in the water is rectangular with its lower third larger and pointed at either end. All other eleven piers are like the second style but smaller in size. Sadly grafitti in big letters marks up the girder sides. Often on my bridge travels beside the Mississippi River I saw trains and train tracks, and much to my delight as a train buff, a train passed while I was here.

According to the Corps of Engineers' old bridge lists, this location had a swingspan, built in 1908 for the then owner, the Great Northern Railroad. It was a two-span Howe through-truss bridge and remained until 1967 when the railbed was raised four feet, the swingspan removed, and the whole bridge made a plate-girder.

It must have been a very active spot indeed early in the 1930's when boats came through, because right next to this turnspan bridge was a lift span on the highway running parallel to the track. What an interesting and exciting place to have been in a Model A Ford when a steamboat arrived with two different moveable bridges to open within 100 feet of each other. My question to the Historical Society was, "How were the bridges opened? Today they have round-the-clock bridge-tenders to do it." She felt that probably someone from the boat would jump off and open, then close the spans. Or a person living close may have been responsible. Pat Hyatt, BNSF administrator, said train personnel may even have gotten out and closed the turnspan if it were open for the boats. He also said they could have had a bridge-tender stationed there. No doubt it is more fun thinking about it, than it would have been experiencing it at the time--the good-old-days syndrome.

Use:
Burlington Northern Santa Fe Railroad traffic

Location:
12 miles west of Ball Club

Style:
12-spans steel deck plate-girder

Length:
Channel span - 115 feet
Total length   - 597 feet

Width:
One track wide

Clearance:
26 feet MLW

Date completed:
1908; originally a swingspan; in 1967 changed to plate-girder and railbed raised four feet

Designed by:
Great Northern Railway

Bridge:
#134.0

Owner:
Burlington Northern Santa Fe Railroad

Burlington Northern Santa Fe Railroad Bridge, Ball Club   *Mary C. Costello*

Ball Club Highway Bridge in Cass County, Minnesota

*T*raveling along US 2, I came upon two bridges beside each other in the town of Ball Club. One was a railroad bridge,(the previous story) the other this US 2 Highway Bridge. Today's Ball Club Highway Bridge is much more modern and attractive than the one I saw. Though it is still two lanes, Westley Djoney said, "MN/DOT lowered the bridge at Ball Club, put on a new roadway, and made it safer in 1987." The railing was changed from an open post style to a solid wall built extending slightly out over the steel girder below. The unusual piers consist of a wall of concrete with an end cap over a single cylindrical leg, which adds much to the design. However, Harold Sandberg, Chairman of the Board Alfred Benesch and Company, Chicago, explained that it is not all about beauty, "The shape of the pier is probably the result of utilizing the existing piers. To accommodate the widening, it was easiest to drive a single pile to eliminate the cantilever. This pile would have to be located far enough away to clear the existing footing." The result is our attractive bridge pier.

The whiteness of the concrete was almost blinding in the afternoon sun--at least the wall and upper part of the pier where the high water hadn't dirtied its beauty. In front of the abutment "wings" is stacked large white and light-colored riprap, adding a great deal to the textural beauty.

But this is not the first time the bridge has changed design. In 1919, there was a vertical-lift bridge in this spot. It was a single span bridge with a 56-foot channel and almost eight-foot clearance. It must have been interesting when a boat came through with both this lift and the nearby railroad swing-span opened to allow passage. It occurred to me that both bridges would have required operators. If hired, one would have been paid by the state and the other by the railroad. Or did a local person do it? Or the boat people themselves? We may never know.

Use:
US 2 highway traffic

Location:
In Ball Club, Minnesota, 7 miles west of Junction 46

Style:
3-span steel beam

Length:
Channel span - 70 feet
Total length - 165 feet

Width:
Two lanes, 46 feet

Clearance:
7 feet MLW

Date completed:
1938; remodeled in 1987; replaced original 1919 vertical lift span

Designed by:
Unknown

Bridge:
#5760 Cass County

Owner:
Minnesota DOT

US 2 Highway Bridge, Ball Club

Mary C. Costello

225

All Mississsippi River Bridges are interesting and important to me but this Highway 9 Bridge/Dam combination is especially so, because I've met its designer, David Morrill. He said he couldn't wait to see my report on his bridge. He is proud of his design, as he should be; a design complicated, yet beautiful in its simplicity and totally functional.

The area was very noisy when I arrived at the bridge, because of the rushing water from the dam below. Although there are six spans to the bridge, only four sections of the dam below seem to generate water. The round columns or piers are set in heavy rectangular block-like bases 25 feet apart. In the darkened underside of the bridge starting from the middle to the back are four sets of steps--one on either side of the pillar-piers. There are more steps outside up the hilly bank on the right, some with railings, for the maintenance people I would imagine. The water from Lake Winnibigoshish thrashed and turned white as it dropped 19 feet before going under the "slab" bridge.

The 14-inch-thick concrete bridge deck is a supporting member of the present bridge, unlike anything I have seen on the Mississippi.

The original bridge, built in 1918, was narrower, with a deck of rough patchwork of asphalt when close to its demise, a raised plank walk, but basically a steel beam span. The dam had wood framed openings through which the river gushed dropping only ten feet, all very different from what we see today.

Nearby, as I visited the site, was a plaque telling the history of the dam and bridge, saying that the first timber-dam was built here in 1898; the second dam and bridge were finished in 1918 and remodeled in about 1970. Today's structure was completed in 1991. The US Corps of Engineers, St.Paul District, is responsible for the dam and reservoir.

Originally the dam was meant to raise the water level and store Spring run-off. It no longer serves that purpose.Today its purpose is for limited flood control, for wild rice and for recreational use.

There was a small park and recreation area beside the bridge where I found a table under roof and ate my lunch out of the sun. As I did so, I watched a kingfisher dive into the clean water below the dam three times from wires above. He got his meal.

Winnibigoshish in Ojibway language means "miserable, wretched, dirty water." At the time the lake was named by the Ojibway it was marshy and shallow, and could have warranted that title possibly, said the historian for the upper Mississippi River.

As I was studying and sketching, a rather large man in an olive-colored, perspiration-soaked coverall walked up to me. He had just finished fishing and had a large Northern in his net. He was very friendly. He said his son was studying to be an artist--his reason for stopping perhaps. Formerly he lived in Council Bluffs, Iowa. We Midwesterners seem drawn to the Mississippi.

This unusual combination bridge and dam is 170 miles away from the river's source at Lake Itasca and is just one of the more unusual bridges we will see. However, this one is by far the greatest engineering feat.

Use:
CSAH 9 crossing the dam

Location:
East end of Lake Winnibigoshish

Style:
6-span thick "concrete slab" span

Length:
Channel span - 28 feet
Total length   - 169 feet

Width:
2 lanes, a single 6-foot walk, 46 feet total

Clearance:
19 feet MLW

Date completed:
1991; replacing 1918 steel beam span, remodeled 1975; originally an 1898 timber dam

Designed by:
David Morrill, with Alfred Benesch & Company, Chicago, Illinois

Bridge:
#5358 Itasca County

Owner:
US Army Corps of Engineers

---

* The Mississippi River passes through a number of large lakes in the north, which was a revelation to me when I started my research--Lake Bemidji, Cass Lake, as well as Lake Winnibigoshish in the far north to name a few, and Lake Pepin below Red Wing.

Itasca County Road 9 Bridge, Lake Winnibigoshish

Mary C. Costello

221

The Third River Road Bridge in the Chippewa National Forest is an access road for the US Forestry Service not a public bridge. "Out west this bridge would be forbidden to the public," said Cliff Hill, an engineer with the US Forest Service. "However, here in the east it is allowed but not encouraged."

Not knowing any of this, I was puzzled to see a sign that said "Closed next 7 miles" on the two-lane forest road. I thought they must be doing road work, but I saw none. I found the bridge, but the water wasn't marked as the Mississippi River nor were there any plaques. It did seem strange. Lots of heavy construction trucks crossed, nothing else.

The bridge is a new-looking concrete girder span over a narrow Mississippi. Like the "teenage" river, its two piers have that youthful appearance, tall and slender. Each pier consists of three large, round, concrete pillars much bigger than the telephone-pole-size ones that have been on bridges leading here. At the top there is a thick concrete cap to hold them in place.

The girders look concave below the extended road. The Third River Road Bridge has a "three-line flat tube" railing with I-beam shaped posts of unpainted galvanized metal. Each pipe is attached in front, not through the posts. I could see the bottom of the river here, clean and clear, and a fish jumped out of the water as I sketched.

The previous construction serving the US Forestry here was a 9-span trestle bridge with a three-plank wooden railing and timber deck. In pictures even the approaching road was unpaved. This bridge was abandoned when the new one was built farther north and east. The old bridge burned down in 1975.

When I returned the next year, I went down the embankment to get a better view. Since no one was around, I left my car unlocked. This was a mistake because I had hardly descended the difficult, weedy embankment when I heard young voices above. Fearing for my open car, I hurried back up the steep incline.

When I got to the top, I saw a couple and their teen-age boy and girl. They asked if I were a biologist or scientist and were disappointed when I said no. They were looking for eagle nests and hoped I might help. The Trexlers were from New York. He was a professor of physics and she a librarian. They were interested in my writing, suggesting several books with a cross-country theme. If ever I were in New York, they invited me to stay with them. For a non-public bridge, the Third River Road Span became very public this day.

Use:
Access bridge for US Forest Service

Location:
4 miles northeast of junction with County Highway 10 on FSR 2171 in Chippewa State Park

Style:
3-span precast concrete girder

Length:
Channel span - 61 feet
Total length   - 182 feet

Width:
2 lanes, 33.8 feet

Clearance:
18 feet MLW

Date completed:
1972; replaced 1926 7-span trestle bridge which burned down in 1975

Designed by:
Howard Clement, U.S.F.S., Milwaukee, Wisconsin

Bridge:
#L9488 in Chippewa National Forest

Owner:
U.S. Government Forest Service

Unique feat:
Not a public bridge; for forestry use only

U.S. Forest Service "Third River Road Bridge," Beltrami County   *Mary C. Costello*

223

Bridge Near Knutson Dam, County Road 39 in Beltrami County

*T*he Mississippi River travels under Beltrami County Highway 39 after leaving the 5-mile-wide Cass Lake and rushing over Knutson Dam. The railing and the piers on this modern-looking, concrete girder span are different. In the sun the 10 inches or so of road projecting beyond the girder cast a deep shadow below. Only the girder edges catches the light. The two piers each have an upper cap of concrete about 40 inches deep, cut off at the corners, resting on hexagonal columns.

The bottom of the girder adds what looks like a belt on the outside of the bridge and the road edge projects a shadow below. The railing has steel posts fastened outside the bridge deck. For the horizontal rail there is a three-sided shape with flanges. All are in unpainted galvanized steel. The blue-grey appearance is attractive with the white concrete and blacktop road.

From my measurement, the clear river is about 59 feet wide and the marshy area alongside takes about another 23 feet. Brown rice and tall lavender and white scented wildflowers fill the banks.

The area is dotted with resort cabins, a signal that it is inhabited at least in the summer. This is in (unorganized) Brook Lake Township, about 100 miles from the source of the river going almost due west. Contrary to the belief that the Mississippi travels south, up here it does unusual things like going first north then east or west, but never straight, always in tortuous twists and turns.

Use:
CSAH 39 traffic

Location:
East side of Cass Lake on Highway 39

Style:
3-span precast concrete girder

Length:
Channel span - 61 feet
Total span   - 183 feet

Width:
2 lanes plus shoulders, 32 feet

Clearance:
9 feet MLW

Date completed:
1959, replaces 1918 span

Designed by:
Robert E. Erickson, Engineering Company, Minneapolis

Bridge:
#7198 in Beltrami County

Owner:
Beltrami County

Beltrami County Road 39 Bridge, Near Knutson Dam

Mary C. Costello

225

County Road 33 Bridge in Beltrami Co.

*H*ighway 33 Bridge lies between Lake Andrusia and Allen's Bay--two more lakes that the "Father of Waters" flows through. A bearded uniformed man gave me directions to it. Five miles ahead he indicated by holding up his fingers, five. The bridge was six to eight miles farther on the highway. I crossed the bridge and went down the sandy road next to it to park.

Here was another quite generic precast concrete beam span with a double-grooved solid concrete parapet and two 10-pole piers of steel and concrete, anchored in a long rectangular cap of concrete. This day the river was quite busy with three or four boats--an outboard-motor boat went under the bridge with a family of five and then an open-aired houseboat whose passenger waved.

On my last visit I recall a different bridge--a five-span rustic looking low, greyed natural wood, single board railing with heavy 4 x 6 posts. Round pilings with cross bracing served as piers. It was a steel beam bridge having a 22-foot blacktop deck, about half the present 43-foot width road.

But what I remember mostly is when I started to leave the newer concrete bridge, my car got stuck in the sand. I used sticks, bark, cardboard and anything I could find to try to get traction under my tires, but nothing worked. I was getting frustrated because I knew I could not be seen by passing traffic from above. I prayed and help came almost immediately. An old Native American grandfather and his young grandson came walking down the rutted sand-filled road from the highway. He offered to help and he tried pushing and only wore himself out several times before he announced he'd go for help. It seemed a long time to me (probably 20 minutes) and he was back with two young men, I believe, his sons. One drove and the other pushed my car. In a matter of minutes, I was free. I gave them $14., all the cash I had, not much reward for saving a woman in distress, but I was most grateful.

Use:
CSAH 33 traffic

Location:
Between Lake Andrusia and Allen's Bay

Style:
3-span precast concrete beam

Length:
Channel span - 55 feet
Total length   - 168 feet

Width:
2 lanes, 43 feet

Clearance:
5 feet MLW

Date completed:
1995; replaced a 1930 steel beam span with piling bents

Designed by:
Edwards and Kelsey

Bridge:
#04519 in Beltrami County

Owner:
Beltrami County

Beltrami County Road 33 Bridge, Between Lake Andrusia and Allen's Bay

Mary C. Costello

227

County Road 8 Bridge, South of Wolf Lake, Beltrami County

Seeing a bridge under construction is an exciting experience, and going back when it is finished almost makes one feel we had a part in it. This is what happened with this latest Highway 8 span.

When I arrived in July it was a busy place. The mud-tracked, officially-closed road had cement and dump trucks going back and forth in front of my red Datsun. As I waited my turn, no one questioned me. Around the curve closer to the bridge the paved road ended. In a clearing beside it was a large pile of smoldering pine trees that had been cut to make way for the bridge--this on a day when the temperature was in the 90's. Also on the ground but nearer the water were a working-crane, five huge precast concrete girders and a giant sandpile. Directly in front of me were the wooden forms for the freshly poured southern abutment, and in the middle of the river were the two finished piers, with five more girders spread out in place between them.

A 7-foot ladder leaned against one of the 6-foot-high girders close by a man giving directions. He soon appeared on land, and we talked. He was the bridge engineer. I don't know how he crossed the water, but I know he wasn't wet. He told me that each of the 15 girders (five more were on the other side waiting) weighed 45 tons. The river here was 5 feet deep at the most and was 200 feet wide. He explained that the preceeding bridge had been built in 1923. Finally, he gave me the name of a man who has followed the new bridge building and destruction of the old, Jim Eltrom. "He lives close by and has all his life," he told me. "His parents came in 1913 before the first bridge was built, so he is vitally interested."

I tracked down Mr. Eltrom's home only to find he was out guiding some fishermen. I met his wife and his pet ferret and saw his 21-point deer and 12-point white-tailed buck heads on the wall. I wish I could have met him; he has been written up in National Geographic. He had shot his own leg off when he was trying to protect his family against a pack of wolves.

When I returned the following summer, the bridge was all put together. It was simple, with no walks or lights, only a wide two lanes. There were nine sets of silver-colored, metal-encased concrete legs on each pier which were driven into the river bed. The beautiful white concrete pier cap, girders and low wall on the bridge were all in shadow because of the evening hour. I stood on the new sod and was about to take a picture when I heard a "slushing" sound in the water. It was a man and his 4-year-old daughter in a yellow plastic paddleboat. The little child cried because she didn't want to go under the "big" bridge. I called to him and said it looked like fun, thinking it would help. It didn't. They returned without going under on the other side of the river behind a blanket of rice stands.

Use:
CSAH 8 traffic

Location:
Between Andrusia and Wolf Lake

Style:
3-span precast girder

Length:
Channel span: - 100 feet
Total length   - 306 feet

Width:
2 lanes, 43 feet total

Clearance:
10 feet MLW

Date completed:
1987, replaces a 1923 truss span

Designed by:
KBM Incorporated, Grand Forks, North Dakota

Bridge:
#04513 Beltrami County

Owner:
Beltrami County

Beltrami County Road 8 (old) Bridge, South of Wolf Lake

Mary C. Costello

229

County Road 8 Bridge, North of Wolf Lake, Beltrami Country

"*T*he Crookedest Great Waterway in the World" [3] does some intestinal twists in Beltrami County after passing through Wolf Lake. County Highway 8 turns west and crosses the river twice, the second time with this 1992 concrete beam span. The bridge is a duplicate of the last one over Highway 8 except it is 85 feet shorter in length, with not as many legs in the piers and no doubles. It is a shame that all bridges are being built alike today. Most bridge differences are in the piers. Again Harold Sandberg wisely noted, "Standardization produces economy. Only 'signature' bridges are designed differently."

I remember the old pony truss that was here on my first visit. I had to drive two blocks beyond (to the next crossroad) because of a wire fence on the edge of the road. It was misting when I walked back. There was a low, black-painted truss on either side of the road, called a pony truss or half-through. In front of them was a white fence of three long steel rods, 155 feet long, without a post or a break midstream resting on a six-inch-high curb. Except for the blacktop being rough, people probably drove over the bridge without realizing that they had crossed a bridge. It had one pier underneath that I never saw because of the weather and the fencing preventing me from going down.

Rice stands took up a great part of the river then as they do today. To one side of the bridge is a beautiful collection of trees. The middle tier were mostly Grant Wood types with a few conifers for spice. In the background were the stately sugar pines. At the ends of the bridge were the typical "hazard" signs," having black and yellow diagonal stripes. When I began my research, I thought these were an indication of a "bridge ahead," but when I inquired of the county engineer, I found they are used for any hazard. The direction of the diagonal points to where the danger is, such as, the bridge. I also found that some counties use black and white; it is up to the county. The green and white "Mississippi River" sign, on the other hand, is universal--understood and appreciated by all viewers for the "Father" that it is.

Use:
CSAH 8 traffic

Location:
0.4 mile east of junction with County Road 25

Style:
3-span precast concrete girder

Length:
Channel span - 72 feet
Total length   - 222 feet

Width:
2 lanes, 47 feet total

Clearance:
10 feet MLW

Date completed:
1992; replaced October 1931 2-span pony truss

Designed by:
Erickson Engineering

Bridge:
#04517 County

Owner:
Beltrami County

Beltrami County Road 8 (new) Bridge, North of Wolf Lake

Mary C. Costello

PART Five

PART *Five*
Rails To Rocks

Within a two-block area on the Mississippi River in Bemidji are three bridges, two of them railroad bridges though soon there will be but one. These rails are the last to cross the Mississippi before the "Rock Bridge" at Lake Itasca, the end of our climb. Between these rails and rocks is a variety of terrain for the small, but always respected, Mississippi to pass.

From Lake Irving (directly below Lake Bemidji) to Iron Bridge Canoe Landing is a wetland forest, making a dense canopy over the wandering stream with homes, cabins and farms quite visible. Then the Mississippi stream develops finger-like curves on the way to

Pine Point Landing near Rice Lake and its wild rice stands that Native Americans have harvested for hundreds of years. Swamps and fast-moving water, along with a rapids, illustrate some of the variety before Coffee Pot Landing. Black bear, bobcat, timber wolf, badger and otter are seen on land by canoeists in this area of the river. Narrow and winding, the river passes through some private farms both wooded and clear to a low wooden dam and then to Wanagan Landing, beyond which the river becomes shallower, Inside Itasca State Park the Mississippi River is in its wilderness state, twisting and turning until it reaches its beginning--its source and our destination.

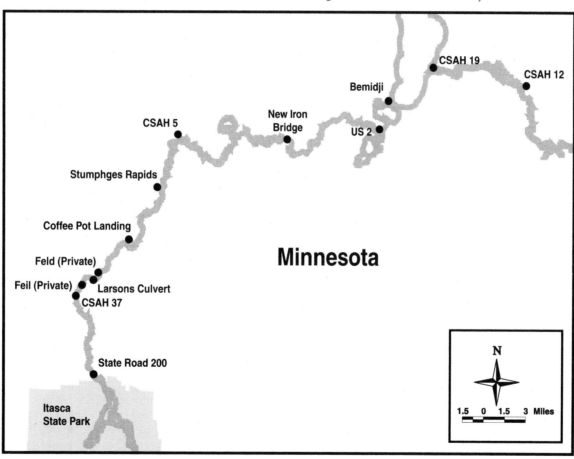

County Road 12 Bridge, Near the Dam East of Bemidji, Minnesota

I was delighted to see this Highway 12 Bridge. It is a special design, aesthetically-pleasing, a "signature" bridge over the Mississippi River. Its beauty can truly be appreciated here.

Before I came to the bridge I heard rushing water from the hydroelectric dam which is northwest of the bridge. The dam was much bigger than the one below Lake Winnibigoshish and also of masonry construction. It has five sections, two of which were closed to the water. The other three made an impressive waterfall.

When I arrived at the bridge a short distance down the highway, I was interested in the vertical-ridged concrete outer surface, called "the breakaway treatment", given to the abutment and road's outer edge. The designer told me that a colorant was added to the concrete to give the surface not only the corrugated texture but some added color and interest. The girder, which was almost hidden underneath, is made of weathering steel. It was brown repeating some of the color in the textured outer concrete walls. The sad part is that not many people see what is unique about a bridge when crossing in their car. But here the designing engineer has added a wall of texture at the bridge end and a see-through parapet, allowing better viewing of the river. However, the canoeists can see and appreciate the entire bridge design and exterior finish.

The railing is different (similar to #1 bridge). It is officially called an "ornamental metal railing" but consists of heavy square steel posts bolted to a 9-inch curbing. In each section three lengths of 3-inch square tubing run horizontally and are spaced about 8 inches apart at the top and 20 inches apart below. The balusters in the lower space are nine thin vertical tubes for strength and protection. It is an attractive all-black railing. However, there are no sidewalks, so Harold Sandberg said that with this railing there must be high curbs for deflecting cars. He indicated that the railing is designed for "people-pushing-on-it load" only. Cars need more.

There is only one pier under the bridge. It is pure white and is a very angular "W" shape, with a cap extending to the edge of the girder.

There is riprap below and beside the bridge. Trees and shrubbery are behind the span. The water was not very rough nor was it perfectly smooth on this cloudy July day. It allowed the bridge to be special.

Use:
CSAH 12 traffic

Location:
East of Bemidji, Minnesota

Style:
2-span continuous steel beam

Length:
Channel span - about 70 feet
Total length   - 140 feet

Width:
2 lanes, 39.6 feet total

Clearance:
11 feet MLW

Date completed:
1975

Designed by:
Strgar-Roscoe-Fausch, Incorporated, Wayzata, Minnesota

Bridge:
#04511 Beltrami County

Owner:
Beltrami County

Beltrami County Road 12 Bridge, Near Dam East of Bemidji

Mary C. Costello

237

County Road Highway 19 Bridge East of Lake Bemidji

*T*he two things I remember concerning this Highway 19 Bridge really have nothing to do with the bridge--one is the rough drive to get to it and the other is the tall bird I saw on the way. A librarian at Bemidji University, who traveled the route daily, told me to go north around Lake Bemidji to get to the bridge because the road south was closed. More than the distance, I remember the unpaved road east of the lake. It was rough and left to bake rock-hard in the sun. For several miles I saw no one else on the road, nor any houses or buildings. I was getting "worked up" inside when the road changed.

Near the bridge the road became level again. It was here I looked east and saw a brown crane in an open sunburnt field next to a stream, the river, I presume. I had not seen a crane in its natural habitat before, so I stopped to take a picture.

When I arrived, I noticed that there were no people, cars or signs of life, no rice beds or even wildflowers growing. It was a lonely quiet place. I was surprised to find such a new bridge. Built in 1984, it is a precast concrete "bulb tee" girder bridge, a new type girder at the time. The girder was shaped like the letter "T" with a bulb at the end of the vertical when seen from the end. These long concrete forms are placed side by side with the crossbars touching, thereby making a solid surface. The top is then covered with a bituminous surface. The innovative style was invented by a concrete company. "Only time will tell how well it withstands wear. It was an expeditious method for building this busy bridge," said Westley Djoney. The only part of the new girder visible is half the T cross plus a thick ledge at the bottom,"the bulb".

Riprap, under the low bridge below the abutment wings, is neatly contained and the grass well-groomed. The two piers are simple deep elongated ovals of concrete for a cap, supported by eleven legs of shiny steel-only the first and last angle or batter.

The bridge roadway has a concrete wall which, from the outside, has two horizontal grooves-very common on Minnesota bridges even today. There appears to be a utility pipe on one side of the span above the bulb. The only other notable feature was the seven drainpipes evenly spaced hanging below the road's outer edge. I have been informed that roads on both sides of the bridge have been replaced, so no more rough rides.

This span replaced an historic bridge called the "Riverside Highway Bridge," built in 1914, which had only two spans and a 70-foot channel opening.

We are definitely now in Indian territory. Only Indians lived here until about 200 years ago when the white man came to explore and hunt for the source of the Mississippi River. Early settlers found this lake, Lake Bemidji, was named after an Indian phrase meaning "lake crossed by water," referring to the Mississippi River which passes through it. An Indian related this story to the pioneers and became known as the Chief Bemidji. This bridge location could be where his family and he lived--where the river exits the lake.

Use:
CSAH 19 traffic

Location:
East side of Lake Bemidji as the Mississippi exits the lake

Style:
3-span precast concrete "bulb tee" girder span

Length:
Channel span - 61 feet
Total length   - 183 feet

Width:
2 lanes, total 44 feet

Clearance:
13 feet MLW

Date completed:
1984, replaces bridge built 1914 historic "Riverside Highway Bridge"

Designed by:
KBM Incorporated, Grand Forks, North Dakota

Bridge:
#04514 in Beltrami County

Owner:
Beltrami County

Beltrami County Road 19 Bridge, East of Lake Bemidji

Mary C. Costello

239

Paul Bunyan[1] Snowmobile Trail Bridge, North of Bemidji

*L*ike a fancy bracelet stands the former Burlington Northern Bridge across the Mississippi River's exit from Lake Bemidji. It is a wooden trestle span with a very shallow super-structure, just a block from the Highway 19 Bridge. It sits on the very edge of Lake Bemidji through which the Mighty River cuts a three-mile path from the southwest lake entrance to this northeastern lake exit.

Called the "Mississippi River Outlet Bridge" by the Corps of Engineers in 1935 when the Minnesota and International Railway owned the bridge. It has 16 wooden trestles some hidden by the trees. Each trestle is composed of 5 wooden pilings with cross bracing. Steel sheeting 1/16 of an inch thick covers the side of bents #5 through #8 because of the winter ice action. The openings between the pilings gives the delicate jewel appearance. It had a simple metal railing.

Railroad Bridge #98 has changed hands a number of times-from the "Minnesota and International Railway" to the "Northern Pacific" and then to the "Burlington Northern," who completely rebuilt it just after their 1970 merger. I didn't see any trains on the bridge because, Mr. Russell D. Link, Burlington Northern Bridge Engineer in St. Paul, said, "Minnesota has purchased the bridge for a snowmobile trail."

Yes, Minnesota Department of Natural Resources bought the railroad bridge for pedestrian purposes, resurfaced it in 1991 without tracks, then in 1996 redecked it horizontally with 320 3x8 inches boards twelve feet long. In addition, a five-and-a-half-foot tall wooden parapet, made mostly of 2x8's spaced, has been added, along with two fishing openings (one on each side), a sloped wooden ramp at each end with paved trails on both ends. It is used in the winter time for snowmobiles, as well as bicycles and walkers in the summer, but no other motorized vehicles or horses are allowed.

Foreground waterlilies and deciduous trees hanging over the narrowing waterway as I sketched from the highway bridge, made the old railroad structure, the dull grey sky and the distant Bemidji look much more interesting.

Use:
Snowmobile trail, fishing, walking and biking

Location:
Northeast side of Lake Bemidji

Style:
15-span open-deck timber stringer with trestle bents

Length:
Channel span - 19 feet
Total length   - 237 feet

Width:
Single track originally, 12-foot deck now

Clearance:
13 feet MLW

Date completed:
1971, year after BN merged with NP; original span built 1901 for M&I; rebuilt in 1920 and 1937; NP merged with M&I in 1942; 1980 rebuilt[2] last BN train crossed in 1985; MNDOT bought and resurfaced without tracks 1991; redecked in 1996 for recreational purposes

Designed by:
Burlington Northern, standard trestle

Bridge:
No number; #98 was old M&I railroad number

Owner:
Minnesota DNR

Paul Bunyan Snowmobile Trail Bridge, North of Bemidji

Mary C. Costello

Minnesota Highway 197 Bridge, Entrance to Lake Bemidji

Paul Bunyan Road south of Lake Bemidji took me right to the bridge. It was raining and I pulled into a liquor store parking lot and asked the surprised proprietor permisssion to park there.

This is one of the few times on my trip that I saw the river really rough and the first time I saw what I thought was the current reversed. Instead of the river going into the lake, it appeared the lake was rushing into the river. An engineer from Bemidji told me the wind was playing tricks on me and blowing the surface water so that it looked that way. I watched a mother duck and her young going toward Lake Bemidji. This is the way the river was going, yet the ducks were struggling against the wind. They then decided to cross over to the opposite side from me and started rocking across the waves. "Father Mississippi" was very small, only about 100 feet wide, but mighty. It was not a time to be on it in a canoe.

The Department of Natural Resources in Minnesota caters to canoeists, especially from here north to the Mississippi's source at Lake Itasca. For that purpose there are steps down to the water and a concrete "boat access point," just one of five around Lake Bemidji.

From a 1930's postcard I saw how the bridge appeared then. It had a heavy concrete post and baluster railing, street lamps in the four corners and heavy, but plain, Italianate brackets under the deck at the pier ends. It was pleasing.

The bridge I saw in front of me had a solid bridge wall in a deep tan-color cement with a two-pipe metal railing above. The brackets below were gone and the cement color of girder and piers was whiter. The pier ends appeared flat and angular, not rounded or pointed as I might expect to prevent eddies from forming. However, the two piers were sliced back where the water met them. Perhaps this does the same thing.

There were trees on both sides of the small river here, four other bridges to my back, and a hazy city skyline above the bridge to the front. Nothing else was visible because of the continuing rain.

Use:
Minnesota Highway 197 and local traffic

Location:
Southwest of Lake Bemidji where the Mississippi enters Lake Bemidji

Style:
3-span concrete deck girder

Length:
Channel span - 39 feet
Total length   - 172 feet

Width:
4 lanes, two 6-foot sidewalks; 66 feet total

Clearance:
9 feet MLW

Date completed:
November 1934, remodeled 1969

Designed by:
Minnesota DOT

Bridge:
#5316 Beltrami County

Owner:
Minnesota DOT

Minnesota Highway 197 Bridge, Entrance to Lake Bemidji   *Mary C. Costello*

243

Old Midway Road Bridge in Bemidji

*T*he date the Old Midway Road Bridge was built, 1917, tells me it is too early to be an Art Deco [3] style design. The designer, a reinforced concrete company, attained beauty on the old bridge with textured areas and color in the concrete.

The design emphasis is on its three arches, built-in railing and its pier ends. The 40,60,40 foot concrete arches have a wide band of deep tan-colored masonry above each. The lower areas have been carefully "bush hammered" [4] for texture. The tiny shadows picked up thereby darken the appearance of the color. The light tan sections are smooth and in relief. All exposed surfaces of the concrete, by the designer's plan, were smoothed by hand-rubbing with a carborundum brick, thus eliminating any imprint of the form--joint, grain, or board mark. This interest in detail shows true pride in one's work.

Instead of the open spandrel that is often seen in Minneapolis bridges, this structure has a smooth triangular shape in that closed space above the arch. The pillar-turned-pier between arches is edged with texture. The center rectangle and half-cone shape at the bottom of both are smooth, and therefore, a lighter concrete color.

The other interesting pattern on the bridge is on the railing. The guard-rail is an integral part of the bridge and has the same relief pattern both inside and out. Its top is a six-inch-deep concrete cap, below which are seven narrow, round-cornered horizontal rectangles, spaced evenly and raised, in a background of the same finish. On top of this sturdy concrete parapet is a simple pipe railing for greater safety. Sadly, the old lamp posts with their globes are gone, sealed off in 1922.

This old two-lane arched bridge, which cost only $15,000 to build, is a beautiful structure and one for which Bemidji can be proud. It would seem historical preservation is in order. But the bridge has a new life to live. A former city engineer told me that the Old Midway Road Bridge will become a part of the city trailways for pedestrians and bikes in 2003, but will carry vehicles until then.

Use:
Local traffic today, but for people and bikes only after 2003

Location:
In Bemidji southwest of Highway 2

Style:
3-span reinforced concrete arch

Length:
Channel span - 60 feet
Total length   - 168 feet

Width:
2 lanes, one 3-foot sidewalk; 33 feet total

Clearance:
13 feet MLW

Date completed:
1917

Designed by:
Standard Reinforced Concrete Company, Indianapolis, Indiana

Bridge:
#2366 in Beltrami County

Owner:
City of Bemidji

Unique feat:
Great detail and textures on bridge exterior

Old Midway Road Bridge, Bemidji

Mary C. Costello

245

Canadian Pacific Railroad Abandoned Bridge in Bemidji

I stood on the tracks of the former Soo Line Railroad Bridge to study this confusing bridge situation--four bridges within a block distance--the Old Midway Bridge (just discussed), and three railroad bridges (one of which has been removed since). Like its neighbors this railroad bridge has a timber beam super-structure and trestles for a substructure. Its strength comes from these trestles, which are many--fourteen I counted. The space between the bents is for all practical purposes closed to boats because of bracing between trestles. Thus, there is only room in the center channel (an opening 30 feet wide by ll feet high at normal water level) for canoes or small boats to navigate.

The trestles consist of five, in some cases six, poles fastened together with 2x12's, which support the "rail" road with its heavy creosoted ties and long freight trains. Beside the track on both sides is a four-foot walkway madeup of 1x6 boards painted white.

The only visible metal on this structure, besides the center span and tracks, is the railing. It runs on both sides of the bridge and consists of 3-feet-long angle-iron posts, fastened to a flat triangular plate at the bottom, attached to the floor braces. The actual handrail is a single 1 1/2 or 2-inch pipe.

Prepared for the need, the railroad had stacked railroad ties on the ground near the bridge end where I stood. These they call sleepers. As I observed this, three rather rough-looking men crossed the river on this bridge's boardwalk. I was concerned for a minute. Perhaps they were working for the railroad or were looking to "ride the rails". In any case, they disappeared, and I turned my attention to the next bridge.

Today the bridge is abandoned and the tracks are mostly gone. The city of Bemidji is contacting the railroad to acquire it to demolish it. The city engineer told me that it will be gone by 2003 when the "197 Corridor" [5] will be complete.

Use:
Abandoned railroad bridge

Location:
In Bemidji between Lake Irving and Lake Bemidji

Style:
14-span open deck wooden trestle

Length:
Channel span - 28 feet
Total length   - 209 feet

Width:
One track, two walkways, 20 feet total

Clearance:
11 feet MLW

Date completed:
l931; built originally in 1910, 244 feet long; 2 spans filled-in 1929; pilings redriven in 1931 reusing steel span and shortening to its current length; almost completely rebuilt in 1963; last Soo Line train crossed in 1990; destined to be demolished by 2003

Designed by:
Milwaukee, St.Paul & Sault Ste. Marie Railway

Bridge:
#P-370.34

Owner:
Canadian Pacific Railroad

Canadian Pacific Railroad Abandoned Bridge, Bemidji

Mary C. Costello

BNSF Railroad Bridge Nearest Lake Irving, in Bemidji

This is the first railroad bridge under which the Mississippi River flows. Coming from the south, as we are doing, it is the last. This very active bridge has a long history. In 1898 the Great Northern Railroad was the first to come to Bemidji and built a bridge on this very spot. In 1905 or 1907 the Minneapolis, Red Lake and Manitoba Railroad rebuilt the bridge here. Next the Northern Pacific owned the road and rebuilt the span in 1952. But the Burlington Northern acquired the Northern Pacific Railroad and the bridge in 1971. In 1995 the Sante Fe and Burlington Northern merged and own the bridge today.

My first view of the Burlington Northern Santa Fe Bridge was through the arch under the Old Midway Road Bridge. I saw the trestle pilings for two different structures, beside each other, under that low curve. It is hard to believe there could be four bridges so close to each other in the space of 1 1/2 blocks. With the Midway span in the way and the railroad bridges having no high superstructures, I saw nothing else till I walked over the deck-arch bridge to the other side. Here were the two railroad bridges. This Burlington Northern Bridge was the longer, the one farthest south, and the busier.

A train was crossing the bridge when I arrived on the scene. It was a long Burlington Northern Santa Fe freight. My best view was from the Canadian Pacific Railroad (former Soo Line) tracks which were inbetween, so there I stayed.

This channel of the Mississippi River between the Bemidji and Irving Lakes widens here next to Lake Irving, and the bridge crosses at an angle more than the map indicates. For these reasons, the span is longer than its neighbor. According to R.D. Link, Bridge Engineer with Burlington Northern Santa Fe, this railroad bridge has two numbers 90.5 and 94 reflecting the destination. The former number is on the line to Grand Forks and the latter to International Falls.

There are thirteen trestles or groups of pilings in the water under the bridge. Each trestle is composed of five piles connected with diagonal planks. The ones next to the channel span have extra shoring, are double strength or ten pilings each. Across the channel span only and under the deck is a 30-foot long steel I-beam for added strength where boats could hit the bridge. I was impressed with the strength and condition of what I saw. The Burlington Northern Santa Fe, Bridge has a simple railing of black metal.

This was three days after the rain and the river had calmed down. The Mississippi was showing her placid side, flowing in the right direction, with only surface ripples. There were some lily pads, a few flowers and marsh grasses on both sides of the river. There was nothing to tell the world that this bridge was a first.

Use:
BNSF Railroad trains

Location:
On the edge of Lake Irving in Bemidji

Style:
12-span open deck timber pile trestle

Length:
Channel span - 30 feet
Total length   - 196 feet

Width:
One track, 12 feet

Clearance:
8 feet MLW

Date completed:
May 1952 by NP; 1898 the GN built first span; then the MRLM rebuilt in 1905 or 1907; BN bought out NP in 1971 and became owner

Designed by:
Northern Pacific

Bridge:
#90.5 and 94

Owner:
Burlington Northern Santa Fe Railroad

Unique feat:
First railroad bridge today in the north to cross the Mississippi River based on its position; and first bridge in Bemidji in 1898

BNSF Railroad Bridge nearest Lake Irving, Bemidji

Mary C. Costello

A brown duck was sitting on a rock in the Mississippi about 8 feet off shore when I arrived. He probably enjoyed the weather much better than I because it was misting. I had come down back roads from the University of Bemidji where I had stayed in the dorm the night before. This bridge was in what seemed an out-of-the-way place.

This generic bridge with concrete deck, parapet, girder, and piers is like most of the rest they are building today over the Mississippi River. The one thing that is different is the rounded pier-cap end is extended up the girder to the deck. The bridge it replaced had not as much beauty, but so much more character.(See drawing insert.)

The old Yellowhead Road Bridge, which I visited in 1986, was built in 1915. It had low trusses, called pony or half-through trusses, on each side for strength. The single pier in the middle of the two-span bridge was different. This support consisted of a square column under each side of the bridge with a deep concrete cap connecting them. At the bottom of the upstream end, was a sloping rounded addition to make the impact with the river gentler. The abutment was like a high retaining wall of concrete straight up from the edge of the river. The roadway between was asphalt.

The black Warren style trusses had heavy outside steel beams but the inner diagonals and verticals were lighter in weight with open slots in the middle. The angle-iron railing was secured inside the trusses as a sturdy unit.

The surprising part of this bridge was that it was a "one-lane" span only 17 feet wide. It was too narrow for cars to pass one another on the bridge. It didn't seem that that occasion would arise very often as the bridge was not a busy thoroughfare. Black and white diagonal hazard signs were posted on all four corners of the bridge but I don't remember any other notice except a ten-ton limit for vehicles. (Raspberry Island Bridge, St. Paul is the only other public "one laner" on the Mississippi)

The lone duck left. I didn't see him go. I continued north on the river which is really south here--on a river that is thought to go south but is actually going north in Bemidji. To us this sounds confusing, but to the duck everything is clear.

1915 Span

Use:
Local traffic

Location:
Southwest Bemidji below Lake Irving

Style:
2-span concrete beam span

Length:
Channel span - 86 feet
Total length   - 174 feet

Width:
Two lane, 38.5 feet

Clearance:
10 feet MLW

Date completed:
2000; original 2-span pony truss built 1915

Designed by:
Erickson Engineering

Bridge:
#04520

Owner:
Bemidji Township

Yellowhead Road Bridge, Below Lake Irving

Mary C. Costello

251

US 2 By-Pass Bridges in Beltrami County, Minnesota

*I*t was a rainy day. I was a block away on Yellowhead Road Bridge when I first saw this attractive set of bridges. The US 2 By-Pass Bridges are very modern. They are concrete--girder, parapet and roadway. The bridge appears to almost double the width of the river in its length because of the marshes on the sides looking like land. Though I couldn't see the second bridge, the reflections in the water and two piers indicated that there were two, one for each direction of traffic.

The piers seem to be "he-man" style (broad shoulders tapering to the waist). On a closer look, they don't have the height or brawn, just the stretched-out-arm look on a sturdier body. It is the outside wall that is the most interesting and unusual. The railing has a grooved vertical texture which gives the bridge character. County Road 12 Bridge (#109) has the same finish called "the breakaway treatment." The only break in the horizontal line of the bridge comes with two vertical silver downspouts at the end of the first quarter and the third quarter of the girder.

Looking down the calm river beyond the bridge, all I could see were trees lining the low banks. They were in various sizes and shapes but all very green. The river was like a path in the forest, curving out of sight--very picturesque.

My second visit a year later involved other people. I pulled off US 2 after crossing the bridge to park. Almost immediately a highway patrolman in an unmarked car pulled up behind me. I explained my project and told him I wouldn't be long. He was nice and left me alone to work. While examining the outside bridge texture, I looked down and saw a flat-bottomed rowboat coming with a young father, grandfather and three children. I asked how the ride was, but they had just "put in." Another boat went under the bridge with a couple and two children, but they were motorized and could only wave--more friendly river people.

Use:
US 2 and 71, a Bemidji by-pass

Location:
Southwest of Bemidji

Style:
2-span precast concrete girder

Length:
Channel span - 92 feet
Total length   - 186 feet

Width:
2 lanes, wide shoulders; 41 feet total

Clearance:
9.5 feet MLW

Date completed:
1980

Designed by:
Clark Engineering, Minneapolis

Bridge:
#04013 and 04014

Owner:
Minnesota DOT

US 2 By-Pass Bridges, Beltrami County

Mary C. Costello

Beltrami County Road 11 Bridge, Minnesota

*T*his was an area of dogs, children and nice homes. I was on the outskirts of Bemidji on US 71. County Road 11 intersects with 71 and the bridge is but a block or two away. The county highway bridge was only 75 feet long and looked quite modern with a blacktop road and a concrete side. Underneath it had two all-wooden piers. The pile legs facing the river's current were wrapped in metal painted a blue-gray. This protection helps to ward off and break up ice.

The railing posts were I-bars bolted to a steel railing having the appearance of an open box. These posts were securely fastened to the bridge side extending the full depth of the bridge. They were painted the same blue-gray and had a concrete curbing below.

At the entrance to the bridge were the yellow and black diagonally-striped rectangular signs which at first I thought meant "bridge," but actually mean "hazard."

The water was low and the spot quiet except for birds singing. I was glad to be done for the day and ready for supper and the night at Bemidji State University. I arrived about 6:15 and just made it, with 15 minutes to spare, before they stopped serving.

The library was open after I finished eating, so I xeroxed plat maps and tried to find more information on Mississippi River Bridges. There was nothing written. I called a professor of history from the university to see if he knew anything historical or human interest-wise about the Mississippi River Bridges. He had never thought of it and knew nothing.

The rest of the evening I spent quietly in my room organizing notes, then took a shower, called my husband and went to bed.

Use:
CSAH 11 and local traffic

Location:
One mile south County Road 7 outskirts of Bemidji

Style:
3-span precast concrete girder, called "channel span"

Length:
Channel span - 25 feet
Total length   - 75 feet

Width:
2 lanes, 26 feet total

Clearance:
8.5 feet MLW

Date completed:
1959; replaced old 1926 wooden Ritchie Highway Bridge [6]

Designed by:
Erickson Engineering

Bridge:
#04502 Beltrami County

Owner:
Beltrami County

Beltrami County Road 11 Bridge, Outskirts of Bemidji   *Mary C. Costello*

Grant Valley Township, County Road 7 Bridge, Minnesota

*T*his was last bridge on this trip and one of the hardest to find. I drove into Bemidji on Highway 8 and stopped for help. Going down a side road I found a family in their backyard. The woman couldn't help, but her husband asked a truck driver on the phone for directions. They were long and complicated so I wrote them down. Out of town and out on the highway again I stopped at a gas station to be sure I was right. The young attendant said his uncle just built a bridge on his property across the Mississippi 30 miles away. I got his uncle's telephone number and thus added another bridge to my already long list--a second private span.

A woman repairing her fence along the highway told me that I had passed the bridge--"two dirt roads back." It was quite a ways back but I found it, turned on it, and the bridge was right there in a dip in the road.

The river was very narrow here, the bridge was small with no piers, just one span in what has now become the norm double grooved wall, concrete deck, 2-lane girder support--looking very pretty in the late afternoon sun with shadows on it and riprap under it.

In contrast to this span was the rustic 1916 weathered grey bridge I had seen on my first visit to this spot. It was a four-span all-timber trestle bridge. The five piles for each trestle were widely spaced with long heavy crossbars. The timber deck was the first I'd seen all the way from New Orleans--using 3-inch-thick planks laid horizontally. The crude abutments consisted of 12-inch beams stacked edge to edge to the height of the embankment under the deck and around the corner where uneven vines of ivy hid most of what was underneath. Heavy pilings were driven into the water to prevent slippage of these boards. The railing had a new 2x8-inch board railing and 4x6-inch posts. Yes, I think this bridge was ready for replacement, though I felt very safe when crossing it.

A River Level Gauge shed beside the wooden bridge served my needs as well as the U.S. Geological Department who keep such records. It was a place from which to photograph the bridge crossing. Looking down from this shed's porch I saw the clean river and long brown grasses looking like a lady's tresses. They were attached to the riverbed and followed the contour of the shallow river bottom moving gracefully in the quiet water. Across the river were rice beds and behind the bridge a dying elm. There were lots of healthy trees with a few houses and farms closeby. However, no one else was out; it was supper hour.

Use:
Grand Valley Township traffic

Location:
One tenth of a mile south of Junction County Road 7 in Grant Valley Township 146

Style:
One-span precast concrete girder

Length:
Channel span - 90 feet
Total length   - 91.5 feet

Width:
One lane, 35 feet

Clearance:
5.5 feet MLW

Date completed:
1997; originally 1916 all timber trestle span

Designed by:
Beltrami County

Bridge:
#04518

Owner:
Grant Valley Township

Beltrami County Road 7 Bridge, Grant Valley Township

Mary C. Costello

257

"New Iron Bridge", County Road 7, Beltrami County

I drove to the "Old Iron Bridge" and found nothing left but the approach. Three striped barricades kept people from driving into the river. I later inquired as to why the high, old iron truss span was not preserved. "It is too costly to maintain such a bridge and to protect it from vandalism," said Westley Djoney, Assistant Highway Engineer, in Bemidji.

The new bridge, built to replace it, is 1/4 mile farther east on County Highway 7, up a hill and around a curve. The new span is not iron trusses, but girders of steel with a concrete parapet--very modern, straight and low.

The bridge's greatest assets are its two deep wedge-shaped piers which, like a boat's bow, cut the water smoothly. The Highway 7 Bridge has a weathering steel continuous girder, about 30 inches deep, with its expected rust-colored finish. Its color is a beautiful contrast to the pure white concrete of the rest of the bridge. The roadway edge extends only a few inches beyond the double-grooved concrete bridge guard-wall. A series of square, silver downspouts help drain the bridge of water and add a vertical line to the exterior. From inside, the bridge has a wide, two-lane roadway and the wall is concave-shaped. Because the bridge crosses the river obliquely, the wall ends appear to stagger.

Especially enjoyable was the flora growing along the river's shores. There were red and purple clover, yellow Bryd Trefoils and a puffy yellow plant, called Ladies Slippers. I was really enchanted with the latter's shape and beauty, but later found it was the trefoils that are the basis for architectural design. Stylized trefoils are used in concrete on one of the buildings at my alma mater, Marycrest International University in Davenport. They also have been used in church pew decoration in both Gothic and Renaissance periods.

I spoke to a canoeist at the site. He, his father and his son were about to launch their boat, but helped me become oriented with my map. I found interesting that the canoe route from Itasca to Bemidji is maintained with the license fees from canoeists. There must be lots of canoeists.

Because the day was clear and sunny, and the river quiet and slow, I was amazed at what I saw in the water under the bridge: a thing of beauty, a joy to behold, a positive sign, a good omen--a rainbow.

Use:
Rural traffic

Location:
2.1 miles northeast of south county line

Style:
3-span bolted steel continuous beam

Length:
Channel span - 70 feet
Total length   - 189 feet

Width:
2 lanes plus; 39 feet total

Clearance:
5 feet MLW (estimated)

Date completed:
1981; replaces old iron truss span three blocks away

Designed by:
Erickson Engineering, Minneapolis, Minnesota

Bridge:
#04512 in Beltrami County

Owner:
Beltrami County

"New Iron Bridge" Beltrami County Road 7 Bridge

Mary C. Costello

259

Beltrami County Road 5 Bridge

What is different about this Highway 5 Bridge? The answer is threefold. The surroundings are different, the road surface is not the normal concrete or blacktop and the bridge style is fairly new.

But first a bit of history. In 1966 a truck carrying wood pulp hit the old "Solway Highway Bridge", as it was known for its proximity to the town. A cable, used for strength on the span, was weak, broke and the bridge collapsed sending the wood pulp into the river. The truck, however, hung on the edge luckily for the driver.

I remember being on the shady forest road and seeing the sunny clearing ahead where I knew the "Highway 5" bridge should be. All of a sudden a furry black bear cub came out of the forest onto the shaded highway. He was not close enough to be hit, but was close enough to be seen well. I was the only car on the two-lane highway at the time. The bear looked in the direction of my car, then lumbered across the road into the trees.

The sun was beating down creating 100-degree temperatures when I found the bridge, but I hardly noticed because of my distracted state. The bright sun made the white precast concrete hard to view. Though the bridge style looked no different from others I'd seen, I've since been told it is a "channel span,"(also #118) used on bridges anywhere from 20 to 60 feet long. Matt Lang, MNDOT engineer in charge of inventory, told me the parts are precast concrete short-legged letter U's, inverted and used side by side across the bridge. Each is about 38 inches wide, 21 inches deep and 31 feet long. On top of this base is placed dirt and the surface to be used-in this case, gravel. The bridge outer edge had a plain concrete band about 20 inches deep but high enough to form a curbing inside. It could easily be mistaken for a beam or girder span.

The railing is galvanized steel, unpainted and the posts are I-beams. The parapet parts are bolted together and fastened on the outside of the bridge. The abutments are at least 8-inch thick beams flush with the river bank. In the water are two short trestles, piles driven into the river bed and braced with diagonals. Metal shields on the upstream piers protect them from ice and debris.

I love the sun and warm weather, but it felt good to get back into the shade of the forest, enroute to Stumphges Rapids.

Use:
County Road 5 traffic

Location:
1.5 miles south of junction with Highway 10,

Style:
3-span precast concrete "channel span"

Length:
Channel span - 31 feet
Total length   - 69 feet

Width:
2 lanes; 29 feet total

Clearance:
6 feet MLW

Date completed:
1967, replaced "Solway Highway Bridge"

Designed by:
Erickson Engineering, Minneapolis, Minnesota

Bridge:
#04505 Beltrami County

Owner:
Beltrami County

Beltrami County Road 5 Bridge

Mary C. Costello

Stumphges Rapids Bridge, Hubbard County, SFR 84

I had spent an hour looking for Stumphges Rapids Bridge, driving along the State Forest Road even into the forest on a rutted path. An elderly berry picker of whom I asked directions was unknowing, interested only in her blueberries, now at their peak. "If you can't fight them, join them," so I quickly learned to identify and pick the tasty delicacy. However, after filling my watercup with berries, I gave up to again look for the elusive bridge.

Five miles back at a junction between two roads in the forest, I found a gas-station/tavern. My heart beat a little faster as I opened the door and stepped from the bright noonday sun into the cool darkness. As my eyes became adjusted, I saw there were only one customer and the attendant behind the bar. I ordered a glass of 7Up and asked where Stumphges Rapids and bridge were located. I had been very close but needed to go farther west. Armed with new directions, I finished my drink, thanked them and left.

Without further delay I found the bridge. No one else was around. The only sound was a dripping drain pipe and for the eyes there was a display of red clover and Queen Anne's Lace.

This bridge, a different type construction, is called a "timber slab." It is of an older style, requiring many man-hours to build. The bridge deck has outer edge forms like those used in pouring concrete. The bottom of the deck is reinforced with wood and the inside filled alternately with planks and gravel What appears to be 2x4's laminated together on edge lie in a tire-track position along the bridge deck. The rest of the space is filled with fine gravel and sand. What results is four bridge-length tracks about 14 inches wide alternating with about 10-inch-wide strips of the aggregate. "Woe be to you" if you get off track when crossing by car. I guess you could continue on the gravel as long as it is under both tires.

The remainder of the bridge is weather-treated wood except for the galvanized steel railing. The silver railing is bolted through two 6x8's fastened together on the outside of the bridges as parapet posts. Near the bottom, a wooden curbing is attached to wide wooden blocks at each post leaving plenty of space between for drainage of water and snow.

The abutments are stacked wooden beams recessed into the bank at the bridge ends. These are held in place with 8-inch-diameter piles. The abutment sides wing out but gradually drop to river level. A single pier in the middle of the span is composed of pilings cross-braced and a 12-inch square cap above.

I saw no sign of the rapids, but that is not surprising with all the twists in the river. Now that I look at the map, it appears to be half a mile farther south from this, the narrowest Mississippi I've seen so far--38 feet.

Use:
State Forest Road 84 and local traffic

Location:
North of Stumphges Rapids on Forest Road 84

Style:
2-span "timber slab"

Length:
Channel span - 22 feet
Total length   - 40 feet

Width:
Narrow 2 lanes, 15.9-foot roadway

Clearance:
3.5 feet MLW

Date completed:
1982

Designed by:
E.D. Wolhowe

Bridge:
#R0038 Hubbard County

Owner:
Minnesota DOT

State Forest Road 84, Stumphges Rapids Bridge, Hubbard County　　　　　*Mary C. Costello*

263

"Coffee Pot Landing" Bridge, Near Clearwater County Road 40

As legend has it the title "Coffee Pot" has been given this canoe landing bridge because many years ago an older couple at a wayside rest area nearby wanted to make people feel welcome and always had the coffee pot on to serve when visitors stopped. Whether true or false, there can certainly be no more attractive spot on the Mississippi to relax and "to put on the coffee pot."

Located close to the intersection of County Roads 40 and 9, the bridge is a "canoe access point," a very picturesque spot with a place nearby for parking and camping. The single span is identified as a "Town and Country Bridge," commercially built, with a 10,000 lb. maximum capacity--or so says the attached plaque. Its reddish-brown steel is of the "weathering" kind. It rusts only to a point, leaving an attractive color, which suits the Coffee Pot name.

This steel footbridge is a beautiful addition to the natural setting. The bridge spans the narrow, approximately twenty-foot-wide river in a gentle curve. The deck consists of 2x10 inch boards on a metal-braced frame. The 30-inch high railing is a structural element of the bridge "classifying it as a pony truss" rather than an arch bridge, wrote Harold Sandberg as he critiqued my bridge copy. Although the diagonal or cross members that brace the bridge below the deck are not visible on the sketch, they are there.

The railing is divided into twelve sections with narrower steel cross-bracing in each division. The approaches are built up with soil for greater bridge clearance. Under the bridge is irregular white and light-colored riprap. This strong contrast of white with the red as well as the varied greens of the trees and bushes are color complements to inspire any artist.

Not only canoeists, but also snowmobilers use this area. In the past "each winter season a snowmobile bridge was placed across the Mississippi at the snowmobile trail-crossing and removed again in the spring," says Ben Thoma. He continued, "This is on the Itasca to Bemidji snowmobile trail but at an area on the river that is dangerous most winters." Today, however, the new steel arched bridge is strong enough and wide enough for the snowmobiles and the SV-200 (a wide tracked vehicle, the weight of a loaded pick-up truck, used to maintain the trail). Therefore, the temporary bridge "built to get this rig across the dangerous ice at Coffee Pot," is no longer needed.

The 20-inch-deep clean river water was moving rapidly but quietly this July day. The campgrounds and picnic area were empty. I heard only the fish jumping. At the end of the land build-up, were fresh water springs rising out of the river's edge. If I could pick one spot on the Mississippi to transplant to my backyard, it would be the "Coffee Pot Landing" bridge.

Use:
Part of recreational trail for horseback riders, hikers and bikers; no motorized vehicles except snowmobiles in winter

Location:
Canoeists river access point and campsite at junction of County Roads 9 and 40

Style:
Single span steel pony truss footbridge

Length:
Channel span - 20 feet approximately
Total length - 50 feet

Width:
10 feet wide

Clearance:
9 feet MLW

Date completed:
1985

Designed by:
Town & Country Bridge Company

Bridge:
No number

Owner:
Minnesota DNR, Park and Recreation or Trails and Waterways

"Coffee Pot Landing" Bridge, Clearwater County

Mary C. Costello

Clearwater County Road 40 Bridge

*H*allelujah! I could see the bottom of the Mississippi River! True the river isn't very wide here (maybe thirty feet) or very deep (ten inches, perhaps), located only 14 miles by river from the source. It is, however, still the Mississippi, and its water is very clean and clear. It is such a joy to see, coming from a location, as I do, on the more mature river that is clouded with silt. I was standing on the shore by the end of the Highway 40 Bridge and could actually see small rocks on the bottom. The river was very calm and reflected the under part of the bridge, piers and rich blue sky. In the bridge's shadow, even the camera "picked up" the rocky river floor.

Highway 40 Bridge is a wooden (treated timber) construction and had the appearance of one of the strongest built I have seen. It is the second "timber slab" span, where the deck is framed-in and the bottom reinforced with wood. The deck surface here is blacktop. All that can be seen of the bottom form is the 12-inch-deep beam on the outside edge.

The low, sturdy parapet gives the bridge character. Fifteen 8x10-inch wooden posts are bolted in perfect lines, one with the other. They are secured in three places--to the bridge frame, to a continuous curbing of wood with long narrow drainage cuts, and finally to the thick 5x10-inch beam railing.

The two piers consist of reddish-colored tubular steel legs capped with a twelve-inch beam the width of the bridge. These pilings are covered with weathering steel--the reason for the ruddy color. The span extends fifteen feet beyond the apparent water's edge and beyond a wall of large hand-placed rocks. The water between is a low marshland.

This rugged structure has no protection from the sun, although farther down the highway on the south are two forests side by side--the County Memorial Forest and the Mississippi Headwaters State Forest.

Perhaps because of the heat, the highway had little or no traffic while I was there. A few wildflowers, wild rice and rocks edged the young river. The birds were away in the shadow of trees. Even the fish knew where it was cooler.

Use:
CSAH 40 traffic

Location:
Clearwater County, near County Road 2

Style:
3-span "timber slab"

Length:
Channel span - 30 feet
Total length   - 90 feet

Width:
2 lanes; 34 feet total

Clearance:
6.5 feet MLW

Date completed:
1982

Designed by:
Clearwater County Highway Department

Bridge:
#15509 Clearwater County

Owner:
Clearwater County

Mary C. Costello

Clearwater County Road 40 Bridge

267

Kenneth Felt Private Bridge, County Road 2

In 1896 Richard Felt built the first bridge over the Mississippi River this far north, about four miles from the headwaters. Mr. Felt was a homesteader on land adjacent to the baby river at this point and built the bridge from rough sawn tamarack trees in the vicinity. A little over a hundred year later his grandson has built a duplicate span with the same kind of trees, from the same area, on the same spot. Ken lives on part of the original Felt homestead, but it is owned for the last 50 years by Ralph Kjorlien who lives in New Jersey. It was Mr. Kjorlien who wanted the bridge to get access to more of his property across the river.

It was not an easy process getting permission to build over the Mississippi, it took two years or more. But since it was to replicate an historical bridge at the site, it was allowed. Required was an allowance of at least three feet of clearance for canoers, but four or five feet would be allowed in their plans. With the help of his neighbor, Ernest Bode, Ken Felt completed the attractive span on the 25 July 1998.

The bridge is even stronger than the original, because beneath the steel deck is a steel semi-trailer bed that is ten inches deep. The main bridge timbers are 25 feet by 10 inches by 16 inches, very strong to withstand man and nature. The test of the tamarack's durability is shown in the remnants of the original bridge Ken found in the riverbank.

Interesting is the fact that the boards were sawn in Felt's own sawmill--both for the original bridge and the present one. This, of course, would make it more convenient for building such a project; but not everyone would have the ambition. A plaque has been installed at the end of the bridge stating the history of the unique and attractive span.

There was a ribbon cutting ceremony on that special opening day, at which Kjorlien and family from the east, plus Ben Thoma, naturalist from Itasca State Park attended. Ben Thoma presented maps and survey sheets from 1900 showing the vegetation of tamarack and spruce primarily, and indicating the bridge built by Richard Felt. It was a part of a survey started in April and completed in October of the whole river down to the Gulf of Mexico. My book is a similar survey of the whole river's bridges 100 years later but in reverse direction.

Use:
Family, public vehicles and pedestrians

Location:
Four and a half miles from Lake Itasca entrance off County Road 2

Style:
Wooden kingrod truss

Length:
40 feet

Width:
12 feet

Clearance:
5 feet MLW

Date completed:
July 1998; replica of 1896 bridge on same location, by pioneer, Richard Felt

Designer:
Richard Felt, duplicated by his grandson 100 years later

Bridge:
No number

Owner:
Ralph Kjorlien, New Jersey

Unique feat:
Original span was first bridge built on Mississippi River near headwaters, 1896

Kenneth Felt Private Bridge, Clearwater County Road 2

Mary C. Costello

Larson's* Culvert, Clearwater County Highway 2

I first learned of "Bob Larson's Bridge" from the proprietress in the Itasca State Park Post Office/Store, just outside the park's north entrance. They said the bridge was at the Larson farm on County Road 2, a few miles down the road. I totally missed it that day, but I came back four days later to find only the highway "hazard" sign. That was all I saw of a bridge. The yellow and black sign was near a house set back on the west side of the road. There were several mailboxes on the roadside; on one I noted the names "Francis and Janice Feil." Mr. Feil was reroofing with two other men and told me, from the rooftop, where the Larson's bridge used to be and where its replacement culvert is, and he proposed I look at his property in the back.

I did what he suggested and in that order. The walk down the neighbors hill to the concrete abutments from the old bridge was among tall weeds and grasses. Guarded by a large elm, the bridge remains had the tree's lacy shadows dancing about, making it a pleasant place to be except for the "unknowns" under foot. The meandering Mississippi was on the other side of the concrete bridge remnants. The old bridge spot is in a gully, far below the since moved county road of which it used to be a part. The abutment remains looked like a tombstone, in dedication to what used to be.

Today's culvert is under County Highway 2, slightly northeast of the old bridge. It is like a squared highway tunnel divided in the middle with a foot-thick wall, each opening eight feet high by eight feet wide. The previously quiet-seeming river roared as it curved into the culvert. It was as though it saw itself in a new light. The twisting, splashing sounds resounded again and again off the walls and ceiling, appearing to forecast the mightiness of a river "on its way."

Following Francis Feil's advice. I then went behind to his farm where the infant river had cut its way through the rocky land.

Use:
Allows the river to flow under CSAH 2

Location:
About 8 miles from the Source in Clearwater County

Style:
Concrete double box culvert

Length:
Channel span: - 8 feet
Total length: - 93 feet

Width:
Two 8-foot openings

Clearance:
6 feet MLW

Date completed:
1939; replaced an 1896 or 1897 truss bridge

Designed by:
Clearwater County Highway Department

Bridge:
#113

Owner:
Clearwater County Highway Department

---

*The culvert and bridge have been called Robert Larson's because they were closest to his property. They are county owned.

Larson's Culvert, Clearwater County Road 2

Mary C. Costello

271

Francis and Janice Feil's Private Mississippi River Bridge

When the Mississippi River is high in the Spring, it is extremely fast and treacherous. When it is dry, it is unsafe because of the rocks on the bottom. This is the demeanor of Ol' Man River in Clearwater County and on the Francis Feil property. To save fording the often unpredictable and deeply trenched river, the Feils have built a vehicular bridge across.

I was not expecting to hear what I did when I stopped on County Highway 2 to ask about another bridge. Mr. Feil said that he had a bridge he'd bet I didn't have on my list. "Take the roadway back and you'll see the bridge I built."

Following his direction, I found a sturdy wooden span. It was a delightful bit of architecture to have on one's own property--a bridge over one of the best-known rivers in the world. I drove over it and was glad it was short, since there was no railing. However, once I was across I couldn't get back without turning around. I wasn't about to back over the bridge so I turned around under a tree in the Feil's yard, and parked near the bridge.

The bridge roadway was about 22 feet long made of 3-inch thick planks laid horizontally with space between for drainage. The ends of these boards have 2x6's to anchor the floor more securely. That raised two-inch lip was the only reminder that you were on the edge of the small bridge.

I climbed down a steep little path right at the end of the bridge. From there I saw the heavy stringer that went from one bank to the other. In the water was an 8-inch-diameter pole with a timber attached to shore up the bridge beam .

The water was beautiful and clear. It seemed to be moving very fast, foaming as it went over rocks. There were lots of rocks, little trees and wild growth on the sides of the stream. In fact, there was so much shade from the bushes, plants, etc. that I could see only filtered sun, and that in infrequent spots. The sound of the water enhanced the sound of birds and insects one hears in such a habitat. I really envy Mr. and Mrs. Feil their little bridge and piece of this infant Father of Waters. In the Minneapolis Star of October 20, 1954, was an article about a "Lost" bridge over the Mississippi River. It had no road leading to it, not even a path could be seen from the air. The Carl Gustafson's were the owners, it said, and "Mrs. G's" uncle, Ole Peterson, built the bridge.

"On no road, and listed on no army engineers' survey, the bridge of timbers and planks crossed the river where it is just a few yards wide, a few miles from Lake Itasca, from which the Mississippi flows north before beginning the huge arc which takes it south to the Gulf of Mexico," said Bob Murphy in the article. The bridge was discovered from the air when they were taking a bridge census for a state highway publication. The Feils have since purchased the property from the Gustafsons and rebuilt the span, a bridge sometimes called the "Mystery Bridge."

Use:
Private approach to Feil's farm

Location:
11 miles from the source by river, or 6 1/2 miles by road, County Highway 2

Style:
Single span wooden beam

Length:
Channel span - 12 feet
Total length   - 22 feet

Width:
1 lane, 12 feet total

Clearance:
6 feet MLW

Date completed:
1981; replaced 1920 span;
originally, 1896, Peter Bergquist bridge located here

Designed by:
Ole Peterson, uncle of Mrs. Gustafson, owners before Feils

Bridge:
No number

Owner:
Francis & Janice Feil

Unique feat:
One of three privately-owned bridges (Inver Grove Railroad/Highway Bridge #19, and Felt Bridge #125)

Francis and Janice Feil's Private Bridge, Clearwater County Road 2   *Mary C. Costello*

273

County Road 37, Barrel Arch Bridge

*O*n my first visit I saw another bridge here. Just one mile off County Highway 2 on Highway 37 was the second highway bridge over the infant Mississippi outside of Itasca State Park. I drove the gravel, hilly highway seeing no one, so I was surprised to have a woman pull up beside me in her car as I photographed the small bridge. She volunteered to get her husband who was born and raised in this area, to help me with the bridge history.

While she went to their farm down the road, I looked around. The bridge was a simple beam span resting on concrete abutments. The parapet, in rather run-down condition, consisted of vertical triangular steel posts with angle iron railings.

Lavonne and Ernest Bode returned in their beautiful cream-colored car to help me. He told of the past. The Red River Timber Company cut all the Norway pine when it was allowed and left the jack pine, which are straggly looking. They floated the logs down the river past this point. This didn't seem possible today because the water table was low. He said that springs come up in spots on the river's edge. "People get fresh water from these springs for home use," said Ernest.

The river here is about 30 feet wide and the view spectacular. It was the view that recalled for Ernest that as a child of four or five, he was washed down the river here by the current and almost drowned.

The Bode's insisted I see the Vekin's Dam and spillway, a relic of upper Mississippi logging days. They led the way to Carl Eastlund's 72 acres, a mile closer to the river's source. Eastlund showed us the dam. The river, hidden among the trees, rushed down the rocky hill to the wooden dam. On the bottom was a huge, flat-sided boulder jutting out of the water, "today often used as a diving board," said our host. Here the water collects to an eight to ten-foot depth. In logging days, the water was stored to move logs downstream.

The following year I was back and a new Highway 37 Bridge had been built. It is a precast "bebo arch". Harold Sandberg, Chairman of the Board of Alfred Benesch and Company, informed me that a culvert has a bottom and is usually 25 to 30 feet maximum. This is a barrel arch bridge though commercially called a precast "bebo arch". It is a type invented by a Minnesota firm. "A single line of concrete arch shapes, 40 feet in diameter and about four-feet wide, touches down on cast-in-place piers," said Matt Lang, MNDOT. The average passerby would not realize that there is a bridge here. The only indications on the widened road above are a low "flair and bury" steel guard rail on the roadside, and, if one looks, the small river back among the pines. To appreciate the bridge one must go down the high embankment next to the small Mississippi stream and bridge wings. The ends of the thirty-foot-wide tunnel-like arch are finished with decorated concrete. Recessed into the masonry are the bridge number and year built. In the two corners are triangles with five sun-like rays exoding. The whole character of the area is less rustic, more formal.

Use:
CSAH 37 traffic

Location:
9 miles from the source in Clearwater County

Style:
Precast "Bebo Arch" or barrel arch bridge

Length:
Channel span - 31 feet
Total length   - 78 feet

Width:
30 feet

Clearance:
13 feet MLW

Date completed:
1987; replaces 1925 steel beam span

Designed by:
Commercially designed

Bridge:
#95483

Owner:
Clearwater County Highway Department

Barrel Arch Bridge, County Road 37

Mary C. Costello

275

First Highway Bridge Outside Park, Minnesota Highway 200

When a child is recognized for accomplishments, parents are proud and happy. I felt the same pride and joy seeing the special treatment given the first bridge outside of Itasca State Park. The Minnesota Highway 200 Bridge has a rustic exterior in rough-cut cedar to suit its location and setting. Just any design would not suffice, as Lloyd Larson, Bridge Engineer in Bemidji, informed me. The Minnesota DOT Bridge Engineers felt the bridge should be wood and have an arch design, "even if used only in the non-structural sense." Therefore the bridge is a steel girder cut in an arch shape and made of a special steel-and-copper alloy that maintains a rusty brown color. The all wooden exterior facing has vertical lines in the "valance" over the river opening, in the "parallel wings" on the sides and in the "curtain walls" going under the bridge.

With canoeist in mind, a 5-foot clearance under the-bridge was planned at normal water level. Canoeists appreciate this span the most, since they see it from all sides. The 29-foot-wide newborn river is only two miles from its source. Highway travelers see only the normal concrete deck and the inside of the concrete parapet.

In the stillness as I drew,I could hear the river talking. That is how I found the bridge. I thought it was located closer so I had walked .7 mile from the Lake Itasca Post Office. I followed the sound of rushing water. Arriving at the "canoe access area," three of my senses were immediately stimulated. My eyes enjoyed the bridge design as well as cattails and rice growing in the shallow water. My sense of smell was awakened by some white-colored, sweet smelling wild plants on the sloping bank. I picked some to permeate my car for the remainder of the day. Finally, the refreshing sounds of the river that attracted me in the first place as it flowed from the park and then echoed under the bridge had my auditory sense working overtime. With the speed of the water ranging from 0 to 10 on this July morning, it was probably moving at 2 mph here headed north.

As the river curved out of Itasca State Park evergreen forest, it was strange to see, a solitary young tree standing in the water, one of Mother Nature's strange whims. The Mississippi River is unique and so is this Minnesota Highway 200 Bridge.

Use:
Minnesota Trunk Highway 200 traffic

Location:
.7 mile west of Itasca State Park's north entrance

Style:
1-span steel girder, under wood surface, arch apparent

Length:
Channel span - 24 feet
Total length - 46 feet

Width:
2 lanes, wide shoulders; 50 feet total

Clearance:
5 feet MLW

Date completed:
1982, original 1919 steel beam span, remodeled in 1937

Designed by:
Glanton Engineering Company

Bridge:
#15002 in Clearwater County

Owner:
Minnesota DOT

Unique feat:
First Mississippi River trunk highway bridge; special aesthetic treatment; located two miles from the source.

First Highway Bridge Outside Park, Minnesota 200

Mary C. Costello

277

Culvert Inside Itasca State Park

The first Mississippi River crossing in Itasca State Park at the North entrance is the "cattle-pass"[7] culvert. It was new in late 2001 in a clearing. The park crew removed the tall trees, white spruce and balsam fir mostly, and undergrowth on the river banks before installing this new concrete archway. The sketch is from the south side where the water enters with a narrow 20-foot-wide stream and is calm and quiet. However, if one were to cross the road and go down the other side, or canoe through the culvert, one would see the rushing water foam as it exits into a much larger pool, about 100 feet across.

The pool into which the culvert discharges is left-over from the days in which a logging dam was at this location. When the logs went down the sluice-way, they had a fairly deep pool to enter so as to avoid hitting bottom and causing a pile up, says Ben Thoma, park naturalist. I find this an interesting bit of history.

The previous metal culvert was a dangerous item for canoeists due to the metal fasteners that pointed down from the top and sides. This was part of the reason for replacing it; the other and more important was the erosion of the roadway above.

On my first visit to the park I had missed the culvert and had to make a second trip to find it hidden as it was among trees and underbrush. When I located it, I climbed down the steep embankment on the north side and watched the water come through the six-foot-wide flat-bottom culvert onto a metal apron. The force of the river gushing out of the cylinder and rolling off the end of the metal into the stream created foam and a curled wave. The foam, collecting on the far side of the apron near some rocks and a log, builting up to a 6 or 7-inch mound that sat looking dried out. The fast mainstream water was traveling in a v-shape with beads splashing into the air, until it gradually settled into the regular river-flow pattern. The still waters farthest away from this action collected algae in surface patches. About 30 feet out from the culvert, the river returned to a smaller size, but the activity had expanded it to half again its original width.

The funniest event on my Mississippi journey happened here. A small slick brown muskrat came from the trees by the road on the west side of the culvert. He came up over the top and down to within 18 inches of me before looking up. When he saw my face, he immediately went behind the metal to hide. Several seconds later he came out for "a double take". I had been quiet. He couldn't believe I was there. He left the way he came but in greater haste.

As I left the Culvert, I realized I had just witnessed the little river, the "Mitchisipi", as the Indians called it, heading out of its birthplace for its journey to the Gulf.

Use:
CSAH 38 in park

Location:
North end of Itasca State Park

Style:
"Cattle-pass" precast concrete culvert

Length:
80 feet

Width:
6 feet

Clearance:
5 feet MLW

Date completed:
November 2001; after a 1930's metal culvert; which replaced a bridge; originally the site of a logging dam

Designed by:
A commercial design

Culvert:
No number

Owner:
Clearwater County Highway Department

Culvert Inside Itasca State Park

Mary C. Costello

Snowmobile/Bicycle Trail Bridge, Itasca State Park

*O*riginally built for snowmobiles in 1969, today the Snowmobile Trail Bridge is used for bikes and maintenance trucks as well. The 146-foot long wooden bridge is also sturdy enough and wide enough for the heavy trail-groomer that must cross it during the snowmobile season. Connie Cox, Lead Naturalist, told me that it was "designed to be historically accurate and aesthetically pleasing."

Walking along the .4 mile trail from the Culvert Road Bridge, headed toward the Mississippi's source, we cross three different spans, the first of which is the Snowmobile/Bike Trail Bridge. (The other two, a footbridge and a log, are subjects for the next two stories.) This bridge is a 3-span timber beam bridge. The horizontally laid floorboards are weather-treated, as is the railing. Four 3-inch diameter logs form the 3-foot 4-inch high parapet with sturdy 6-inch diameter posts every 3 to 4 feet. Twelve-inch log beams brace the bridge from below. Its rustic appearance suits the abundantly lush growth setting. Standing on the deck looking in either direction I could see the winding river was lost behind greenery less than 100 feet away.

Ben Thoma, Naturalist and Historian for Itasca State Park, informed me that since the new bike trail was built, bike use has greatly increased. "Some 150 rental bikes are out on user-days, but most campers who ride bring their own bikes. I would estimate that on peak days, there might well be over 300 to 500 bikes in use within Itasca State Park." The bike trail is available for walking and biking which might

have to change in the future. The major problem on the bike trail is bikers hitting trees and other bikers. The Snowmobile/Bike Trail Bridge is well utilized both summer and winter.

This 1979 span was in excellent shape when removed so was stored, then reused on the Heartland Trail between Park Rapids and Walker.

The reason for the longer replacement span was to provide a better surface at both ends for bicycle traffic during the summer.

Use:
Snowmobiles, bikes and pedestrians

Location:
On the north end of the Bicycling/Hiking Trail in Itasca State Park

Style:
3-span timber beam

Length:
146 feet

Width:
11 feet 4 inches

Clearance:
4.8 feet at MLW

Date completed:
1996; replaced 1979 span; which replaced 1969 bridge

Designed by:
Itasca State Park Crew

Bridge:
No number

Owner:
Minnesota DNR Park and Recreation Division

Snowmobile/Bike Bridge, Itasca State Park

Mary C. Costello

281

Footbridge on Headwater Trail in Itasca State Park, Minnesota

*O*n "Headwater Trail", a short distance from the headwaters outlet of the Mississippi River, is this neatly constructed rustic bridge. Built of logs from the park, it is the most used footbridge on the whole Mississippi with 600,000 plus visitors per season.

It was here I began my Mississippi ventures and set the pattern for this book--taking pictures first, then immediately sketching. Most people stopped to watch the fast moving water flow and see the fish, rocks and pebbly bottom. It is amazing how clear the water is.

The bridge is a single span beam style, with approximately 12-inch-diameter log stringers underneath. The floor boards run horizontally but are notched where the railing supports meet the floor. The parapet is made of redwood stained pine. There are 12-inch posts under each of the bridge corners to support the heavy bracing above. The railing consists of five 6-inch log posts with a handhewn point at the top and two 4-inch poles for railings. Flat boards under the deck fastened against the posts on either side add stability. To complete the structure, square timbers are stacked to form the abutment.

The little river is shallow, maybe 9-inches deep. Cattails and large riverrock spice up the south side of the stream. To the north, bushy trees hang over a widened pool, then completely hide the curving water a short distance away.

The flat-cut stone on the bank/shoreline are stones which were installed as the curbing in the old headwaters parking lot by the CCC crews in the 1930's. They are reject construction-monument stones from the Cold Springs, Minnesota, Granite Company, stored at the park-shop area until utilzed here in the early 1970's to retard erosion and to provide a better way for visitors to actually go down to the river. The old bank was being eroded from overuse by the headwaters visitors," Ben Thoma, Park Naturalist, informed me.

People often fish from the footbridge in the small river which may have more fish in it today than at the time Henry Schoolcraft determined that this was the true source of the Mississippi River. I thought of Schoolcraft and his Indian guide well over 150 years ago, looking down, possibly even wading down, the picturesque stream rippling in the breeze. The view truly is beautiful, limited though it may be, because the river turns again.

Use:
Headwater trail crossing for hikers and bikers

Location:
In Itasca State Park on the Headwaters Trail about a block from the source

Style:
1-span log beam bridge

Length:
22.5 feet

Width:
6.4 feet walkway; 8-foot total

Clearance:
31 inches MLW

Date completed:
1966

Designed by:
Itasca State Park Maintenance Crew

Bridge:
No number

Owner:
State of Minnesota DNR, Division of Parks and Recreation

Unique feat:
Most used footbridge across the Mississippi; over 600,000 visitors per season

Footbridge on the Headwater Trail, Itasca State Park

Mary C. Costello

283

Return Loop Footbridge in Itasca State Park

*I*n 1991 a new bridge was added to the five other spans in Itasca State Park. This 177-foot long bridge created a different crossing for a route back to the Mississippi source through the wooded area on a 6 1/2-foot-wide elevated boardwalk. The boardwalk levels off the dirt path and elevates on both sides of the bridge where the ground slopes to the river making easier and safer walking. The walk has a 3-inch wooden curb but no handrail except by the bridge, still it is safe and dry even in high water.

This bridge allows visitors access to the other side of the river--the west side of the Mississippi otherwise only briefly viewed after crossing the rocks at the source. "It created a return loop for those who walked across the rocks, or access to the other side of the river for those who didn't want to cross the rocks,"said Connie Cox, Lead Naturalist in Itasca State Park.

The Return Loop Bridge reminds one of the early historic bridge from the 20's and 30's, says Connie. It is constructed with 6-inch logs as posts and as diagonal bracing at each end. The 3.5 foot railing is composed of two rows of 4-inch logs bolted on, going the full length of the span. Three 13-inch wooden beams support the bridge, and 2x6 decking laid horizontally completes the structure. The bridge is 5-feet wide with a bench installed at one end (not shown). It was built in 1991, the year of the 100th anniversary of the park.

Besides damage protection from erosion, compaction and vegetation, "another purpose of the boardwalk was to direct traffic along the picturesque river's edge, thereby relieving pressure on the main access bridge just north." Previously--"people came and went over the same bridge. This created very congested conditions. They also wanted to follow the course of the river, thereby damaging the stream bank where this boardwalk now is," explained Mrs. Cox.

What a pretty picture this bridge makes against the pine tree backdrop and the small blue river reflecting all.

Use:
Pedestrian return loop to source

Location:
North of Itasca State Park, 10 yards from Source

Style:
Single span timber beam

Length:
29 feet over water, but 177 feet with approaches

Width:
5-feet, plus railing

Clearance:
3 feet at MLW

Date completed:
1991

Designed by:
L. Markell, Minnesota DNR Park and Recreation Division

Bridge:
No number

Owner:
Minnesota DNR Park and Recreation Division

Return Loop Footbridge, Itasca State Park

Mary C. Costello

285

"Single Log" Footbridge on Headwaters Trail

*T*his "first" bridge after the outlet of the Mississippi River is made from a single log, or perhaps more accurately, "half-log". About 80 feet from the Mississippi's beginning, this flat-side-up log is 30 feet long resting, recessed, on short logs at each end for added height and steadiness. The maintenance crew in the park have constructed it to survive high water. In 1986, a heavy rain carried the log downstream some three to four hundred feet where it came to rest at a sharp bend in the river channel.

Placed near the Great River's source, this "log" span provides a means for the visitor to cross the river without removing shoes or being in danger of falling off slippery rocks. It was first put in use in 1968, and has been replaced several times since. The last time was with this longer, higher and treated-wood log. However, after a heavy rain in August, there was only 1/2-inch clearance under it. It was then that Ben Thoma, Park Naturalist, commented, "And we thought it was high enough so as never to wash away again."

There is no railing so that one can really feel they are "walking the plank."

Use:
Safe path across the river near source

Location:
Slightly northwest of the outlet on the Headwaters Trail

Style:
1-span, half a wooden beam

Length:
30 feet

Width:
20 to 22 inches

Clearance:
20 inches at MLW

Date completed:
1987, replaced washed-away 1979 log; original log placed 1968

Designed by:
Itasca State Park Maintenance Crew

Bridge:
No number

Owner:
Minnesota DNR, Park and Recreation Division

Single Log Footbridge, Itasca State Park

Mary C. Costello

287

Bridge of Rocks at Lake Itasca, Source of the Mississippi

When does a row of rocks become a birthing place? When the Mississippi River leaves Minnesota's Lake Itasca, "Ol' Man River" is born.

The very first bridge across the Mississippi River is a row of rocks at Lake Itasca separating the river from the lake. Henry Rowe Schoolcraft discovered this "true source" on the 13th of July, 1832. (The name "Itasca" is a "portmanteau" or a merging of two words, in this case the Latin "VerITAS CAput," meaning "true head or source.") In 1939, the Civilian Conservation Corps built the "Rock Bridge". "It was an effort to stabilize the marsh area where previously the location of the river channel was dependent on ice break-up each Spring," said Ben Thoma, Park Naturalist. The CCC put a concrete footing at the edge of the lake, then rock over that. However, only the top layer of rock,--looking very natural,-- shows, for the small river to work its way across and around.

I arrived about 9:30 a.m., paid to enter the park, and drove to the source after a side trip to the lodge museum and gift shop. A naturalist accompanied me to the spot where the river starts. It was still early, so no one else was there. A log placed across the river a short distance away had been washed downstream in a recent seven-inch rain. My guide said the stick we threw into the water would arrive in the Gulf of Mexico in 30 to 35 days, depending upon the many variables of its journey.

I took off my aerobic shoes and socks, rolled up my pant-legs and waded across the infant stream. The river was about five inches deep and twelve feet wide. (In August of 1988 it rose to 48 feet wide with the rains.) The water was quite cool, though the sun was beating down.

A family arrived and the three boys started across the rock bridge. One fell into the water from the slippery rocks, and everyone laughed. A much larger group of people had now formed. Men, women and children alike were crossing on the varied-size rocks.

Near the rock bridge was a nine-foot tree stump with a poetic statement carved into it: "Here 1,475 feet above the ocean the Mighty Mississippi begins to flow on its winding way 2552 miles to the Gulf of Mexico." Behind the bark-bared trunk was the lake with wild rice and cattails growing in a wedge shape. It was the rocks separating the lake and the river that announced "Here the Great River begins!".

Use:
The rocks indicate the start of the Mississippi and stabilize the outlet.

Location:
North end of Lake Itasca

Style:
Rocks on concrete foundation with the center lower for water discharge

Length:
24 feet long rock walk

Width:
3-5 feet wide rockway

Date completed:
1939

Designed by:
Minnesota State Park Design Office

Bridge:
No number

Owner:
Minnesota DNR, Park and Recreation Division

Unique feat:
Beginning of the great Mississippi River

The inscription on the marker reads:

HERE 1475 FT.
ABOVE
THE OCEAN
THE MIGHTY
MISSISSIPPI
BEGINS
TO FLOW
ON ITS
WINDING WAY
2552 MILES
TO THE
GULF
OF MEXICO

Rock Bridge at Lake Itasca, Source of the Mississippi River   *Mary C. Costello*

289

STAIRWAY OF WATER

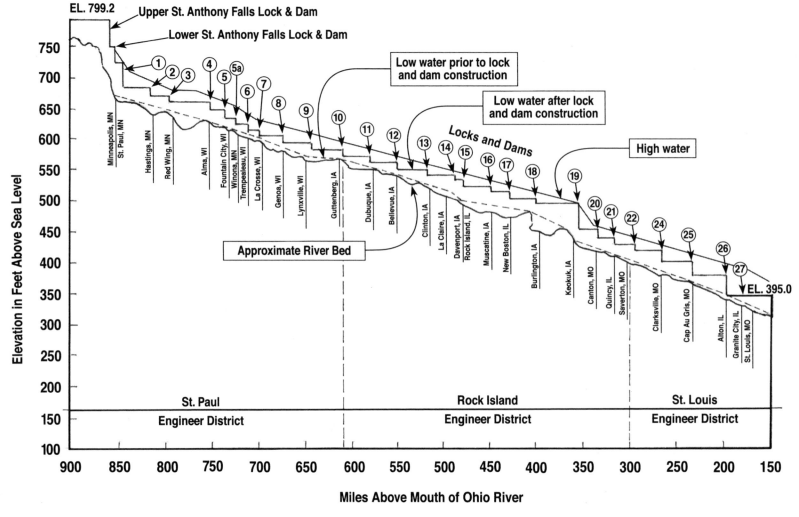

The schematic drawing above represents only a part (750 miles) of the Mississippi River. There are approximately 600 miles more above Minneapolis to the source and 1,200 miles more below St. Louis to the mouth. Those areas have no locks and dams. It is most interesting that the illustrated drop in the river elevation shown is 420 feet in a distance of 669 miles.

The Corps of Engineers supervises the "stairway" in each of three areas--St. Paul, Rock Island and St. Louis. The only district that Volume II is concerned with is the top almost 300 miles. (Volume I covers the other two districts.) Studying the "steps" please note: The irregular lower line and the space below it are the river bed and the earth below it.

The Corps explains that this is not totally accurate since distortion results when you reduce to this small scale. The broken line represents the river at low water before the locks and dams were built. Transportation at these times was curtailed for some distances. The locks and dams now form a series of lakes (called pools) seen as stairs in which a 9-foot depth is maintained in the river channel during low water conditions. The gates in each dam are adjusted to keep the proper water depth but are never completely closed. Finally the top line is at flood stage where the gates are open and the water flows freely.

Diagram is courtesy of the Army Corps of Engineers.

NOTES

PART ONE

1 Stephen Hill, Manager of Projects in the United States for the Canadian Pacific, explained the placement of the new through-plate-girder by barge and removal of the old span by the same means. Because I didn't understand, he explained it simply saying," by taking water out of the lift barge it becomes lighter and higher in the water raising new parts into position. Conversely, by adding water to the barge it sinks and the old members can be removed under the span safely."

2 The only "privately-owned-for-profit bridge" on the Mississippi River has done well. By charging 75 cents a car, the owner, Mr. Al Roman of Chicago, has kept the span open and saved hours of driving time for scores of people between St. Paul Park and Inver Grove since 1982 . However, the most recent news is that the bridge has been closed since 1999 and is not likely to open again after finding a beam with problems. Though Mr. Roman is willing to repair any problem, some inspectors feel it is still not safe, though others disagree. The bridge still exists with all its history, but the future isn't looking good.

PART TWO

1 It took one or two men to open and close the Omaha Swingspan in the early days (1860's) which had a lever or two (removable bars) in the middle of the bridge floor to push around in a circle like a capstan to move the gears. " It is that initial push to start the movement," that is the hardest says a friend who has done it. Two people make it easier.

2 The Minnesota DOT will probably not be building more arch bridges because they are more expensive than girders or even cable-stayed designs. Cable-stayed bridges have the tower or pylon but not the heavy piers needed in the arch design.

3 Colonel Charles C. Smith, chief engineer of the Minneapolis Union Railway Company, chose the site below the falls for the Stone Arch Bridge. He designed the bridge where he felt it would be protected from log and ice jams and would have a better foundation, with the falls sandstone base, and for less money. Hill approved the Colonel's plan. Smith was assisted by another engineer, a master mason and a master carpenter in building the Stone Arch

4 I later found that the trackless spur (not shown but referred to) followed the shoreline until it crossed the Mississippi to Boom Island. This bridge has an interesting history. (see #47)

PART FOUR

1 Delta is the fourth letter in the Greek alphabet, a triangle, which is what these piers appear to be, though upside down with the point down in the water.

2 From a distance the Palisade water tower appeared as a giant "Dry Idea" deodorant bottle sideview. It has a broad base tapering to the point at which the cylindrical water-tank begins. I liked its appearance.

3 This a quote from the book by Willard Price, The Amazing Mississippi.

PART FIVE

1 Because of Minnesota's history in logging, many Minnesotans are endeared to this giant lumberjack's legend and name things after him. Huge statues of Paul Bunyan and Babe, his blue ox, stand on the southwestern shore of Lake Bemidji built in 1937. Bemidji, as well as Akeley, Minnesota, both claim to have the honor of his birthplace. The city of Akeley has his gigantic cradle and the largest statue in the U.S. of Paul Bunyan on his haunches with his axe and an open hand on which a person can sit. Aleley was once a booming lumber town. (See Introduction for more)

2 In 1980 the Burlington Northern Railroad was given to understand that a new wood products plant was coming north, so they rebuilt this bridge. That plant did not materialize and by 1985 the bridge saw its last train cross.

3 The Old Midway Bridge has such beautiful colors and textures created by the reinforced concrete company that at first I thought it was Art Deco. However, besides being built too early for that 1925 period, the type of design is different. With Art Deco decoration is achieved by dividing smooth surfaces into shapes by line or carved motifs. The Old Midway Bridge on the other hand uses mostly textures and subtle color changes in concrete to create its beauty.

4 Bush hammering is a process of texturizing a surface accomplished by using a hammer with a serrated face (notched or toothed like a saw) on the concrete surface. (Old Midway Bridge, Bemidji #113)

5 The "197 Corridor" is a Bemidji city plan to widen the State Highway 197 and to include better access, improved trail access, replace the Mississippi River Bridge and stabilize Lake Bemidji shoreline. At least some should be accomplished by 2003.

6 Westley Djoney, Assistant Highway Engineer in Bemidji in 1987, said that the Ritchie Highway Bridge was an old wooden bridge named after the County Highway Commissioner Ritchie who lived near the bridge. It was torn down in 1959 when the present bridge was built.

7 A "cattle-pass" culvert is, as the title suggests, a type of commercial culvert often used by farmers to allow animal passage under a road to another pasture. In the Itasca State Park case, it is a precast concrete culvert that was put together on the spot for canoes and water to pass through.

BIBLIOGRAPHY

Books

American Waterways Operators. 1982. Big Load Afloat. Washington, D.C.: American Waterways Operators Incorporated.

Billings, Henry. 1961. Bridges. New York: The Viking Press.

Bissell, Richard. 1973. My Life on the Mississippi or Why I Am Not Mark Twain. Boston: Little, Brown & Company.

Butterfield, C. W., and George A. Ogle, compiled. 1884. "Railroads and Boat Landing. The History of Crawford and Richland Counties, Wisconsin. 645-46. Springfield, Illinois: Union Publishing Co.

Cortright, Robert. 1994. Bridging. Tigard, Oregon: Millcross Litho.

DeLony, Eric. 1992. Landmark American Bridges. Manufactured in Mexico.

Dupre, Judith. 1997. Bridges, A History of the Worlds Most Famous and Important Spans. New York: Black Dog and Leventhal Publishers.

Gies, Joseph. 1963. Bridges and Men. Garden City, New York: Doubleday and Company, Incorporated.

Gottimoeller, Frederick. 1998. Bridgescape, The Art of Designing Bridges. New York: John Wiley & Sons, Incorporated.

Historic American Engineering Record (HAER). 1986. Behemoths: The Great River Bridges of George S. Morison. Loveland, Colorado: Fraser Design.

Madson, John. 1985. Up On the Upper Mississippi River: An Upper Mississippi Chronicle." New York: Schocken Books.

Plowden, David. 1974. Bridges, The Spans of North America. New York: W. W. Norton and Co.

Price, Willard. 1963. The Amazing Mississippi. New York: The John Day Co.

Salvadori, Mario. 1980. Why Buildings Stand Up, or The Strength of Architecture. New York: W.W.Norton and Company.

Steinman, D. B. 1953. Famous Bridges of the World. New York: Random House.

Twain, Mark, 1917 edition. Life on the Mississippi. New York: Random House.

U.S.Coast Guard. 1984. Bridges Over the Navigable Waters of the U.S.: Gulf Coast and Mississippi River System Commandant Publication P16590. 2, 75-80.

Warren, G. K. Brevet Major General. 1878. Report on Bridging the Mississippi River Between St. Paul, Minnesota and St. Louis Missouri. 2nd ed. Washington, D.C.:Government Printing Office.

Reference Books

Book of Knowledge, 1963 ed, s.v. "explorers of North America, and "the flight of Black Hawk."

Collier's Encyclopedia, 1993 ed., s.v. "bridge."

Compton's Encyclopedia, 1982 ed., s.v. "bridge."

Encyclopaedia Britannica, 15th ed., s.v. "bridge."

World Book, 1993 ed., s.v. "bridge."

Journals and Journal Articles

Long, Donna Tabbert. 1993. "Meandering Minnesota"s Scenic River Road." Home and Away (pp. 21A - 26A)

Morison, Elting E. "The Master Builder." Invention and Technology Magazine. (Fall 1986): 34-40.

Nickell, Dr. Frank and Dr. Susan Swartwout. Big Muddy, A Journal of the Mississippi River Valley. Winter 2000: 86 pp.

Russell, Helena, editor. Bridge Design and Engineering. London, England. (Issue 14), First Quarter 1999: 75 pp.

Trowbridge, Arthur C. "The Mississippi in Glacial Times." The Palimpsest 40 (July 1959): 257-12Palimpsest , May 1922, 133-141.

Newspaper Articles

"Aerial Photo Reveals Lost Bridge."The Minneapolis Star, 20 October 1954.

Borck, Craig. "A Lift Operator's Life Has Its...Ups and Downs." St. Paul Sunday Pioneer Press, 27 May 1973.

"Bridging the Mississippi." The Palimpsest, May 1922, 133-141.

Brown, Dee. "The Day the Iron Horse Crossed the Mississippi. The Chicago Tribune, 22 May 1977, Perspective Section, 1 & 2.

Hiebert, Gareth. "32-Ton Bridge Is His Elevator." St. Paul Sunday Pioneer Press, 13 January 1963, 1,7 and 8.

"Savor the Sun on a Minnesota Journey." Minnesota Explore, Minnesota Office of Tourism, Spring/ Summer 1997, 1 & 2.

Wiedrich, Bob. "A Bridge Stands A Test of Time." The Chicago Tribune. 30 April 1975.

Other Material

Allan, T, and Donald Jackson, compiled. 1977. "Bridge Truss Types: a guide to dating and identifying." Twelve-page Technical Leaflet #95, May. For the American Association for State and Local History, Nashville, Tennessee.

Ashton, David & Associates of Baltimore, Maryland. "Building Types: Bridges." James Goode & Company, Architectural Books. 1997 Catalog. Washington, D. C.

"Bemidji, Spirit of the Great River." Bemidji Area Vacation Guide, Courtesy of the Minnesota DNR.

Breining, Greg and Linda Watson. 1977. "A Gathering of Waters, A Guide to Minnesota's Rivers." Minnesota DNR, Government Publication, St. Paul, Minnesota.

Corps of Engineers, St. Paul District. "The Upper Mississippi River Nine-Foot Channel." Folded pamphlet with diagram, 'Stairway of Water.'

Frame III, Robert M. 1988. " Statewide Bridge Survey Inventory Form." (8 pages) State Historic Preservation Office, St. Paul.

"Headwaters River Trail." 1998. Mississippi Headwaters River Trail (in 6 sections), (Map and information), Mississippi Headwaters Board, Walker, Minnesota.

Hill, Stephen. 2002. "Replacing Five Trusses With Eight TPG's at Tomak, Sub Bridge 283.01." (CP Publication) Minneapolis, Minnesota.

"Land of Legends, Birthplace of the Mississippi River." (Promotion) Bemidji Chamber of Commerce, Bemidji, Minnesota.

Mississippi River Canoe Route, Lake Itasca to Cass Lake. 1983. (Map and information) Minnesota DNR.

"Queenpost and Queenrod Trusses; Description of Kingrod Trusses." 1908 International Correspondence School Manual.

Westbrook, Nicholas. 1971. "A Guide to the Industrial Archeology of the Twin Cities.

Interesting Reading

Arpy, Jim. 1983. The Magnificent Mississippi. Grinnell:Iowa Heritage Gallery/Publications.

Curry, Jane. 1983. The River's in My Blood: Riverboat Pilots Tell Their Story. Lincoln: University of Nebraska Press.

Dorsey, Florence. 1947. Road to the Sea: The Story of James B. Eads and the Mississippi River. New York: Reinhart & Co.,Inc.

Glazier, Willard. 1887. Down the Great River. Philadelphia: Hubbard Brothers, Publishers.

Jackson, Donald C. 1988. Great American Bridges and Dams Washington, D.C.: Preservation Press.

Peterson, William J. 1967. Mississippi River Panorama , by Henry Lewis. Iowa City: Clio Press.

1968. Steamboating on the Upper Mississippi. Iowa City: State Historical Society of Iowa.

Roba, William, ed. 1987. William F. Cody 1846-1917: Buffalo Bill, The King of the Border Men. Davenport, Iowa: Service Press, Inc.

Russell, Charles E. 1928. A-Rafting on the Mississip'. New York: Century House Americana.

GLOSSARY

Abutments--heavy supports at the extreme ends of a bridge; receive thrust from an arch or strut; retains earth under roadway approach.

Adolescent piers--(my term) for concrete piers that appear youthful with narrow arms and tall slender body.

Anchor arm--part of a cantilever span that reaches between the shore abutment and the pier.

Arch bridge--a curved structural member spanning an opening. One of the oldest type bridge. The early ones were stone blocks wedged together to form the arch. Today short spans are concrete or wood but long span arches are concrete or steel. Arches can be either above or below the deck. The arch pushes downward and outward against its massive abutments, which must be heavy to resist the thrust. (Types: deck-arch, half-through-arch and through-arch).

Art Deco--a style of architectural decoration developed in 1925 at the Paris "Arts Decoratifs" Exhibition from which the term came. Art Deco decoration is not applied but achieved by dividing surfaces into shapes by line or carved motifs.

Askew--Set or turned to one side. Used to describe bridges with piers and abutments not perpendicular to the span of the bridge.

Baltimore truss--a flat-top Pratt truss with substruts or lower diagonals. Sub-ties above make it a petit. This style began in 1871, through the early 20th century.

Baltimore truss

Baluster--upright support in a railing.

Balustrade--row of balusters topped by a railing.

Barrel arch--a semi-circular arch, same as a Roman arch; like the end of a barrel.

Bascule bridge--earliest of all movable bridges; a counterpoised or balanced drawbridge; swings upward on a horizontal axis, like a trapdoor or an ancient drawbridge over a moat. It may have one leaf or two.

Bascule bridge

Batter--piles at the end of a line angle out to resist horizontal forces such as wind; in thickness from bottom to top.

Beam bridge--simple log or board across supports.

Bebo arch--a commercial name for a barrel arch sometimes used in a culvert as in #128.

Bent--framework on land supporting loads as does a pier.

BNSF--Burlington Northern Santa Fe Railroad

Box girder--a strong box-shaped horizontal member of a bridge; a part on which the weight of the deck is carried.

Bow truss--a tied arch with diagonals serving as bracing and the verticals supporting the deck. This style was used in 1840 and late 19th Century for 70 to 175 foot lengths.

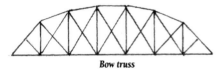

Bow truss

Bridge-tender--a person responsible for opening and closing movable bridges.

Bryd trefoil--a ground cover with small yellow flowers and leaves with three leaflets.

Bulb-tee girder--precast concrete "T" beam with bulb at the bottom of vertical placed so that the ends of the "T" flanges meet forming a row. The solid top thus formed then can be covered directly with a bituminous surface, to expedite construction. (Highway 19 Bridge East of Lake Bemidji, #110)

Bulb "T" cross-section

Cables--thick, strong wire ropes used on suspension bridges. John Roebling, Trenton, N.J., invented wire cable in his back yard and manufactured it in the 1830's. (Later he designed and built the Niagara Falls Railroad Suspension Bridge, 1855, and the Cincinnati Suspension Bridge, 1865; Roebling's son Washington built the Brooklyn Bridge, 1883 after his father's death.)

Cable-stayed bridge--combines features of cantilever and suspension bridges. One or two towers support a balanced section of the deck with cables that reach out at increasing angles from the perpendicular. If there are two towers, the bridge is built out from each and meets in the middle. The cables form a radiating pattern, a fan or a harp, depending upon points on the roadway and the tower at which they are connected. It is a variation of an old bridge style first perfected for use in a long span in Dusseldorf, Germany in 1955.

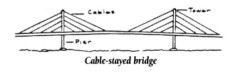

Cable-stayed bridge

Camelback span--section of a bridge with a polygonal top chord having exactly five slopes

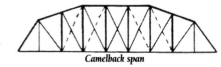

Camelback span

Cantilever bridges-- consist of two independent beams called cantilevers that extend from opposite banks of a waterway. The two cantilevers are joined together above the middle of the waterway. Each finished cantilever is self-supporting, balanced on its pier and braced by triangular trussing. The most famous cantilever is the Firth of Forth Bridge, Edinborough, Scotland, 1889.

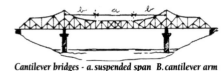

Cantilever bridges - a. suspended span B. cantilever arm

CCC--Civilian Conservation Corps, organized by President Roosevelt during the Great Depression, to put people to work doing civil projects, such as building the concrete footing at the edge of Lake Itasca for the rocks to cross in Itasca State Park

Cedar block surfaced deck--cedar wood used in 6 or 8 inches blocks used on their side in a pattern like brick for a deck surface.

CGW--Chicago Great Western Railroad.

Channel span--section of a bridge that crosses the deepest part of the river; navigation channel. Bridge engineers compare lengths of bridges by the main-span distance, center to center. However, the Corps of Engineers measures this distance without interference to navigation (deducting any part of pier, rock or other obstacle) so that their total "clear" channel span can be as much as 50 feet less than that of the engineers. I have included both distances, "clear" and "total" for all navigable parts of the river.

"Channel span" bridge--precast concrete bridge for short distances made up of "C"shapes. It is light and economical to build. (#118 and #121)

Chord-- one of the principal members of a truss bridge, usually horizontal; at the top and/or bottom.

Clearance--as used in this book's statistics, means vertical clearance, distance between the underside of the bridge and normal water level.

CNW--Chicago Northwestern Railroad

Compression--a force which pushes or squeezes from the outside; one of the stresses put on a bridge.

Concrete Slab--thick concrete deck is a supporting member of this bridge (Highway 9 Bridge at Lake Winnibigoshish, #103)

Corten steel--a tradename by Bethlehem Steel for weathering steel; composed of copper and steel which rusts to a degree and stops, forming a brown color; never requires paint unless there is pocketing of water on or within the members.

CP--Canadian Pacific Railroad

CRI&P--Chicago Rock Island and Pacific Railroad

CSAH--County State Aid Highway

Day Labor System--in 1929 or before where men were hired for the day only, especially unskilled labor. Used in the 15th and 16th centuries.

Deck truss--a truss under roadway. Usually on small bridges or for strengthening suspension bridges since the Tacoma Narrows Bridge failure in 1940.

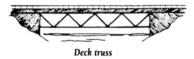

Deck truss

Delta piers--the 4th letter of the Greek alphabet, triangular. (Laurel Street Bridge, Brainerd #82)

DNR--Department of Natural Resources.

DOT--Department of Transportation.

DOTD--Department of Transportation and Development.

Double"T" pier--a pier with concrete in the shape of two "T's" connected at the flanges.

Drawspan or drawbridge--technically a movable bridge that can be drawn up, down or aside to admit or hinder passage. Although today we seem to differentiate between drawbridges as lifting, and swingspans as turning, in the 1860's and 70's, G.K.Warren referred to those that swing as drawspans. Therefore, I will be using "swing," "turn," and "draw" interchangeably. A drawspan is balanced on a pivot pier and turns to allow boats to pass. Its span is measured by including the length of both arms. All drawspans on the Mississippi are railroad bridges.

Falls--refers to St. Anthony Falls which powered the mill in 1823 which ground coarse flour.

Falsework--a temporary scaffolding built of timber or steel to hold a bridge up until it is self-supporting

Flair and bury--a corrugated steel guardrail on which the end is flush with the ground, with no end post.

Flair and bury

Ford--a place in a river crossed by walking or on horseback, usually the narrowest part of the stream.

FSR--Forest Service Road (Third River Road Bridge, #104)

Girder--a strong horizontal member used on edge to bear the weight of a floor or partition. Girders are made of wood, steel or concrete. Girders in iron or steel can be in many different shapes: I or H section, T section, or Z section to name a few.

Girder bridge--a bridge with two or more parallel girders connected by steel beams bearing the weight of the roadway or railroad track.

Guard rail--inner track which prevents derailed train wheels from going further astray if train goes off the main track.

Gusset--a rectangular or triangular insert to give strength or width.

Gusset plate--a metal plate over each meeting place of truss members. The gusset plates, two per kingpost in bridge #1, weigh 51.4 tons each.

Hammerhead piers--what I call "he-man" piers, broad shoulders and base, in concrete. (Lafayette Street, St. Paul #22)

Hangers--cables or steel shapes that hang from an arch or suspension bridge, cable to support the roadway; they help distribute the weight of moving loads more evenly.

Haunch--any deepening of a member over a support, such as the deepened portion of a girder over a pier

He-man piers--(my term) for piers with giant size arms

Hennepin--Fr. Louis Hennepin, first recorded white visitor who named the falls after his favorite saint, St. Anthony of Padua.

HNTB--Howard Needles Tammen and Bergendoff, consulting engineers.

Humpback truss--a term used by bridge workers; synonymous with camelback; truss with convex top chord.

I-beams--beams in the shape of the letter "I" with flanges top and bottom; a standard shape used in bridge construction both in steel and precast concrete. (Two 36-inch-deep I-beams 50 feet long will carry a train.)

Iron range--Cuyuna Iron Range, near Aitkin, has a high manganese content. These open pit mines are now abandoned and mostly filled with water. Vermilion and Mesabi are other ranges.

KBM Inc.--engineering company in Grand Forks, North Dakota. The original owner Keith Barry MacKichan died but the employees have continued for several generations using his initials only. They have designed a number of Minnesota's bridges (#107 is one.)

Kingpost--a vertical bridge member connecting the apex of a triangular truss with the base; also a small triangular-shaped wooden bridge type with origins in the Middle Ages. (#125)

Length--in this book, the total bridge length including approaches, usually.

Liftspan--towers on either side of the moveable section and large pulleys raise the bridge to the height needed to clear passing boats. It is a vertical motion rather than horizontal as are swingspans. A bridge-tender controls it from the ground. (Hastings Lift Railroad Bridge #17 and the St. Paul, CNW now UP Lift Span # 24)

Log-booming--an industry in mid-to-late 1800's that cut and floated logs down the Mississippi River. Boom Island was the location of one such business and reason for its name.(Boom Island Back Channel Bridge, #46)

M&I--Minnesota and International Falls Railroad

Melan ribs--a man by the name of Melan designed a special method of constructing concrete arches using a light metal arch encased in cement, avoiding the need for scaffolding. The result is stronger and easier in some locations. (Third Avenue Bridge, #40)

MLW--Mean Low Water, or normal water level, used in statistics for vertical clearance.

Moment--the tendency to cause rotation about a point or axis because a force is acting on a member

MRLM--Minneapolis, Red Lake and Manitoba Railroad (BNSF Railroad Bridge Nearest Lake Irving in Bemidji, #115)

MSAS--Minnesota State Aid Street

M.St.P&S.Ste.M.--Minneapolis, St. Paul and Sault Saint Marie Railroad

Nicollet--a French explorer in America, 1598 to 1642. An island and a bridge are named after him in Minneapolis

NP--Northern Pacific Railroad

Oxbow--bow-shaped bend in the river.

Parapet--low wall or railing.

Parker truss--a common type truss; essentially a Pratt truss with an arched upper chord or c camelback having five slopes. C.H. Parker designed it; popular in the mid-to-later 19th and 20th Centuries (former US 169 Bridge at Aitkin, # 88)

Pennsylvania or Petit truss--arched top chord with a standard Pratt truss and added sub-struts and sub-ties for added strength. Called Pennsylvania because the Pennsylvania Railroad used this truss extensively from 1875 to the early 20th Century.

Pennsylvania or Petit truss

Pier--an intermediate support under a bridge; heavy column or columns used to hold up a bridge.

Pile--a long slender stake driven into the ground to carry a vertical load; used as a base (footing) under piers.

Pile and trestle bridge--a braced framework of piles for carrying a road over a depression or water; dates back to the time of Julius Caesar; a kind of beam bridge popular especially in military engineering, erected quickly and easily; for shallow quiet water with clay or fine-grained soil bed.

Pivot pier--a wide central pier supporting a horizontal ring girder on which the turnspan rolls as it is rotated parallel to the channel. There are two types: rim-bearing span which is supported entirely on the ring girder; and a center-bearing span which pivots on a large bronze center bearing and is merely stabilized by the ring.

Plate girder--a built-up beam strengthened by riveting and welding together a combination of steel plates and angles; for long spans requiring deep strong sections.

Pony truss--a half-through truss with short side trusses; too shallow to have overhead bracing.

Pool--two distinct meanings: in the South, the water area where the river hits the bank and erodes to the bottom; in the North, the water area between dams on the river.

Portal--entrance to a through-truss bridge.

Portmanteau--the merging of two words into a third. The Latin "Veritas Caput" meaning "true head or source" was shortened by Schoolcraft into the last four letters of the first word and first two letters of the second, "Itasca".

Pratt truss--a strong, simple straight-forward truss with vertical compression members and diagonal tension members; patented by Caleb and Thomas Pratt in 1844. Virtually the standard American bridge form from 1890 to 1925.

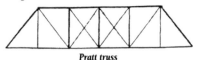

Pratt truss

Prestressed concrete--created by imbedding a series of parallel high-grade steel wires tightened for a powerful compressive stress through the full length of a concrete beam. More economical than reinforced-concrete, prestressed concrete can use up to 50 percent less steel and 25 percent less concrete to make slender and graceful modern bridges; widely used after 1950.

Protection cell--generally speaking is wooden or metal pilings in a circle filled with big gravel, covered with concrete, along the bank to deflect towboats.

Protection pier--a barrier that juts out from a pivot pier; wooden pilings filled with riprap to guide boats and protect the pivot pier.

Rainbow arch--not a technical term. It is a high-rise arch, not Roman or semi-circular.

Relief--the projection of sculptured figures or ornament from the background. The kinds of relief are named according to the amount of projection. "High relief" is half or more than half the natural thickness of the figure. "Low or bas relief" is slight, as on a coin.

Reinforced-concrete--steel rods placed in the part of the beam which is under tension. Extensively used for buildings in Chicago. Used previously for shorter span bridges, like road crossings. Current drawback is need for extensive field labor to build forms.

Riprap--irregularly shaped chunks of limestone which line river banks to minimize current and wave erosion that would otherwise wear away the wall and destroy its effectiveness.

Rope/Tow Ferry--commercial service using a boat or raft for transporting people across the river using a rope and pulley system.

River level gauge shed--a small building used for measuring the water level especially important during a drought or flood.

Scour--result of river current hitting the bank or pier; whirl-pools circle downward and dig deep holes in underwater sand or ground. To minimize this, piers are set with the current. On a river without dams, the normal river bottom scours. In the life of a bridge the normal bottom may lower significantly and the pier footings must be placed deeper to account for this.

Segmental arch--in architecture an arc less than a semi-circle.

Segmental concrete--a box-girder in 10-foot pieces, in post-tension. (Wabasha Street Bridge #26)

SFR--State Forest Road (Stumphges Rapids Bridge, #122)

Sheer Boom--if there are two protection piers by a bridge, the second would be called a "sheer boom"; also describes a floating structure that guides the river traffic into the proper channel to pass through the drawspan.

Sheer Fence--is a long extended construction, as much as 500 feet long, which floats. Its purpose is to protect and is built at an angle to help deflect a moving object, boat or barge. Sheer means to turn aside from a course. It is a long compression member by a river bank.

Shoal--water having little depth or shallow water.

Slab bridge--a reinforced road which supports itself; no girders or other superstructure used. (Lake Winnibigoshish Bridge, #103)

Sleepers--railroad ties piled by the side of the track

Slip form--the form is pulled or raised while the concrete is placed.

Slough--an inlet from a river.

Span--part of a bridge between two piers.

Spandrel--area between the exterior curve of an arch and the horizontal deck above.

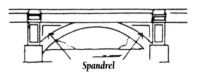

Spandrel

SR--state road.

Steel--material used in building bridges; made by refining molten pigiron. More ductile than iron, wood or stone; withstands the effects of impact and vibration. Strongest bridge material--20% stronger than wrought iron. Flexibility makes steel ideal for suspension towers.

Stereoscope--an instrument that gives three-dimensional effect to photographs viewed through it. It has two eyepieces through which two slightly different views of the same scene are viewed side by side.

StPMM--St. Paul Minneapolis and Manitoba Railroad (Jim Hill owned, #40)

Strahnet--strategic highway network or defense highway system close by military bases, designed to connect the base to the interstate highway network for speedy deployment of the Armed Forces in an emergency. There are 15,000 miles nationally. (Camp Ripley Bridge, #79)

Stringer--a longitudinal member extending the length of the bridge panel to support the deck.

Struts--members that connects straight parallel columns or the like. They do not carry weight but serve to brace other members.

Suspended span--in a cantilever bridge the last span inserted between the two cantilever arms, completing the connection.

Suspenders-- see hangers.

Suspension bridge-bridge with roadway that hangs from steel cables supported by towers. Primitive man accidentally and then purposely built suspension bridges. Best bridge style for long distances.

Suspension bridge

Substructure--part of bridge below the deck; pier and footings.

Superstructure--the portion of a bridge above the pier.

Swingspan--another term for turnspan or drawspan; movable span that turns on a vertical axel or pivot pier; requires considerable space in which to turn.

Tamarack tree--an American larch, yielding a useful lumber. Coniferous tree usually found in swamps, tough durable wood.

Tension--a force which pulls the ends of an object apart.

Through-truss--a truss bridge on which the roadway goes under the superstructure; carries its traffic load level with the bottom chord.

Tied arch--a steel arch in which the bottoms of the rib are tied together by a strong girder. The tied arch is a self-contained unit.

Timber slab--an older style construction where the forms, as for concrete, are laid on the outer edges. The bottom of the deck is reinforced and the inside is filled with wood and gravel. Two-by-fours are fastened together in a tire-track position and the rest filled with fine gravel. (#122 and #124)

TKDA--Toltz, King, Duvall, Anderson and Associates Incorporated, Engineers, Architects and Planners.,

TPG--through plate girder

Truss--a frame made in the shape of a triangle; the most rigid form of framework.

Truss Bridge--one in which a series of triangles is used in simple or complicated superstructures. The main members of a truss are either stiff, heavy struts or posts or thin flexible rods or bars. Common truss designs are Pratt, Warren or Parker.

Turnspan--see swingspan

Truss beam--beam constructed by lacing sides together.

Vertical lift--see liftspan

Vierendeel truss--a truss with no diagonals, having only squares or rectangles. It is not used as much because it is not as strong; but can be used in part, for example, in the center of a span where the stress is not as great, or in buildings for the open space it creates. (Used in part on Inver Grove Railroad/Highway, Privately owned bridge #19)

Vierendeel truss

Warren truss--a simple straightforward design whose diagonals are alternately placed in tension or compression. Designed by Captain James Warren, a British engineer, in 1848 and quickly adopted by American bridge designers; still used by present-day bridge engineers.

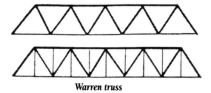

Warren truss

Weathering steel--a mixture of copper and steel which stops rusting after a certain point; like Corten steel but without the tradename given by Bethlehem Steel Company.

Web--consists of entire area between the top and bottom chords of a truss bridge. The part that lies between the flanges is the web; or the verticle portion of any member

Wing dam--a navigation structure built out from and often perpendicular to the river bank, to increase the flow of the river in main channel.

WPA--Work Projects Administration; started under President Franklin Delano Roosevelt to put men to work during the Great Depression. A part of the National Recovery Act, NRA. In effect 1935 to 1943.

Wrought iron--a tough, malleable and relatively soft commercial form of iron used for railway bridges between 1850 and 1890.

MISSISSIPPI RIVER RAILROAD BRIDGES IN MINNESOTA

Bridge Number on the River	Railroad Bridges	Date	Converted to path	Page
3	CP Main Channel Bridge, LaCrosse	1876		8
4	CP East Channel Bridge, LaCrosse	2001		10
5	CP French Slough Bridge, LaCrosse	1998		12
17	CP Vertical Lift Bridge, Hastings	1981	1871*	36
19	CRI&P (former) Railway/Highway Bridge, South St. Paul	1895		40
21	UP "Beltline" Bridge, St. Paul	1982		48
24	UP Lift Bridge, St. Paul	1913		54
28	UP "Omaha Swingspan" Bridge, St. Paul	1916		62
33	CP High Bridge, Minneapolis	1902		72
37	NP (former) Pedestrian/Bike Bridge, Minneapolis	1924	1999	80
40	BN Stone Arch Pedestrian/Bike Bridge , Minneapolis	1883	1994	86
45	BNSF East Channel Bridge, Minneapolis	1893		96
46	BNSF Main Channel Bridge, Minneapolis	1893		98
50	BNSF North Channel Bridge, Minneapolis	1884		106
52	CP "Camden" Bridge, Minneapolis	1905		110
66	BNSF Bridge, St. Cloud	1892		142
73	CP Bridge, Bowlus	1907		156
74	BNSF Bridge, South Little Falls	1990		158
76	BNSF Bridge, North Little Falls	1891		162
79	BNSF Railway/Highway Bridge, Fort Ripley	1931		168
83	BNSF Bridge, Brainerd	1984		180
89	Soo Line (formerly) Pedestrian/Bike Bridge, Palisade	1910	1988	182
96	BNSF Trestle Spur Bridge, Grand Rapids	1953		206
101	BNSF Bridge, Ball Club	1967	1908**	216
111	BN (formerly) Snowmobile Trail, North Bemidji	1971	1996	240
114	CP Bridge (abandoned)	1931		246
115	BNSF Bridge, Bemidji	1952		248

In 1871 the present vertical-lift bridge was built as a swingspan.
**In 1908 this girder bridge was constructed as a swingspan.*

In Minnesota, 27 of the 135 bridges were built by railroads. In the lower river, 20 of the 86 bridges were railroads. Of the overall 220 bridges on the Mississippi River, almost 1/4 were railroad spans.

The two volumes of "Climbing the Mississippi River Bridge by Bridge" area history of bridges and the people who built and used them. From the simple crossing of the infant stream by stepping stones or by walking on a log without handrails, to traveling the great, wide, long, famous bridges and almost every kind in between, Mary Costello adds the human touch. Bridges and people are inseparable. She sees with the eyes and hearts of those who build them, use them and love them.

She is dedicated to her task even to becoming a tenacious detective. Who could imagine losing a Mississippi River bridge? Read these books and become a bridge addict. Wonder why bridges are built? And why they die? Learn to appreciate the ingenuity that they represent.

Harold R. Sandberg, P.E.,S.E
Chairman of the Board
Alfred Benesch & Company
Engineering Consultants
Chicago, Illinois

This is the only modern day compilation of pertinent facts about all the bridges on the Mississippi River--from the marshes of Minnesota to the mouth in Louisana and it comes with realistic, accurate sketches of each structure.. As such, it is highly recommended as a valuable source of information for the layman, as well as a useful starting point for the serious researcher. Mrs. Costello has done the bridge engineering fraternity a real service by gathering all this information in these two volumes.

William B. Conway
Modjeski and Masters
Consulting Engineers
New Orleans, Louisiana

No bridge engineering library would be complete without this book.

Patrick Cassity
J. Muller International
Bridge Engineering Consultants
Chicago, Illinois

DISCLAIMER: *All clearances on the bridges are approximate and vary with the water level day to day. Owners are not responsible if the clearances are different from quoted.*